How Should We Rationally Deal with Ignorance?

This book addresses two questions that are highly relevant for epistemology and for society: What is ignorance and how should we rationally deal with it? It proposes a new way of thinking about ignorance based on contemporary and historical philosophical theories.

In the first part of the book, the author shows that epistemological definitions of ignorance are quite heterogeneous and often address different phenomena under the label "ignorance." She then develops an integrated conception of ignorance that recognizes doxastic, attitudinal, and structural constituents of ignorance. Based on this new conception, she carves out suggestions for dealing with ignorance from the history of philosophy that have largely been overlooked: virtue-theoretic approaches based on Aristotle and Socrates, consequentialist approaches derived from James, and deontological approaches based on Locke, Clifford, and Kant. None of these approaches individually provide a satisfying approach to the task of rationally dealing with ignorance, and so the author develops an alternative maxim-based answer that extends Kant's maxims of the *sensus communis* to the issue of ignorance. The last part of the book applies this maxim-based answer to different contexts in medicine and democracies.

How Should We Rationally Deal with Ignorance? will appeal to scholars and advanced students working in epistemology, political philosophy, feminist philosophy, and the social sciences.

Nadja El Kassar is Professor of Philosophy, with a focus on theoretical philosophy, at the University of Lucerne, Switzerland. Her research interests include social and feminist epistemology, philosophy of perception, and philosophy of mind. Recently she has published articles on ignorance, epistemic injustice, and intellectual self-trust.

Routledge Studies in Epistemology
Edited by Kevin McCain, *University of Alabama at Birmingham, USA* and Scott Stapleford, *St. Thomas University, Canada*

Seemings and the Foundations of Justification
A Defense of Phenomenal Conservatism
Blake McAllister

Trust Responsibly
Non-Evidential Virtue Epistemology
Jakob Ohlhorst

Rationality in Context
Unstable Virtues in an Uncertain World
Steven Bland

Seemings
New Arguments, New Angles
Edited by Kevin McCain, Scott Stapleford, and Matthias Steup

The Epistemic Injustice of Genocide Denialism
Melanie Altanian

Misinformation, Content Moderation, and Epistemology
Protecting Knowledge
Keith Raymond Harris

How Should We Rationally Deal with Ignorance?
A Philosophical Study
Nadja El Kassar

For more information about this series, please visit: www.routledge.com/Routledge-Studies-in-Epistemology/book-series/RSIE

How Should We Rationally Deal with Ignorance?
A Philosophical Study

Nadja El Kassar

NEW YORK AND LONDON

First published 2025
by Routledge
605 Third Avenue, New York, NY 10158

and by Routledge
4 Park Square, Milton Park, Abingdon, Oxon, OX14 4RN

Routledge is an imprint of the Taylor & Francis Group, an informa business

© 2025 Nadja El Kassar

The right of Nadja El Kassar to be identified as author of this work has been asserted in accordance with sections 77 and 78 of the Copyright, Designs and Patents Act 1988.

All rights reserved. No part of this book may be reprinted or reproduced or utilised in any form or by any electronic, mechanical, or other means, now known or hereafter invented, including photocopying and recording, or in any information storage or retrieval system, without permission in writing from the publishers.

Trademark notice: Product or corporate names may be trademarks or registered trademarks, and are used only for identification and explanation without intent to infringe.

ISBN: 978-1-032-45121-3 (hbk)
ISBN: 978-1-032-45122-0 (pbk)
ISBN: 978-1-003-37550-0 (ebk)

DOI: 10.4324/9781003375500

Typeset in Sabon
by Newgen Publishing UK

Contents

Acknowledgments — vii

1 Introduction — 1

PART 1
What Is Ignorance? — 27

  2 The Framework I — 29

  3 Conceptions of Ignorance — 37

  4 Facets of Ignorance — 68

  5 Causes of Ignorance — 108

PART 2
Rationally Dealing with Ignorance — 119

  6 The Framework II — 121

  7 Virtue-Theoretical Answers — 124

  8 Consequentialist Answers — 143

  9 Deontological Answers — 150

  10 The Maxim-Based Answer — 173

PART 3
Applications 197

11 Ignorance in Democracies 199

12 Ignorance and Uncertainty in Medical Contexts 216

   Outlook 231

   References *234*
   Index *256*

Acknowledgments

Trying to make sense of ignorance and human approaches to ignorance from a philosophical perspective is an intriguing task. It is a task that one cannot and should not approach on one's own, and that requires a conducive, respectful atmosphere of genuine interest in humans and their lives. And so it's not enough to think for oneself; one also has to include other perspectives into thinking and still be aware of oneself in the community of these other perspectives. Incidentally, this is my reading of the three maxims of Kant's *sensus communis* that makes up a large part of my proposal developed in this book. I am grateful to many people for inspiring conversations and their interest in discussing ignorance with me, for worrying about pernicious ignorance, for laughing about our attempts at knowing-it-all, for being curious about ignorance, and for taking ignorance seriously without being arrogant.

I am grateful to Lutz Wingert for giving me the space to think freely about ignorance and develop my own position and for always having a good real-life case and the right literature at hand. Many thanks also to my colleagues at ETH Zürich – in particular Rachele Delucchi, Martin Hurni, Jérôme Léchot, Raphael Meyer, Silvan Moser, Vanessa Rampton, and Romila Storjohann – for always being up for discussing philosophy and opening up new perspectives.

I was very fortunate in being able to work on my project with Philip Kitcher at Columbia University in New York in Spring 2017, in a time when ignorance suddenly became somewhat of a hot topic. The discussions with Philip Kitcher and Andreas Ditter, Miranda Fricker, Yarran Hominh, the late Charles Mills, Susanna Schellenberg and Katja Vogt have confirmed and shaped my conviction that ignorance is a deeply human issue that is not a passing trend and that needs to be examined by philosophers and human beings alike.

But it is not just philosophers who have contributed to this study – after all, ignorance is not just an epistemological or philosophical issue – and so I am grateful to these human beings (many of whom work as philosophers) for our conversations about ignorance: Melanie Altanian, Natalie Alana

Ashton, Claus Beisbart, Christine Bratu, Florian Braun, Romain Büchi, Mara-Daria Cojocaru, Matthew Congdon, Dina Emundts, Hannah Fasnacht, Karen Frost-Arnold, Sanford Goldberg, Stefan Gosepath, Josh Habgood-Coote, Karen Koch, Anne Kühler, Martin Kusch, David Lauer, Kristina Lepold, David Löwenstein, Matthias Mahlmann, Anne Meylan, Rebecca Papendieck, Elena Romano, Sebastian Schmidt, Lilja Walliser, Eva Weber-Guskar, Anna Wehofsits, Christian Weibel, and Monika Wulz.

I have presented different versions of chapters of this book at various places and have benefited greatly from the discussions after my talks. Many thanks to the members of Matthias Mahlmann's colloquium at the University of Zurich, the members of Anne Meylan's colloquium at the University of Zurich, and participants in colloquia at the Universities of Basel, Berlin, Bern, Essen, Fribourg, Hamburg, Erlangen-Nürnberg, Münster, and Wuppertal as well as audiences at further events in Berlin, Bern, Cologne, Erlangen-Nürnberg, Freiburg, Madrid, Münster, Villanova, and Zürich.

The original version of this monograph was part of my Habilitation at ETH Zürich, and I am grateful to the four reviewers for taking time to the manuscript and writing their reports. Thanks also to the faculty at D-GESS at ETH Zürich for their inputs when I presented the project to them.

Many thanks to two anonymous referees for Routledge and the editors and series editors for their perceptive comments and support in preparing this book. And thanks to Rosaleah Stammler for kindly guiding me through the publication process.

I am finishing the manuscript as a fairly new professor at the Institute of Philosophy and member of the Faculty of Humanities and Social Sciences at the University of Lucerne. I would like to thank my colleagues for their warm welcome and their interest in my takes on ignorance and on philosophy.

Over the years, my friends have continually had a keen interest in discussing philosophy and theories of ignorance with me – thanks for that!

Finally, I am infinitely grateful to my family for approaching ignorance and doing philosophy with me in the most valuable ways I could ever imagine.

1 Introduction

1.1 Studying Ignorance

Thinking and writing about the questions "What is ignorance?" and "How should we rationally deal with ignorance?" is a transformative experience both philosophically and existentially. I have found that ignorance is everywhere, including philosophy, science and everyday life. I have been very concerned about my own ignorance and other people's ignorance. At the same time, I have become more relaxed about the reality of my own ignorance. I have become more relaxed about admitting my own ignorance – sometimes, at least. And I have learnt to expect the popular proverbs about ignorance. When I mention my topic, almost everyone – philosophers and laypeople alike – cites "ignorance is bliss" and in German-speaking contexts almost everyone cites the saying "Ignorance does not protect against punishment." And everyone is tempted to make a joke about their own ignorance about the topic *ignorance*. But ignorance is not always funny and is not always excusable. And so I have also become impatient with some blatant instances of ignorance.

I hope that these subjective experiences do not give the impression that you will now be reading a text by a philosopher who is tired and exasperated by her work, her topic and other people and sets out to lecture everyone about (their) ignorance. Nothing could be farther from the truth. At the provisional end of this study, I am still excited about ignorance and the question about how we should deal with it because ignorance is a fascinating and important topic and there are so many facets to it. One striking facet is that ignorance can be pernicious but also valuable, ignorance is not per se bad or per se good. Another crucial facet is our attitude, people's attitude, toward ignorance. Ignorance is something that concerns human beings in particular and so it is vastly important to gather, include and recognize their perspectives on ignorance, as well as their attitudes toward ignorance.

And since I think that people's reactions to ignorance and the question how we should deal with it matter to the topic, I continue to be surprised

DOI: 10.4324/9781003375500-1

by how skeptical some philosophers are about the value of the project and the two questions. It was philosophers, and never laypeople, who would ask "Why are you even looking at this topic?" and "Why should we examine ignorance?" And, fortunately, not all philosophers were critical of and skeptical about the value of the project. Many philosophers were very interested in my topic. And, in virtually all cases of telling laypeople about my project, I have met fascination, curiosity and even something that seemed to me something like relief. People seemed relieved that I am addressing a topic that is so relevant to them, personally. Many felt overwhelmed by the amount of knowledge and information available to them, and their own ignorance about things that they should (maybe) know. They wondered whether there is a right to remain ignorant. And they were concerned about the ignorance of other people who base sweeping claims, conclusions and actions on false beliefs and *Halbwissen* (incomplete knowledge).

In fact, our intricate relation to knowledge and not knowing is one central reason why ignorance and how we should rationally deal with it are worthy topics for a philosophical study. We care about knowledge, sometimes for instrumental reasons, sometimes for its own sake. But next to our knowledge we are perpetually faced with our own ignorance and other people's ignorance; there is an infinite sea of ignorance, sometimes invincible, sometimes overwhelming, sometimes surmountable, sometimes detrimental, sometimes benign. Ignorance can be harmful in various ways; for example, it may lead us to wrong decisions; it may keep us from reaching our aims because we work on faulty assumptions; or we may hurt other people because we do not know that our comment addresses a sensitive issue for them. But ignorance can also be useful and valuable. Say, if someone does not know about their partner's plans for a surprise birthday party for them, they would not want to know about these plans because such knowledge would spoil the surprise. Some psychological research suggests that overly optimistic and, strictly speaking, false beliefs about one's chances of recovery are conducive to getting better after being sick (e.g., Taylor and Brown 1988, McKay and Dennett 2009). And some deliberate ignorance may be valuable for individuals (e.g., Hertwig and Engel 2021). Despite these and related positive facets, ignorance often has a persistent negative ring to it. One explanation for this association may be the strong value that societies accord to knowledge and education, *Bildung*. And people often implicitly and explicitly associate ignorance and stupidity, a trait that is hardly ever valued.[1] In this book, I also argue against these simple associations in order to make room for a more nuanced approach toward ignorance.

My hunch is that we care about ignorance because ignorance is natural to human beings and because it can be valuable and disvaluable. We know that we are always ignorant about one thing or another, or even many things, and we also know that ignorance is a natural feature of human beings, human beings just are cognitively fallible. And we know that we cannot overcome all ignorance and that (sometimes) we have more important things to do than to worry about ignorance. So, one might be tempted to take a relaxed perspective toward ignorance – it is just a fact of human lives. And yet, the effects of ignorance – valuable and pernicious – in practical and theoretical lives also keep us from being too relaxed about ignorance. Ignorance is not irrelevant; it is not, as one would say in German, *egal*.

1.2 Approaching Ignorance

Since ignorance is so multifaceted and ambiguous, it calls for a nuanced approach. In my study, I have aimed to develop and employ an adequately nuanced approach. Readers will have to judge whether I have reached this aim. Of course, there are different ways to realize a nuanced approach, one option is to examine the phenomenology and layers of ignorance by looking at related concepts such as innocence, cluelessness, naïveté. I discuss some of these facets in Chapter 4 as symptoms of ignorance.[2] Another approach to the nuances of ignorance is via the linguistics behind *ignorance*. In fact, the approach is fairly obvious for expressions of "ignorance" in German since the layers are even intrinsic to the German terms for "ignorance." Unlike English, German has at least four words connected to the English word *ignorance*: *Unwissen, Nichtwissen, Unkenntnis, Ignoranz*. In addition, there is also one term designated for the *state* of being ignorant or of not knowing: *Unwissenheit*. According to the German standard dictionary, the *Duden*, "Unwissenheit" is "lack of knowledge of a thing; lack of (scientific) education." This additional expression for the state of being ignorant is an advantage of German morphology. *Nichtwissen* is the most neutral of the four terms, it primarily denotes not knowing something. *Unwissen* with its prefix *Un-* that may imply a pejorative meaning and a negative evaluation denotes a negatively evaluated form of not knowing.[3] But note also that the Duden just gives *Nichtwissen* as the meaning of *Unwissen* (Duden). *Unwissen* may be ambiguous. The extension of *Unkenntnis* is similar to that of *Unwissen*. *Ignoranz*, however, is very different from the other terms, it refers to not knowing and not *wanting* to know, being close-minded. And the term *Ignoranz* implies that this state is criticized and reprimanded. The term *ignorance* cannot mirror these distinctions, but I think we can agree that *ignorance* generally is akin to something like *Nichtwissen* and *Unwissen*. At the same time, it can also denote *Ignoranz* but is not by itself limited to *Ignoranz*. In this study, I want to keep *ignorance* as a neutral term and use specifications by adjectives to capture variants such as *Ignoranz*, for example, "close-minded ignorance" or "willful ignorance". So, "being ignorant" is not in and of itself a negative or pejorative statement about someone's state.

Addressing ignorance by way of examining knowledge may be another nuanced approach to ignorance. If ignorance is the negation of knowledge, then all the facets of knowledge will be reflected in ignorance, only in the negated form. For example, if knowledge is justified, true belief, then ignorance is determined by a lack of justification, lack of true belief and lack of belief. But I think that this approach restricts ignorance because it reduces ignorance to being the negation of knowledge and it, thus, does not receive the scrutiny and attention that it deserves. If one wants to examine the relation between ignorance and knowledge, this is certainly one part of the right approach, but not for examining ignorance.

My worry about privative approaches is similar to the worries surrounding biographies and studies of works of famous artists who have famous partners or siblings. Fanny Hensel can be approached as the composer who is the sister of Felix Mendelssohn Bartholdy or as Fanny Hensel, the composer. Of course, her composer brother will be mentioned in her biography and in approaches to her work, but he is not primary. The case of composer and pianist Clara Schumann and her composer husband Robert Schumann is very similar. One can approach her work as the work of Clara Schumann, Robert Schumann's wife, or as the work of Clara Schumann, composer and pianist. Robert Schumann will almost certainly appear in a study of her work, but he is not primary. In the same way, in a study of ignorance, ignorance should be primary and not another related concept, even if the concept is a central concept such as *knowledge*. If one regards ignorance as secondary, one is in danger of saying too much about the related concepts rather than look at ignorance.

Let me emphasize that these remarks do not mean that studies of ignorance cannot learn from knowledge. Or that one must not say that ignorance is lack of knowledge. Quite to the contrary, sophisticated conceptions of knowledge that go beyond traditional justified true belief accounts and that take seriously the epistemic agent as well as the (social) situatedness of the epistemic agent and the impact of context promise to provide insights about ignorance. But I am worried that simplistic conceptions of knowledge will skew our conception of ignorance. And most authors who argue that ignorance is lack of knowledge work with such simplistic conceptions (see for example, Le Morvan and Peels 2016). Haas and Vogt are an important exception because their conception of knowledge includes "the cognizer" (2015) and I do work with some of their claims about knowledge to understand ignorance. Nevertheless, I am generally cautious about approaches to ignorance that derive it from looking at knowledge.

You will see that there is no chapter on truth in this study. And my reasons for this decision are related to the considerations concerning knowledge. Discussions about truth would side-track the study of ignorance. In addition, contrary to some, I hold that one can be ignorant of truths and falsehoods. So, ignorance does not just appear with truth but can also appear with falsehood (see also Chapter 4). And, of course, error as a form of ignorance is closely connected to falsehood. Examining the relation between ignorance and truth and falsehood has to remain for another occasion.

Let me also note that I do not discuss stupidity in much detail, I think that stupidity deserves its own study – for example, as presented by Ronell (2002), Geisenhanslüke (2011) and van Treeck (2015). And ignorance deserves its own study independently from stupidity and any history and connotations that come with this term.

My experiences while working on the project and people's views of the two main questions have also shaped my approach to the questions and my main claims. First, my conception of ignorance is geared to fit real-world ignorance, that is, ignorance as a phenomenon that human beings – we – encounter in our epistemic lives, as opposed to ignorance as some abstract logical state of an ideal reasoner or ignorance merely as some S not knowing that *p*. This shapes Part 1 of the book: What is ignorance? I argue that

> ignorance is a disposition of an epistemic agent that is constituted by (1) beliefs, (2) epistemic attitudes, (3) epistemic character traits, (4) conduct and (5) socio-political structures.

Second, my suggestion for how we should rationally deal with ignorance is supposed to be applicable for all human epistemic lives and addresses real-world epistemic concerns. This shapes Part 2 of the study: How should we rationally deal with ignorance? Ultimately, a Kantian Maxim-based Answer will turn out to provide the best approach. Third, my conception and suggestion must not be unrealistically intellectualized by positing intellectual expectations and norms that finite, non-ideal, rational agents such as human beings cannot ever meet. That is why I put my conception to the test in two applied cases from politics and medicine.

1.3 What Cases of Ignorance?

My study is concerned with *being ignorant* or *not knowing* rather than with the unknown.[4] I am interested in the subjects of ignorance rather than the objects of ignorance. This also entails that I have asked what it means to be ignorant and what are manifestations of being ignorant or of not knowing. The subject is at the center of my study. It is, thus, inevitably

6 Introduction

related to virtue epistemology that also focuses on the epistemic agent (Battaly 2008, 640). But unlike virtue epistemology it does not necessarily argue that "intellectual virtues and vices ... are the fundamental concepts and properties" (Battaly 2008, 640). I do not want to subscribe to any such commitments because I do not want to buy into the virtue ontology that comes with its particular historical backdrop. And not everything about ignorance is reducible to virtues and vices.

This is also why I do not discuss Donald Rumsfeld's famous statement about "known unknowns" in more detail. Rumsfeld explained at a press conference on February 12, 2002, before the start of the Iraq war that

> there are known knowns; there are things we know we know. We also know there are known unknowns; that is to say, we know there are some things we do not know. But there are also unknown unknowns – the ones we don't know we don't know.

Rumsfeld's taxonomy – which, it has to be noted, is not as ridiculous as commentators have made it seem – is a taxonomy of objects of ignorance and does not address the ignorant subject. Daniel DeNicola contextualizes Rumsfeld's statement helpfully and he notes that there are actually four forms of knowns and unknowns, not just the three forms that Rumsfeld mentions – Rumsfeld does not mention number 4:

1 known knowns: what I know I know
2 known unknowns: what I know I don't know
3 unknown unknowns: what I don't know I don't know
4 unknown knowns: what I don't know I know.

(DeNicola 2017, 40)

Rumsfeld's conjecture has made the distinction well known beyond the borders of philosophy. Errol Morris has even directed a documentary, *The Unknown Known* (2013), about Rumsfeld's political career that centers on his statement at the press conference.[5] But DeNicola points out that the distinction has been familiar in epistemology *before* Rumsfeld's press conference; for example, it has been noted by Ann Kerwin in an article on medical ignorance, published in 1993. My study is interested in understanding the state a subject, say, Rumsfeld, is in when they don't know that they don't know, or when they know that they don't know.

But what are examples of being ignorant, of not knowing, of not knowing that one does not know, etc.? This is a crucial question for knowing what this book is about. Not knowing that Bern is the federal city (*Bundesstadt*) of Switzerland is a case of ignorance, as is not knowing that Ottawa is the capital of Canada. Not knowing that cruise ships produce high emissions of carbon and sulfur dioxides is another case of ignorance. Here are some more examples – and more context to some of the examples, because, as we will see, context matters for ignorance, too:

a A scientist's ignorance about an as of yet undiscovered method for treating Parkinson's disease.
b The ignorance of someone who does not know that they left their keys to the office at home (until they find out).
c The ignorance of smokers in the 1970s who did not know that smoking causes lung cancer because tobacco companies fabricated a veil of doubt and kept people ignorant.
d The ignorance of someone who has not heard of the North Atlantic Oscillation (NAO) before she hears this term for the first time, and the ignorance of that same person after she has heard the term but still does not know what it is.
e The ignorance of someone who does not want to know a relevant fact. For example, Hannah does not know that cruise ships have high emissions of carbon and sulfur dioxides that are bad for the environment. When her friend Monika tells her about a documentary that says that cruise ships are bad for the environment, Hannah stops her mid-sentence and says that she does not want to hear anything about this documentary. She does not want to know because she does not want Monika to spoil the fun of the cruise trip. Yet, knowing that these emissions of carbon and sulfur dioxides are bad for the environment is important for being able to take the right action against climate change. Note that Hannah may still go on the cruise trip even if she knows about the bad effects the ship's emissions will have. She may know that useful measures against climate change are not restricted to individual actions, but also about systematic and structural actions.
f The ignorance of someone who does not want to know the end of the novel she is currently reading or the series she is watching and therefore avoids all articles and conversations about the novel or the series she has not finished yet. She is deliberately ignorant.
g The ignorance of someone who is curious and wants to know. Kate does not know that cruise ships have high emissions of carbon and sulfur dioxides that are bad for the environment. When her friend Monika tells her about a documentary that says that cruise ships are bad for the environment, Kate is interested in the impact of cruise ships on the environment and asks Monika for more details.

Of course, the list could be much longer. After all, ignorance can be epistemically good, epistemically bad, practically consequential, innocuous, existential and so on. There are myriads of types of ignorance.

8 Introduction

This list gives you an idea what types of ignorance are discussed in this study, and it introduces examples that will return in this study. In addition, it serves as a first clue that ignorance is not a purely epistemological issue, which will be reflected in the conception of ignorance developed later (Part 1).

My main focus lies on propositional ignorance, ignorance of some proposition, some fact or a set of facts, one may say. Such propositional ignorance can also have a very real existential significance, for example, a patient may not know and may not *want* to know whether she will survice her cancer or not. One may not want to know whether one's unborn child has a genetic disorder, and one has a *right* not to know whether one's unborn child has a genetic disorder. We do not know when we are going to die[6] and we do not know what is going to happen tomorrow – we may guess, but we cannot know for sure. Some doctors do not know that the level for blood sugar for patients with diabetes who are more than 60 years old is not the standard 6.0 but is calculated by dividing the patient's age by 10 – a new rule that was introduced a few years ago. The doctors' ignorance is a simple instance of propositional ignorance – as are the other examples in this paragraph–, but it has direct and indirect consequences for the patient's well-being and her life. They are all instances of propositional ignorance with existential impact. I return to discussing medical ignorance in the shape of *medical uncertainty* in Part 3.

Ignorance is also prevalent and central in the sciences and in research. For example, is Big Bang theory the right explanation of how the universe began? Is String theory the right theory for understanding black holes? How does evolution work? What are the causes of this-and-that form of cancer? What are the best ways for treating cancer? What is the mechanism that tells cells to stop growing in organ growth? Scientists and non-scientists have experienced ignorance in science and research manifested and discussed on a daily level during the COVID-19 pandemic. How is COVID-19 transmitted? What's the best medical treatment for severe cases of COIVD-19 infections? And the list goes on.

These topics and questions motivate and *drive* scientific research and researchers. Ignorance, thus, is an engine of science (cf. Firestein 2012). But science is also all about actually dealing with ignorance, for example, in working around ignorance in one's research.[7] In Paleoclimatology, scientists use sediment cores, ice cores, tree rings, cave deposits, etc. to determine CO_2 concentrations, temperatures, precipitation rates, wind speed/direction in previous times, some ten thousand years ago. The sediment cores etc. are proxies for the conditions that one cannot access directly.[8] And in other fields, too, we find proxies as building blocks for research and as ways of dealing with ignorance.

Errors and false belief are two crucial forms of ignorance in science that have shaped and haunted the sciences and they continue to do so. For example, from the 17th to the 19th centuries "Phlogiston" was thought to be the name of a tasteless, colorless gas that escapes when material is burned. It took till the end of the 19th century for researchers to find that there is no such gas. There are numerous additional examples. For example, in medicine, medical practitioners for a long time ignored and rejected evidence that childbed fever is caused by lack of hygiene and can be countered by simple hygienic measures such as hand washing. First studies linking childbed fever and lack of hygiene were presented by the surgeon and obstetrician Alexander Gordon at the end of the 18th century. But it took until the mid-19th century and Ignaz Semmelweis' observation that doctors unknowingly infected women giving birth in hospitals for the findings to be accepted slowly and turned into measures in hospitals (cf. e.g., Carter and Carter 2005, Kricheldorf 2016, O'Connor and Weatherall 2018). According to Hans Kricheldorf's reconstruction, Pasteur's germ theory of infectious diseases was a crucial building block that allowed other practitioners to accept contagion as a cause of childbed fever (Kricheldorf 2016, 116).

Medical practitioners long thought that stomach acid is the cause of stomach ulcers and it took a self-experiment in 1982 by Barry J. Marshall – and the related theory by Marshall and his colleague Robin Warren – to convince the scientific community that bacteria, *Helicobacter pylori*, are the cause of stomach ulcers. The community had thought that bacteria cannot survive in the acidic environment of the stomach and, therefore, dismissed the bacteria explanation.

In astronomy, for roughly 2,000 years scientists have been claiming that the Ptolemaic, geocentric system is correct when, in fact, the heliocentric system is correct. The list of errors and false beliefs is much longer, and it is likely to gain more entries as time progresses.[9]

There are also mistakes and errors in topics studied in the humanities. For example, in her book on homosexuality in 19th-century Britain, Naomi Wolf misinterpreted the legal term "death recorded" in court documents and was led to suppose that homosexuals in the 19th century were executed for sodomy. But in fact, "death recorded" as a legal term does not mean that the person is executed but that they were pardoned (Lea 2019).[10]

In my study, I explain in more detail why error and false beliefs are forms of ignorance and I subsume them under the term *ignorance* (Section 4.5). Suffice it to say for now that false beliefs also co-appear with a lack of relevant true beliefs and knowledge and, in this respect, they are just like "standard" ignorance that is co-constituted by a lack of knowledge – and, on my conception, epistemic attitudes like open-mindedness and close-mindedness; I will say more about this later.

As I have noted at the beginning of the introduction, the motivation for also discussing false belief and ignorance as error is not just philosophical but also quotidian. If I had limited ignorance to lack of knowledge and had excluded false belief and error, a large number of instances of epistemic subjects being ignorant, of not knowing, could not be included in my study, namely, those instances in which a subject does not know some fact p and in its place has a false belief that they take to be true. In order to address real-world, quotidian ignorance, one must include false belief and error in one's discussion.

My focus is on *factual ignorance*, and I do not discuss moral ignorance, normative ignorance or practical ignorance. Moral ignorance is ignorance of moral beliefs or principles (cf. e.g., Rosen 2004, Zimmerman 1997, Harman 2011, Mason 2015, Baron 2016); it is mostly relevant for discussions of blame, blameworthiness and culpability. I have decided to bracket moral ignorance because it would multiply and exceed the scope of the study; the issues related to moral ignorance and dealing with it, are different from those of propositional ignorance. This is for another occasion.

Practical ignorance as "ignorance constituted by a lack of know-how" (Nottelmann 2016, 33) is often contrasted with propositional ignorance. Especially when propositional ignorance is equated with lack of know-that. I do not discuss practical ignorance in this book because one would need to inquire into the relation between the practical and the propositional and because practical ignorance (just like propositional ignorance) does deserve its own study.[11]

1.4 Methodological Assumptions

My study is influenced by socio-epistemological assumptions, questions and topics. I regard ignorance as a social epistemological phenomenon and study the social dimensions of ignorance. And therefore, I assume that we cannot understand ignorance and reactions to ignorance by only looking at the mind of the agent. Instead, ignorance can also be co-constituted by social and institutional structures. That is why studying ignorance, and how one should rationally deal with it must also include the subject's surroundings, their communities, their social conditions. The epistemic subject is, thus, a social agent, situated in social communities (cf. Goldberg 2017a). Like other authors in social epistemology, my work is open to input from other disciplines, such as sociology and psychology (cf. Kusch 2010).

My approach to ignorance also belongs with *revisionary epistemology* because I have found standard conceptions of ignorance to be ill-equipped for ignorance as a real-world phenomenon in the lives of real, non-ideal, epistemic agents and for addressing the question of rationally dealing with ignorance. Revisionary epistemology criticizes existing conceptions of epistemological concepts and proposes an alternative conception. For example, for *knowledge*, "a revisionary project starts by arguing that what knowledge should be differs from what knowledge is. It then proposes that we revise our account of knowledge accordingly" (Fassio and McKenna 2015, 755–756).[12] I criticize existing conceptions of ignorance, for example, ignorance as lack of knowledge or ignorance as lack of true belief, and argue that ignorance should be understood as composed of a doxastic component, an agential component and structural components. This alternative conception of ignorance is what I call an *Integrated Conception of Ignorance* because it brings together what is correct in existing conceptions of ignorance and at the same time avoids their shortcomings.

Because it aims to develop a suggestion for how human beings can improve how they address ignorance, my approach to how we should rationally deal with ignorance also belongs with *ameliorative epistemology* (cf., e.g., Ahlstrom-Vij 2013a, 1–5). I will focus on addressing *one's own* ignorance, in particular.

In addition, I employ *empirically informed conceptual analysis*.[13] My discussion of the "standard" conceptions of ignorance shows that a mere conceptual analysis of the term does not get at the real-world phenomenon "ignorance" – one needs to include and acknowledge that ignorance is a social phenomenon and a disposition of epistemic agents who are socially embedded. In the process of proposing a conception of ignorance, I consider studies on ignorance and related phenomena, for example, in psychology and medicine, as well as ignorance as a phenomenon manifested in reality and experiences of ignorance.

In addressing the question of how one should rationally deal with ignorance in Part 2, I have found it fruitful to dig into *historical answers* to the question – and, despite initial appearances, there are a number of implicit and explicit suggestions for rationally dealing with ignorance. We can learn from this history. I have focused on answers by Aristotle, Plato/Socrates, William Clifford, John Locke, William James and Immanuel Kant. But the list of authors who have also put forward implicit or explicit proposals for the second question is much longer and includes René Descartes, Baruch Spinoza, St Augustine, Nicholas of Cusa, Francis Bacon, Friedrich Nietzsche. I hope that in reading this introduction and Part 2 of the study that develops my answer to the "how to deal with ignorance" question, it becomes clear how the authors that I have chosen come together to pave the way to an appropriate answer for rationally dealing with ignorance. – In my work I have not come across any suggestions regarding ignorance by *historical* female philosophers; I am sure that I am just currently ignorant about relevant works by *historical* female philosophers and hope to be informed by more knowledgeable readers. Recent years and advances in feminist philosophy and critical race theory have seen many new significant philosophical contributions on ignorance by women, for example, Lorraine Code (2004, 2014a, 2014b), Linda Alcoff (2007), Cynthia Townley (2011), Gaile Pohlhaus (2012), Katja Vogt (Haas and Vogt 2015), Elinor Mason (2015), and so this is not an all-male study.[14]

My study may also be grouped with what is called *non-ideal epistemology* (cf. McKenna 2023). Non-ideal epistemology is a form of *non-ideal theory*, and the term *non-ideal theory* is mainly used in political philosophy (cf. Valentini 2012, Mills 2017). But *non-ideal theory* also applies to a certain kind of epistemology, epistemology that engages with human beings as non-ideal, fallible rational agents. A text on ignorance – in virtue of its topic – is an instance of non-ideal epistemology because it addresses a non-ideal aspect of human beings. But my text is also a case of non-ideal theory because I acknowledge that human beings are fallible and not rational but often irrational. And, most importantly, I do not ignore the effects of injustice on ignorance from this study; that is another way of using a non-ideal approach (El Kassar fthc). I adopt Quassim Cassam's justification of vice epistemology for my study of ignorance, too: Cassam points out that "a failure to engage with the intellectual vices by which our cognitive lives are blighted represents a failure to engage with the human epistemological predicament" (Cassam 2016, 176). Instead philosophy should address the "day-to-day cognitive lives of most members of the species homo sapiens" (Cassam 2016, 159).

I have found that my approach to ignorance is somewhat similar to what Kathryn Norlock (2019) calls non-ideal pessimism, the view that there will never be ultimate improvement in the actions and behavior of human beings; there is development, but no improvement. Yet, this does not mean that we have to give up doing anything about (epistemic) evil and all the bad things in the world, it just means that one must not think that things are going to get better or be solved at some point in time or by just one measure. In the end, I do not want to call my position pessimist, as does Norlock, I suggest calling it *reflective optimism* in Part 2, but I agree with her on the significance of taking a non-ideal, realist approach.

1.5 "Ignorance" in the History of Philosophy

Etymologically and historically, it would seem that philosophy and philosophers are much concerned with and about ignorance. The etymology of philosophy – *philos* and *sophia*, lover of wisdom – and the fact that, due to Socrates, wisdom has been closely connected to recognizing one's own ignorance might lead one to expect that ignorance is a central topic in philosophy. But this is not the case. Ignorance has been and continues to be a somewhat neglected topic in epistemology and philosophy. In this section, I want to give a brief, necessarily incomplete overview of the history of ignorance in philosophy. For another, complementary history of ignorance in philosophy, see Peels (2023).

Socrates surmises that he is the wisest of all people – Pythia had said so – because he is aware of his cognitive limitations, because he knows that he does not know. And philosophers traditionally aim at being wise – or at least they are said to do so – so they would have to engage with their own ignorance. Socrates does engage with ignorance – his own and other people's ignorance –, for example, in *Philebus* he introduces the following distinction of three forms of ignorance:

> Now, ignorance is a vice, and so is what we call stupidity ... Are there not necessarily three ways in which it is possible not to know oneself? ... The first way concerns money, if someone thinks himself richer than in fact he is. ... Even more consider themselves taller and handsomer than in fact they are, and believe that they have other such physical advantages. ... But an overwhelming number are mistaken about the third kind, which belongs to the soul, namely virtue, and believe that they are superior in virtue, although they are not. ... And again, among virtues, is it not especially to wisdom that the largest number of people lay claim, puffing themselves up with quarrels and pretensions to would-be knowledge?
>
> (Plato, *Philebus*, 1993, 48d–49a)

But such inquiries into forms of ignorance are rare in classic texts. One may also interpret the Socratic method as a way of dealing with people's (interlocutors') ignorance, for example, as in Socrates' dialogue about geometry with the slave in *Meno* (Plato 2010, 82b–86b). But the dialogues mostly address ignorance only in passing (cf. Vogt 2015, ch. 1).

Stephan Meier-Oeser in his entry on ignorance in *Historisches Wörterbuch der Philosophie* (2001) notes that the term for a long time was used without any conceptual specifications. Rather, ignorance is mainly discussed in connection with the will, blame and culpability, for example, in Aristotle's *Nicomachean Ethics*, book 3. With the advent and rise of Christianity the scope of inquiries into *ignorance* changed significantly: it became narrower. Mainly, ignorance was discussed in connection with human inability to know that God exists. And ignorance was introduced as a result of the original sin committed by Adam and Eve by eating from the Tree of Knowledge.[15] Adam and Eve were expelled from paradise and their descendants, that is, all human beings were also punished by being ignorant. In particular, they are ignorant by believing that something that is false is right. Ignorance, thus, is a punishment for the original sin. I cannot adequately address the relation to ignorance as inherited by original sin in this context. Let me just point out that the snake promises that by eating from the Tree of Knowledge, Adam and Eve will be able to recognize good and evil, which is a particular form of knowledge. And indeed, they do acquire moral knowledge, and not just factual knowledge.[16]

St Augustine is explicit about the causal connection between the original sin and ignorance und describes it as the most just punishment, for example, in his *On Free Choice of the Will* (1993):

> And it is no wonder that because of our ignorance we lack the free choice of the will to choose to act rightly, or that even when we do see what is right and will to do it, we cannot do it because of the resistance of carnal habit, which develops almost naturally because of the unruliness of our mortal inheritance. It is indeed the most just penalty for sin that we should lose what we were unwilling to use well, since we could have used it well without the slightest difficulty if only we had willed to do so; thus we who knew what was right but did not do it lost the knowledge of what is right, and we who had the power but not the will to act rightly lost the power even when we have the will.
>
> Indeed, all sinful souls have been afflicted with these two punishments: ignorance and difficulty. Because of ignorance, error warps our actions; because of difficulty, our lives are a torment and an affliction. But to accept falsehoods as truths, thus erring unwillingly; to struggle against the pain of carnal bondage and not be able to refrain from acts of inordinate desire: these do not belong to the nature that human beings were created with; they are the penalty of a condemned prisoner.
>
> (St Augustine 1993, III, §52)

Thomas Aquinas distinguishes invincible ignorance – ignorance of that which cannot be known – from vincible ignorance – ignorance of that which can be known. Only the latter is a sin (Thomas Aquinas 1912–1936, I–II q76 a2).

The connections between religion and philosophy, knowledge and ignorance are also found in the history of curiosity. Hans Blumenberg admirably traces the history of curiosity as a virtue turned vice, then turned virtue (1985, part 3) and his study is a valuable complement of any study on knowledge and ignorance in philosophy and religion. One of Blumenberg's many fascinating observations concerns curiosity's ambiguous status in medieval philosophy. On the one hand, curiosity as wanting to know was a virtue on the Aristotelian framework. On the other hand, St Augustine grouped curiosity with vices. This dilemma has shaped much of medieval discourse on knowledge and epistemology. Nicholas of Cusa's *De docta ignorantia* (1440/1994) can also be read as an attempt to grapple with the two forces by combining the human natural desire to know and the humility of human finiteness (Blumenberg 1985, 354ff.).

Cusa emphasizes how God is infinite and, therefore, finite human beings cannot grasp his existence, but their attempts at getting at the depths of God's existence lead to *learned ignorance* (1440/1994). Some one hundred years later, Sebastian Castellio like Cusa, outlines how ignorance can be acceptable. Sebastian Castellio (1563/2015) carves out a space for doubt and ignorance and he argues that we only have to know what is required for knowledge of God (*Gotteserkenntnis*) and for fulfilling one's duties as a human being (Castellio 1563/2015, 90). He submits that such an attitude leads to religious tolerance.

In the Arabic philosophical tradition, Al Fārābī also discusses the import and significance of ignorance. Al Fārābī distinguishes different forms of ignorance and combines the perspectives on the subject and the object of ignorance. For example, "[i]gnorance about a thing is of two kinds: one of them is ignorance that is noticed as such, and the other is ignorance believed to be knowledge" (Al Fārābī 1986, 79, 14; Al Fārābī et al. 2002, 619). You will see later (Chapter 4) that this distinction is also found in contemporary taxonomies of ignorance, for example, in Jens Haas and Katja Vogt's distinction between preferred ignorance and presumed knowledge (Haas and Vogt 2015). Other distinctions of ignorance in Al Fārābī's work, such as the distinction between "ignorance as absence" (Al Fārābī 1986, 90, 18), "ignorance as negation" (Al Fārābī 1986, 90, 22) and "ignorance as a state" (Al Fārābī 1986, 79, 14) are most probably related to Aristotle's distinction between ignorance as privation and ignorance as error.[17]

Al Fārābī's remarks about ignorance are not limited to epistemological consideration. Ignorance also figures prominently as a trait of an imperfect state: there are immoral, ignorant and errant states, in contrast to the virtuous state. The citizens of the ignorant city "do not know what virtue is" (Booth 2017, 188). Immoral cities know the virtues but do not follow them and errant cities have the false virtues (Al Fārābī 1998, Al Fārābī 2009).[18]

Another crucial discussion of error in the Arabic philosophical tradition is Al-Ghazālī's *The Rescuer from Error*. In this text, Al-Ghazālī relates how he overcame an intellectual crisis in which he doubted all belief. He explains how God's revelation of truths and mystic insight are crucial for knowing God and regaining certainty (Al-Ghazālī 2005, Khalidi 2005).

Many centuries later, René Descartes, Baruch Spinoza and John Locke, too, discuss God's role in human ignorance and error. For Spinoza and Descartes, errors and false beliefs become a problem in their theories because of God's close connection to human beings. Descartes needs to explain how and why human beings have false belief because it is not possible that God has equipped human beings with faulty capacities nor that he would deceive his creations, human beings. The solution for Descartes lies in the will of human beings: the will is infinite and it judges even when it is not able to judge. It oversteps its boundaries, so to say (Descartes 2017, Fourth Meditation). For Spinoza, the problem of errors is particularly tricky and interesting: since our mind is part of God's intellect, having false beliefs would imply that God also has false beliefs, but this cannot be right. So, Spinoza must explain how human beings can have come to have false beliefs. According to Thomas Cook's reconstruction, the solution is that the human mind is not identical to God's intellect but lacks important components of God's intellect and that is how human beings are cognitively limited and commit errors and God does not (Cook 2007, 69–77).

Locke focuses on God having equipped human beings with the rational capacities required to avoid error. Thus, strictly speaking, any error is a sin against God and one has failed to meet a moral obligation toward God. I return to Locke's account in Part 2 to discuss it as a proposal for how one should rationally deal with ignorance.

In the Enlightenment, ignorance has a more prominent role since it is what Meier-Oeser (2001) calls a *contrasting concept* for the Enlightenment program. Human beings are supposed to strive for knowledge, and ignorance appears to hinder this development. *Stupidity (Dummheit)* is a related obstacle (cf. e.g., van Treeck 2015). I discuss Kant's approach toward ignorance and error in Parts 1 and 2.[19]

This brief history of ignorance would not be complete without James Ferrier. Ferrier's 1854 book *Theory of Knowing and Being* is an exception in most of the history of philosophy because he is one of the few authors who explicitly examine ignorance. In addition to epistemology, he studies what he calls *Agnoiology*, theory of ignorance since, as he argues, we cannot engage in ontology without understanding the nature of ignorance as well as the nature of knowledge. Ferrier defines ignorance as "deprivation of knowledge"; ignorance "is an intellectual defect, imperfection, privation, or shortcoming" (Ferrier 1854, 397).[20]

Ferrier's neologism leads to another field in which ignorance has since (and more recently) become central, so-called "agnotology", a term deliberately invented to capture studies of how ignorance is manufactured and maintained (Proctor 2008). Agnotology studies cases of manufactured ignorance, such as the ignorance about the harmful health effects of smoking that was manufactured by tobacco companies The companies created journals that were intended to plant doubts about scientific findings about the effects of smoking and employed further tools for obfuscating relevant scientific results (Proctor 2008, 11–18). Works in agnotology are mainly located in *history of science*, maybe because most of the scholars who use the term and work in this field are historians of science (cf. Proctor and Schiebinger 2008). Some scholars try to relegate work on ignorance from epistemology to agnotology, but as I will argue in the next section, ignorance does belong with epistemology and not with agnotology.

Friedrich Nietzsche is another author who has discussed and examined ignorance, its nature and its value. And readers who are familiar with Nietzsche's work will probably wonder why Nietzsche does not take a more prominent role in this study. Nietzsche aims to rehabilitate ignorance by asking how it is that human beings aim for truth. Why do we aim for truth? After all, sometimes it is better not to know the truth but to be ignorant about it.

> The will to truth that still seduces us into taking so many risks, this famous truthfulness that all philosophers so far have talked about with veneration: what questions this will to truth has already laid before us! What strange, terrible, questionable questions! ... What in us really wills the truth? In fact, we paused for a long time before the question of the cause of this will – until we finally came to a complete standstill in front of an even more fundamental question. We asked about the value of this will. Granted, we will truth: why not untruth instead? And uncertainty? Even ignorance?
> (Nietzsche 2002, 5)

Truth is not the only value that matters, according to Nietzsche. That is how ignorance enters the picture and is recognized as a condition of human life in general.

> We do not consider the falsity of a judgment as itself an objection to a judgment; ... The question is how far the judgment promotes and preserves life, how well it preserves, and perhaps even cultivates, the type. And we are fundamentally inclined to claim that the falsest judgments (which include synthetic judgments a priori) are the most indispensable to us, and that without accepting the fictions of logic, without measuring reality against the wholly invented world of the unconditioned and self-identical, without a constant falsification of the world through numbers, people could not live – that a renunciation of false judgments would be a renunciation of life, a negation of life. To acknowledge untruth as a condition of life: this clearly means resisting the usual value feelings in a dangerous manner; and a philosophy that risks such a thing would by that gesture alone place itself beyond good and evil.
> (Nietzsche 2002, 7)

18 Introduction

I agree with Nietzsche's observation that there are cases in which ignorance is better than knowledge and also that ignorance is an ineliminable limitation of human life. But the context of his observations does not fit with my general approach. Nietzsche argues against Socratic and Platonic faith in reason (cf. Geisenhanslüke 2011, 150), and, as you will see, all of the authors and theories on which I rely value reason highly. And I myself have put *rationally* dealing with ignorance in my formulation of the second lead question. I am interested in finding a way for *rationally* dealing with ignorance. My favored answer goes via reason and rational capacities; it is a rational answer. This disagreement is why I have not included Nietzsche's work on ignorance in this study. He disagrees with a number of background assumptions of my study and authors that I refer to, and bringing the different views together would require tilting my picture and translating between the opposing views. In addition, I am not sure whether Nietzsche would be happy about being brought together with views that he probably takes to be (hyper-)rationalistic. And I cannot include a view that, on some interpretations at least, is anti-rationalistic.

In the 1970s Peter Unger has reminded philosophers of the connection between skepticism and ignorance. He argues that skepticism is right and that "no one ever *knows* anything about anything" (1975, 1, emphasis in original). But this take on ignorance has hardly caught ground. Vogt considers whether skepticism is a way of dealing with the possibility of ignorance (2015), but she does so for classic texts. Other contemporary works on skepticism seldom discuss ignorance.

The last two or three decades have seen increasing interest in other aspects of ignorance. Feminist epistemology has uncovered two facets of ignorance that have always been implicit but seldom discussed explicitly: ignorance as social and political. Ignorance is a feature of unjust oppressive societies – maintaining ignorance about the lives of the oppressed, ignoring testimony by minorities, manufacturing ignorance or also keeping the oppressed out of educational contexts (e.g., Bailey 2007, Dotson 2011, Medina 2013, Mills 2007, Mills 2015, Pohlhaus 2012). Philosophers addressing ignorance as political often also include decolonial and postcolonial theories and studies from history of science and agnotology in their work because these theories share central background beliefs and topics, for example, the intersection between ignorance and power (Tuana 2006, 3).

At approximately the same time, but arguing quite differently, authors rooted in traditional analytical epistemology have begun discussing the nature of ignorance, for example, Rik Peels and Pierre Le Morvan in a number of articles addressing the question "What is ignorance?" (Peels 2010, 2011, 2012, Le Morvan 2011b, 2012, 2013). Peels argues that what he and Le Morvan call the "Standard View of Ignorance" – the view that ignorance is lack of knowledge – is false and must be replaced by the "New View of Ignorance" – the view that ignorance is lack of true belief. The view that ignorance is lack of knowledge is largely taken to be the default conception of ignorance (e.g., Le Morvan 2011a; Zimmerman 2008). One of the aims of my book is to challenge this perception and to argue for a different approach to ignorance (that's the task of Part 1 in particular). Duncan Pritchard (2021) and Anne Meylan (2024) have advanced Normative Views of ignorance that include (normative) expectations in the conception of ignorance, for example, one is only ignorant if one lacks awareness of a fact that one ought to know (Pritchard 2021b). Peels argues for the New View of Ignorance in a recent monograph on ignorance (2023). Since these are the most prevalent views in today's analytical epistemology, I will discuss them in more detail and contrast my proposed conception with these views.[21]

Moral philosophy and political philosophy have also seen increasingly more discussions of ignorance, for example, discussions of culpable ignorance (Rosen 2004, Harman 2011, Zimmerman 1997, 2008, Mason 2015, 2017). But, as I have noted, I will not discuss moral ignorance further in this study.

The feminist, critical race approach and the "traditional" approach to ignorance – ignorance as mere lack of true belief or mere lack of knowledge – are rarely in communication with one another (cf. El Kassar 2018). My study aims to bring the approaches into dialogue and to develop a conception that respects the insights from different philosophical approaches. Only such an integrative approach can do justice to the real-world phenomenon ignorance in our times.

1.6 Does the Study of Ignorance Belong in Epistemology?

I have alluded to philosophers who are skeptical about the value of studying ignorance and in this section, I want to address and disarm concerns about studying ignorance in the context of epistemology.[22] By looking at such criticism and worries we learn more about the scope, place and significance of the topic.

In general, I have found that there are four clusters of criticism of epistemology of ignorance:

1 Ignorance is not an interesting topic for philosophers.
2 Epistemological studies of ignorance are a *contradictio in terminis*.
3 Ignorance does not belong to epistemology but to other philosophical fields.
4 Ignorance has its own discipline, it belongs with agnotology.

20 Introduction

Let me elaborate on the criticism in turns. The first objection is rather common in philosophy and in epistemology. The basic idea is that ignorance is not an interesting topic for philosophers because all there is to say about ignorance is that ignorance is the privation of knowledge. In addition, knowledge is much more striking than ignorance so one should study knowledge instead of ignorance. Take, for example, the following reasoning from a summary article by Le Morvan and Peels on the dispute between the Standard View and the New View:

> Taking ignorance to be the complement of knowledge unifies theorizing about ignorance with theorizing about knowledge in that it seems that insights into the nature of knowledge automatically yield corresponding putative insights into the nature of ignorance. This is because, on the Standard View [i.e., the view that ignorance is lack of knowledge, N.E.], ignorance has no substantive and positive nature of its own. Being purely privative and negational, its nature is completely determined by its contrast with the nature of knowledge. So conceived, the relationship between ignorance and knowledge proves analogous to the relationship between darkness and light inasmuch as darkness is the absence or want of light.
>
> (Le Morvan and Peels 2016, 16–17)

Clearly, this argument is a *non sequitur*. Just because ignorance can be described as the privation of knowledge does not mean that it does not merit independent study. Second, there is more to ignorance than an account of its nature. Third, one may reject the Standard View of Ignorance (as I do). Fourth, the nature of ignorance is not fully determined by its negational character, just as the nature of darkness is not fully determined by its negational relation to light. For example, fear in the dark is more than fear of absence of light.

The second objection argues that there can be no *epistemological* studies of ignorance – it is a *contradictio in terminis* – because epistemology is the study of knowledge and as such it does not include ignorance. Clearly, this argument is also not convincing. I have noted earlier how James Ferrier argues that there can be no ontology if one does not study knowledge *and* ignorance. In addition, epistemology is not restricted to the study of knowledge, it is concerned with the epistemic situation of agents. And clearly, ignorance (co-)determines the epistemic situation of all human agents.

The third objection tries to move ignorance to other disciplines in philosophy, for example, moral philosophy, logic, philosophy of science, feminist philosophy and critical race theory. Ignorance does not really belong in epistemology because it is much more prevalent in these other fields. But there is no adequate argument for any such maneuver: epistemologists

Introduction 21

need to engage with ignorance to understand knowledge, to disentangle human epistemic life, to uncover epistemic norms, etc. Epistemological studies of ignorance are even *necessary* in epistemology because it can fill gaps in epistemology. For example, as we will see, epistemological studies of ignorance can examine the standard twin goals "Strive for truth and avoid falsehood" that epistemologists rely on but fail to examine and relate adequately (Section 8.1). Epistemological studies of ignorance can help epistemology cover omissions and lack of belief, a perceived lack in epistemology since theories of justification only work for beliefs and not for omissions or lack (cf. Riggs 2003). They can also extend epistemology to cover epistemic vices, as does vice epistemology (Cassam 2016).

In addition, the other disciplines like moral philosophy and feminist philosophy focus on selected aspects of ignorance, for example, feminist epistemologies of ignorance focus on ignorance as detrimental, impacting the life of the oppressed, and thus narrow the field of study (e.g., Alcoff 2007, Dotson 2011, Medina 2013). In contrast, socio-epistemological studies of ignorance address fundamental issues about ignorance (e.g., nature, normativity, value) and can regard ignorance as *not* intrinsically negative. In a way, one may say, epistemological studies of ignorance do the groundwork for the other disciplines in philosophy. And, of course, the fields can cooperate to improve their accounts involving ignorance. In fact, they *need* to cooperate, as I will show in Part 1 in my study of what ignorance is.

The fourth objection argues that the study of ignorance belongs with agnotology – the "study of conscious, unconscious, and structural production of ignorance, its diverse causes and conformations, whether brought about by neglect, forgetfulness, myopia, extinction, secrecy, or suppression" (Proctor 2008, 3). This is the natural home of studies of ignorance – as the neologism crafted by Proctor indicates. But this objection overlooks an important detail: Proctor is a historian of science, and agnotology uses the tools of historians, not so much the tools of philosophy, that is, agnotologists study historical sources, they mainly work descriptively, working out a narrative of what happened. In contrast, epistemological studies of ignorance are interested in people's access to the world, their epistemic situation, epistemic agency, and they work normatively, they ask normative questions. Note that this does not mean that historical texts are excluded from my study, in fact, as I have said earlier, I also rely on historical philosophical texts to develop an answer to the question of how one should rationally deal with ignorance. But I do so from a philosopher's perspective and not a historian's perspective.[23]

These objections are crucial and consequential because they are ultimately questions about the legitimacy of epistemological studies of ignorance, questions about who defines what epistemology is. And I insist that ignorance must not be excluded from this prestigious field of philosophy.

1.7 Build-Up

My study has three parts: Part 1 develops a revisionist-analytic answer to the question of what ignorance is. Part 2 is a normative study of how one should rationally deal with ignorance. Part 3 applies the Integrated Conception of Ignorance and the maxim-based approach to rationally dealing with ignorance to politics and medicine.

Part 1 explicates the concept *ignorance* and fills a gap in epistemology by improving on the scarce explorations of ignorance in philosophy. I distinguish logical and empirical conceptions of ignorance. Then I discuss different conceptions of ignorance (Standard View, New View, Normative View). On that basis, I develop a more complex conception of ignorance that captures both its epistemological meaning and relevance, as well as its real-world manifestations (*pace*, for example, Goldman and Olsson 2009, Peels 2010, Le Morvan 2011b). On the new conception, the Integrated Conception of Ignorance, ignorance consists in doxastic components, agential components and structural components.

I use the structure of a medical encyclopedia entry for a syndrome to get at the different layers of ignorance: What is ignorance? How widespread is ignorance? What are symptoms of ignorance? How do ignorant beings live? What are causes of ignorance? This extraordinary heuristic allows me to go beyond the merely doxastic level of ignorance, and include, for example, the phenomenology of ignorance. In addition, it delivers insights about ignorance that are particularly helpful for answering the second question, how we should rationally deal with ignorance. Note that the syndrome-heuristic does not imply that all ignorance is bad. One might be tempted to draw that inference since a medical syndrome qua disease seems to be bad; but this inference is not warranted because a syndrome is a category, not an evaluative judgment.[24]

On the basis of the Integrated Conception, Part 2 discusses what the most sensible ways for dealing with ignorance – in particular, one's own ignorance – are. I start by examining the oft-cited claim that ignorance should be turned into knowledge by discussing the consequences of Aristotle's *Metaphysics* claim that "all human beings desire to know" and asking whether Socratic ignorance is the best way for dealing with ignorance. I dismiss these virtue-theoretic answers because they are imprecise and not adequate for human epistemic practice. After that, I discuss consequentialist answers that suggest looking at results to find the best way for rationally dealing with ignorance; the Jamesian twin goals, "Strive for truth, avoid falsehood", are the primary example of that approach.

Then I discuss deontological answers to how one should rationally deal with ignorance: Clifford's duty to mankind; Locke's view that human beings have an alethic obligation toward God (Locke 1979, Wolterstorff 1996) and the view that there is a duty to know – developed on the basis of Goldberg's notion of practice-generated entitlements (Goldberg 2017b). None of the proposals provides adequate principles for dealing with ignorance.

Finally, I show that Kant's advice as to how one can avoid error in the *Jäsche Logic* (JL, AA IX)[25] and parallel passages on the *sensus communis* in *The Critique of the Power of Judgment* (CPJ, AA V) and *Anthropology from a pragmatic point of view* (Anth, AA VII) is the best suggestion for epistemic agents for rationally dealing with ignorance. The three maxims are "1. To think for oneself. [The enlightened mode of thought] 2. To think oneself (in communication with human beings) into the place of every other person. [The extended mode of thought] 3. Always to think consistently with oneself. [The consequent mode of thought]" (Kant, JL, AA IX 57, my additions in brackets). I develop the Maxim-based Answer from these maxims and from Ernst Tugendhat's remarks on intellectual honesty. By discussing three objections – the Pessimist Objection, the Objection from Those Who Just Do Not Care and the Objection from Overdemandingness, from Arrogant Elitism and from Intellectualization, a cluster of related objections – I further explicate the proposal and make explicit its background assumptions as well as its advantages.

In Part 3, I apply these insights to two real-world issues related to ignorance: democracy and ignorance (politics) and medical uncertainty (medicine). My Integrated Conception which recognizes that ignorance consists in doxastic, agential and structural components shows that ignorance is not a threat to democracy but rather a natural feature of democracy. In medical epistemology, my new conception overcomes the ambiguities between the terms *ignorance* and *uncertainty* and the overly detailed taxonomies in current medical literature. My suggestion for rationally dealing with ignorance also proves helpful for dealing with ignorance and uncertainty in clinical medicine and in patient–practitioner interaction.

In addressing ignorance as well as asking how one should rationally deal with ignorance, I contribute to epistemological studies of ignorance. First, I study ignorance from the perspective of epistemic agents, by considering our dealings with ignorance. Second, I bring together historical insights about ignorance that are often overlooked and contemporary works. Third, I develop a new way of conceptualizing ignorance, taking both epistemological and political considerations into account, aspects which traditionally have been kept separate. By discussing them together, I show that practical considerations feed into epistemology and epistemological considerations feed back into practical approaches.

1.8 Reading Suggestions

Since this is a monograph and we have grown less accustomed to reading whole books and are sometimes interested in just one question or issue in the book, I would like to offer a few reading suggestions for readers. If one is interested in the debate about the nature of ignorance and my criticism of current, analytic approaches to ignorance, one can focus on Part 1. Discussing the facets of ignorance, different instantiations of ignorance, causes of ignorance is crucial for my claim that ignorance is not just cognitive or propositional. The Integrated Conception of Ignorance is developed in Sections 3.5 and 3.6.

If one is interested in seeing what a historically informed, socio-epistemological take on dealing with one's own ignorance looks like, one can skip Part 1 (maybe read Section 3.5 for the Integrated Conception) and start with Part 2. Also, if one is interested in how different epistemological approaches play out with regard to ignorance, Part 2 is the place to go.

And if one is most interested in real-life ignorance and suggestions for dealing with it, one may also start with Part 3 in which I apply the Maxim-based Answer to ignorance in democracies and in medical contexts. For readers who want to get suggestions for further applications, it might be also more useful to start with the application and then look at the theoretical details of the Maxim-based Answer in Chapter 10.

Notes

1 Being stupid or pretending to be stupid may be a constitutive feature of being – playing the fool – and that may be why fools are the only characters who can get away with being stupid. See Van Treeck (2015, 17–22) on the complicated character of the fool (*Narr*) and Geisenhanslüke (2011) on the relation between stupidity, wit and literature.

2 Authors from other disciplines have started to connect innocence and ignorance. For example, Gloria Wekker introduces the term *white innocence* to capture how Dutch society presents itself as color-blind, non-discriminatory but is permeated by xenophobic and racist beliefs, structures and traditions. In developing the notion of innocence, she explicitly connects innocence and ignorance: "The claim of innocence, however, is a double-edged sword: it contains not-knowing, but also not wanting to know, capturing what philosopher Charles W. Mills (1997, 2007) has described as the epistemology of ignorance. ... Essed and Hoving also point to 'the anxious Dutch *claim of innocence* and how disavowal and denial of racism may merge into what we have called *smug ignorance*: (aggressively) rejecting the possibility to know.' (2014, 24)" (Wekker 2016, 17–18, reference adapted, N.E.). Amélie Rives'

spirited criticism of innocence and ignorance as values in the education of girls in the late 19th century provides an interesting insight into the role of ignorance in education (1892). Rives' remarks invite us to consider how these educational values have developed in later and contemporary education.
3 Cf. the entry "un-" in *Digitales Wörterbuch der deutschen Sprache*.
4 Since I argue that ignorance is not just lack of knowledge or lack of true belief, I mostly use the term "being ignorant" rather than "not knowing" to describe the state the subject is in and which I want to examine. "Not knowing" may include implicit assumptions about knowledge being primary for understanding ignorance and so I've tried using it only when it is really appropriate. "Being ignorant" is related to "not knowing," but they are not the same.
5 See also David A. Graham (2014) for a political-historical contextualization of Rumsfeld's statement.
6 See the Belgian movie *Le tout nouveau Testament* (2015) for a fictional rendition of how people would react to learning of their death date and hour.
7 But see also Kourany and Carrier (2019) for the challenges to knowledge production in the sciences.
8 Thanks to Nemiah Ladd for providing this example.
9 For further examples of errors in science, see e.g., Kricheldorf (2016).
10 See Kennedy (2019) for a discussion about the reaction to this mistake.
11 Bondy (2018) has suggested that one could extend my Integrated Conception of Ignorance to cover practical ignorance, but I do not think that there is an easy route from remarks about propositional ignorance to practical ignorance in the sense of lack of know-how. We need to respect the highly evolved debate about know-how (e.g., in Löwenstein 2017) and include their concerns and arguments in any account that wants to address the lack of know-how or lack of practical knowledge. Any further conclusions require communication between the different fields and debates. Peels (2023, 37, 41) lists practical ignorance as one kind of ignorance – with objectual and propositional ignorance as the other kinds.
12 For an exemplary article in such revisionary epistemology, see Haslanger (1999).
13 Thanks to Lutz Wingert for highlighting this approach.
14 There are also historical non-White suggestions on ignorance and how to deal with ignorance, but I have not included them in this study. There is no denying that this is a gap in this study. And it would be arrogant to try to patch up this gap by adding a footnote or paragraph about the literature that is missing from this study. This literature should be included appropriately and not in passing. So I leave any further remarks for another occasion.
15 It is almost ironic that ignorance is the punishment for the act of eating from the Tree of Knowledge.
16 John Milton's *Paradise Lost* considers the ramifications and the context of the original sin committed in paradise in a literary form, for example, by having the devil ask himself why knowledge, the Tree of Knowledge, is forbidden for human beings (Milton 1667/2003, book IV, 505ff.). Thanks to Christian Weibel for indicating this reference.

17 Unfortunately, the relevant passages in Al Fārābī's *Book of Demonstration* are not translated into English. Therefore, I only refer to Alon's entries (2002). See Alon (2002) for more entries on ignorance in the Fārābī-lexicon. And see Hodges and Druart (2019) for an introduction into Al Fārābī's *Philosophy of Logic and Language*.
18 Al Fārābī in his political works argues that the democratic state is the happiest state.
19 See Adler and Godel (2010) for a collection of articles on ignorance in the Enlightenment age, and Bates (1996) for an interesting contribution on error in late Enlightenment France.
20 See Keefe (2007) for a discussion of Ferrier's work.
21 See Silva and Siscoe (2024) for a recent and – I daresay – quite typical example of a contemporary epistemological analysis of ignorance that focuses on the "Standard View" and "New View" and only refers to social and political contexts and implications in a footnote.
22 I avoid using the term "epistemology of ignorance" for my approach because Mills, Alcoff and others use the term for describing pernicious ignorance, epistemologies that employ ignorance in oppression and for maintaining unjust states. My study is not restricted on that kind of ignorance, and so I talk about "epistemological studies of ignorance" and keep "epistemologies of ignorance" for its intended meaning.
23 So, I do not argue that epistemological studies of ignorance must include agnotology. Peels (2023) seems to read my argument in El Kassar (2018) as making that claim. But I do not undertake a study in agnotology; this is epistemology.
24 Thanks to an anonymous reviewer for encouraging me to add this clarification.
25 I follow abbreviations used by the Kant-Forschungsstelle to refer to Kant's work. The *Jäsche Logic* is one exception because it is not included individually in their list; therefore, I use the abbreviation "JL" to refer to it. I refer to the *Akademie Ausgabe* numbering to give page numbers.

Part 1
What Is Ignorance?

2 The Framework I

2.1 A Fundamental Distinction: Logical Conceptions and Empirical Conceptions

In attempting to develop an appropriate conception of ignorance, I propose to start by distinguishing two approaches that address two importantly different kinds of ignorance:

1 The logical conception: ignorance as a concept used in logic.
2 The empirical conception: ignorance as manifested in the real world in the cognition and psychology of real, non-ideal epistemic subjects.

I will often refer to the latter kind of ignorance as *real-world manifestations of ignorance*. Such cases of ignorance are not idealized, not pure, but closer to the messy realities of the epistemic lives of subjects.

This distinction is quite rare in philosophy of ignorance.[1] In fact, to my knowledge, Olsson and Proietti (2016) are the only authors who suggest a similar distinction. They distinguish a formal approach to ignorance and a "descriptive or psychological one" (Olsson and Proietti 2016, 84). What they call a *formal approach* is what I call a *logical approach* or the *logical conception*. Such a formal approach "list[s] the properties of the concept in question (e.g., knowledge and belief) with respect to its content and to its interaction with other concepts (e.g., Boolean operators such as 'and,' 'or,' 'not')" (Olsson and Prioietti 2016, 84).

Epistemologists frequently overlook that ignorance is also discussed in logic, both as a topic in its own rights and in the context of discussions of vagueness (e.g., Williamson 1996, Dorr 2003). This section introduces some examples for logical work on ignorance. It will be a somewhat brief section because there are basic issues surrounding these approaches to ignorance that I acknowledge but cannot solve nor deal with adequately: what is the impact of syntactic or semantic logic results concerning ignorance on epistemological works on ignorance? What is the relation between logic

30 What Is Ignorance?

and epistemology? Answering these questions is too big for this study. But I want to give an example of a logical conception of ignorance so that the distinction can be picked up. In addition, I will gesture toward reasons why logical or formal approaches to ignorance do not provide an adequate basis for addressing the question of how one should rationally deal with ignorance in the way that this study aims to address the question. – This is not necessarily a fault of logical approaches, they just ask very different questions from theories that include ignorance as the state of a thinker. As I have noted above, logical approaches "list the properties of the concept in question (e.g., knowledge and belief) with respect to its content and to its interaction with other concepts (e.g., Boolean operators such as 'and,' 'or,' 'not')" (Olsson and Prioietti 2016, 84). This approach is not as germane to the question of how one, an epistemic agent, should rationally deal with ignorance.

There are only a handful of philosophers working on theories of ignorance today who may be said to pursue the project of determining the logical conception of ignorance. Olsson and Proietti themselves are an exception to this gap, and they refer to a paper by Wiebe van der Hoek and Alessio Lomuscio (2004) which provides a purely formal analysis of ignorance.[2] I will only present and discuss Olsson and Proietti's semi-formal account of ignorance in this section because I won't be talking much about ignorance in the logical sense. Moreover, they do not aim at a formal account but a semi-formal account that may be closer to the approach taken in this book Kit Fine's analysis of "ignorance of ignorance" is another example of a logical study of ignorance (2018).

Olsson and Proietti aim to fill a large gap in the theory of ignorance: they want to develop a (semi-)formal account of ignorance. Their proposal is based on a technical paper by van der Hoek and Lomuscio (2004). Van der Hoek and Lomuscio restrict ignorance thus: being ignorant as to X is "not knowing that X and not knowing that not-X"[3] (Hoek and Lomuscio 2004, 98, in Olsson and Proietti 2016, 82). This definition excludes cases in which the subject does not know that X because she knows that not-X; clearly, she is not ignorant even though she does not know that X, therefore, we do not want a definition of ignorance that cannot exclude this case.

On this basis, Olsson and Proietti develop the following semi-formal account of ignorance. Ignorance involves an agent who does not know whether X or not-X and therefore has X and not-X in her "epistemic space" (Olsson and Proietti 2016, 91). Ignorance thus is defined as follows, where IX stands for "the agent is ignorant about X" (Olsson and Proietti 2016, 91):

$$IX = \text{def}\ (\neg K\ X) \wedge (\neg K\ \neg X)$$

From this definition it follows that ignorance is not simply the absence of knowledge. And as Olsson and Proietti put it: "being ignorant about X does not reduce to not knowing that X" (Olsson and Proietti 2016, 91). They present this finding as showing that "ignorance does not simply come out as absence of knowledge" (Olsson and Proietti 2016, 91). Theirs is a non-reductionist, semi-formal account of ignorance because it does not want to reduce ignorance to the absence of knowledge.

And even though I do agree with the general thrust of the claim, I want to note that Olsson and Proietti do not support this non-reductionist, semi-formal account adequately. They make the result sound more substantial than it is. It is tailored to refute those authors who say that ignorance is absence (or lack) of knowledge, but their refutation is based on some terminological inaccuracies and, thus, appears to be inflated. Olsson and Proietti do not distinguish knowing that X, knowing about X and being ignorant that X, being ignorant about X when these are crucially different kinds of knowing and being ignorant.[4]

With this example of a logical conception of ignorance in place, I turn to explicating the difference between the empirical conception and the logical conception more clearly. The conceptions ask different questions about ignorance and yield different answers to the question of what ignorance is. For example, the empirical conception examines such diverse instances of ignorance as scientists' ignorance about an as of yet undiscovered method for treating, say, Alzheimer's disease, HIV/AIDS, avian flu or someone not knowing that Ottawa is the capital of Canada. These particular instances of ignorance do not have to be obviously interesting and they may even be irrelevant to logical conceptions of ignorance because these conceptions care about the formal, the logical, and not so much about the empirical content and the manifestation side of ignorance.

If, on the other hand, one scrutinizes ignorance on an empirical conception, this implies that ignorance is manifested in the real world in human beings. These manifestations can be very diverse, as I have noted when introducing examples of ignorance. A scientist's ignorance about an as of yet undiscovered method for treating Alzheimer's disease but also the ignorance of someone who has not heard of *emoluments* before she hears that term for the first time, and after she has heard it but still doesn't know what it is. As we will see later, on an empirical conception of ignorance there is room for extending agential ignorance to processes that cause ignorance, and institutional structures that facilitate ignorance and may even be said to count as manifestations of ignorance (Section 3.5).

The distinction between a logical conception and an empirical conception is fairly novel in work on ignorance, but we can quickly see that it is productive. First, it helps us explain apparently incompatible claims about ignorance because we can see that they are based on a confusion about which conception of ignorance the author embraces. Look, for example, at the following two claims:

A Ignorance is derivative of knowledge, that is, knowledge is primary (e.g., Le Morvan and Peels 2016).
B Ignorance is prior to knowledge, for example, before the subject is knowledgeable she is ignorant, or before the physician learns of a new method in vascular bypass surgery she is ignorant of it (cf., e.g., Firestein 2012).

These claims seem to be incompatible: (A) says that knowledge is primary, and (B) says that ignorance is prior to knowledge. But with the distinction between ignorance on a logical conception and ignorance on an empirical conception we can see that the two claims concern two different kinds of ignorance: claim (A) is relevant for ignorance as used in logic, claim (B) is relevant for ignorance on an empirical conception.

Second, the distinction enables us to connect otherwise disparate work on ignorance within different philosophical fields and across different disciplines because we can thus be clearer on what the authors are talking about – the logical conception or the empirical conception – and how their separate claims complement each other – or do not. The distinction is thus key to further conceptualizing disputes about the nature of ignorance, recognizing that the authors working on ignorance may (and do) aim at different conceptions.

2.2 The Syndrome Framework

Let me say something about my framework for approaching *ignorance*. In spelling out the facets and characteristics of ignorance, I approach ignorance as one would approach a syndrome in medical studies. A syndrome is a disease that consists in several interrelated symptoms, for example, as in the metabolic syndrome, a cluster of symptoms that contribute to the likelihood of type 2 diabetes and cardiovascular diseases, or the Takotsubo syndrome, a temporary heart condition. The presence of the relevant symptoms indicates and confirms that the patient suffers from the syndrome. However, for many syndromes not all symptoms have to be present for the syndrome to be diagnosed in a patient. This feature is one of the central reasons for analyzing ignorance as a syndrome. As we have seen earlier in the examples of ignorance as an empirical concept, the features, characteristics and aspects of ignorance can be very different. For example, ignorance of which the subject is not aware and ignorance of which the subject is aware are very different as regards the self-reflexive awareness, but they are still both cases of ignorance. And talking about ignorance as a syndrome provides a framework for capturing and acknowledging these differences.

Let me emphasize that by using the syndrome framework, I do not pre-judge ignorance as intrinsically bad, disvaluable or even as a disease. Ignorance can be valuable, and it is one of the aims of this project to leave room for valuable ignorance and not restrict it to a bad (epistemic or moral) state. A syndrome is interesting for this study of ignorance because it is a phenomenon that has different symptoms that can be present but do not have to be conjointly present for the syndrome to obtain. And a syndrome is not an intrinsically bad or pernicious state. A syndrome is a special type of phenomenon, and it is special because of its relation to its symptoms. There is no simple relation of necessary and sufficient conditions between the symptoms and the syndrome and this kind of relation, I submit, also holds between ignorance and its constituents.[5]

We will see that the symptoms of ignorance are not restricted to lack of knowledge but concern the whole epistemic agent. Another advantage of this framework is that we can go beyond the so-called standard conception of ignorance as lack of knowledge and get at the *texture*, the details of ignorance. This is because by treating ignorance as a syndrome, the agent who is "affected" by ignorance comes into the center of attention. As I have noted in the Introduction, my aim is to examine ignorance as a state of subjects and not as an object. The study is of being ignorant rather than of the object of ignorance – *Unwissenheit* rather than *Unwissen* in German.

I do not follow the build-up of entries for syndromes in medical encyclopedia, but many of the areas covered in medical encyclopedia will also appear – adapted to the philosophical topic – in this discussion of ignorance. These entries cover the following issues:[6]

1 Definition. A general description of the topic of the entry.
2 Epidemiology. How widespread is the disease?
3 Symptoms. What are the symptoms of the disease?
4 Pathophysiology. How do human beings with the disease live?
5 Diagnosis. How does one diagnose and identify the disease?
6 Etiology. What are the causes of the disease?
7 Treatment. How can the disease be treated?

Obviously, there are limits to this heuristic for analyzing ignorance and I do not adhere to it without reflection. The most important limitations are that ignorance is *not* a medical condition and that ignorance is not something that must be treated. In this study, I am looking for ways of dealing with ignorance, but I am not looking for a *cure*. As we will see, ignorance is pervasive and necessarily present in human lives – in being human – so the idea of *curing* ignorance is nonsensical. Some ways of dealing with ignorance may be regarded as offering "treatments" – not a cure that eradicates ignorance and leads to some state of not-ignorance. But I do not want to overstretch the syndrome heuristic and the related metaphor: I am not looking for a treatment of ignorance. That means that the second question of how we should rationally deal with ignorance will be addressed outside of the syndrome framework.

Despite these limitations, this somewhat extraordinary frame has significant advantages. If I frame ignorance as a syndrome, it should be clearer that this study is about ignorance as a state of human beings, and not about ignorance as an object.[7] Second, since every encyclopedia entry has a definition, a first sentence that collects the most salient features of the topic of the entry, viz. ignorance, it provides a framework for pitting different conceptions of ignorance against each other as competitors for the definition. And third, by asking questions about the symptoms of ignorance, we can capture different facets of ignorance, for example, the structure of ignorance, different kinds of ignorance, causes of ignorance. In addition, by capturing ignorance in terms of a syndrome, the question of *dealing with ignorance* is always implicitly and sometimes explicitly present in Part 1 already and forms the basis for the different suggestions for rationally dealing with ignorance in Part 2.

Fourth, by using the framework, we get to further details of ignorance that are crucial in understanding ignorance and suggesting how one should deal with it. By detailing the epidemiology, the symptoms, the etiology, etc. of ignorance, I can assemble the components, features, measures and tools that we require for addressing the question of how we should deal with ignorance. We need to know what kinds of ignorance we are dealing with and what features we are dealing with, etc. and this is what we can get at by employing the medical encyclopedia framework and the syndrome framework. I have already gone through the anamnesis – in the medical sense –, by looking at examples of ignorance in the Introduction. Now let's turn to definitions of ignorance to get the right conception of ignorance in view. The aim of the following chapters in Part 1 is to provide an overview of (cognitive) conceptions of ignorance and to develop an appropriate conception of ignorance that will provide the basis for the question of how we should rationally deal with ignorance.

Notes

1 Outside of philosophy of ignorance, there are other examples of distinction between a logical and a psychological concept. For example, Andrew Chignell

in a paper on Kant's concept of justification makes a similar distinction between assent as a "psychological concept" and judgment as a "logical concept" in Kant's epistemology (2007, 35).
2 It might seem that the Standard View and the New View of ignorance also belong with reductionist logical approaches to ignorance. The Standard View reduces ignorance to a lack of knowledge – Le Morvan's view – and the New View reduces it to true belief – Peels' view. Both authors talk of offering *definitions* of ignorance (e.g., Peels 2010, 57, 59, Le Morvan 2011b, 335), and, second, both proposals look like descendants of Aristotle's privation account of knowledge. Especially the Standard View can be said to make very similar claims. See this passage about the implications of the Standard View noted above: "Insights into the nature of knowledge automatically yield corresponding putative insights into the nature of ignorance. ... Being purely privative and negational, its nature is completely determined by its contrast with the nature of knowledge" (Le Morvan and Peels 2016, 17). But the two views do not belong with logical approaches to ignorance since Peels and Le Morvan talk about "the nature of ignorance" (Le Morvan and Peels 2016, 12), about "what it *is* to be ignorant" (Le Morvan and Peels 2016, 12, emphasis in original), and this means that their theories belong with empirical conceptions of ignorance.
3 Hoek and Lomuscio use φ instead of X.
4 Further problems are in view for Olsson and Proietti with regard to their list of features of ignorance:

a Ignorance is a (cognitive) state, not a (cognitive) process (Olsson and Proietti 2016, 83).
b Ignorance does not come with an emotional or volitional component (Olsson and Proietti 2016, 84).
c Ignorance does not come in degrees because knowledge does not come in degrees (Olsson and Proietti 2016, 85).
d Ignorance is a passive attitude because it can be independent of the agent's knowledge of alternatives (Olsson and Proietti 2016, 92).

The first claim (a) about ignorance being a (cognitive) state is later reformulated by Olsson and Proietti as referring to a state understood as "a particular configuration of the epistemic space" (Olsson and Proietti 2016, 91) of an agent.

First, the features of ignorance are not developed formally, which is unfortunate even for a semi-formal account. Second, it is not clear where these features of ignorance come from and what the basis for these claims about ignorance is. They appear to be only stipulations.

Olsson and Proietti also do not offer sufficient arguments for (b) and (c); they just present them as obviously true when looked at in comparison with another attitude – doubt. Ignorance, unlike doubt, does not have an emotional or volitional component, and ignorance, unlike doubt, does not come in degrees. In the first case the strategy may work: their definition of ignorance does not include an emotional or volitional component, unlike doubt, which, according to Olsson and Proietti's construal, contains the agent having the issue in doubt on her "research agenda" (Olsson and Proietti 2016, 94).

But in the case of (c) where ignorance is said to not have degrees, there is not enough argument for that. The only argument they offer is that knowledge does not come in degrees either, but obviously, they cannot avail themselves of this argument because they take themselves to have shown that ignorance is not absence of knowledge. Why should the standards of knowledge apply for ignorance, if ignorance is not just absence of knowledge?

Note also that van der Hoek and Lomuscio, on whom Olsson and Proietti rely in their formal account, allow that there are degrees of ignorance and they consider that those degrees could be captured in a "spectrum of concepts," for example, A has no information at all, or A regards a fact to be "more likely to be true or false but still contemplates the possibility of the fact being false" (van der Hoek and Lomuscio 2004, 99–100). It is thus not clear why we should suppose that there are no degrees of ignorance, even on a semi-formal (logical) approach.

Since it is unclear how the four features are related to the semi-formal definition of ignorance as not knowing X and not knowing that not-X, the worries and objections against the features of ignorance given by Olsson and Proietti do not necessarily affect the definition of ignorance. But Olsson and Proietti's contribution to the formal approach to ignorance would seem to be, in effect, fairly uninformative, because the major insight is one they take from van der Hoek and Lomuscio. Let me emphasize that the rest of their paper does contain a novel and valuable discussion of how one should define doubt and the relation between doubt and ignorance, which I cannot address in this context. In this respect their contribution is innovative, but it is not sufficient as a semi-formal non-reductionist account of ignorance.

5 Thanks to an anonymous reviewer for inviting me to say more about the use of the term "syndrome" in this book.
6 The order may change and there may be more distinctions (e.g., more on biochemistry), but this doesn't matter for my study.
7 Cf. the German distinction between *Unwissen* (object) and *Unwissenheit* (state of ignorance).

3 Conceptions of Ignorance

This chapter is devoted to formulating a conception of ignorance that captures ignorance as a real-world phenomenon manifested in human beings as they are. I will frame this issue as the task of determining the first sentence for an entry for the syndrome *ignorance*. This rather metaphorical frame may be surprising to some readers, but it is useful for illustrating why it matters which definition or conception of ignorance we employ. It is what forms the basis for everything we say about, do with and do about ignorance. When Sally Haslanger distinguishes different answers we may want from asking "What is racism?" and from asking "What is knowledge?", she shows why it is important to have an answer – a conception – that fits to what we want (Haslanger 1999, 2017). And since I'm interested in ignorance as a real-world, cognitive phenomenon, "what we want" is important for the answers that can be given to the question "What is ignorance?"

For most philosophers, I dare say, "What is ignorance?" looks like a simple question with a simple answer. Their answer is: Of course, the first sentence that gives a general description of ignorance should be: "Ignorance is lack of knowledge," or the closely related "Ignorance is absence of knowledge." They would go for this definition because that is how they put ignorance. There is ignorance when there is no knowledge. Today, authors standardly state that ignorance is lack of knowledge or lack of true belief. I have already revealed in the Introduction that I will not accept this definition of ignorance, but there is no denying that it currently is the standard position.

Nevertheless, there is ample reason for contesting the status of "ignorance is lack of knowledge" as the standard position, and, thus, as the hypothetical first sentence on ignorance. The claim that ignorance is lack of knowledge is rejected by other conceptions, for example, quite explicitly, by the defenders of what is called the New View who say that "ignorance is lack of true belief" (e.g., Peels 2010, 2023).

There are further legitimate claims to defining ignorance by other accounts and so in this chapter I review different conceptions of ignorance and treat them as candidates for the definition. The following conceptions of ignorance will be discussed:

1 Reductionist propositional conceptions: Standard View and New View
2 Agential conceptions of ignorance: Normative View and Epistemologies of ignorance
3 Structural conceptions of ignorance
4 Integrated Conception of ignorance.

My proposed conception is the Integrated Conception that recognizes ignorance as a multifaceted phenomenon.

3.1 Reductionist Propositional Conceptions

Reductionist propositional conceptions reduce ignorance to lack of knowledge or lack of true belief. They focus on propositional ignorance and on the doxastic character of ignorance. The most prominent reductionist views are the Standard View – ignorance is lack of knowledge – and the New View – ignorance is lack of belief. Rik Peels defends the New View of ignorance, but he accepts that there is more than propositional ignorance and even notes that

> the nature of ignorance is … to be in a state of propositional ignorance (i.e. to lack propositional knowledge or to lack true belief), to be in a state of objectual ignorance (i.e. roughly, to lack objectual knowledge), or to be in a state of practical ignorance (i.e. to lack practical knowledge).
>
> (Peels 2023, 37)

But the New View is a view about propositional ignorance (as we will see later) and does not combine with objectual ignorance or practical ignorance. Peels recognizes that strategic ignorance is not reducible to propositional ignorance and also involves practical ignorance, but the New View is limited to propositional ignorance. That is why this approach fits the heading "Reductionist propositional conceptions," together with the Standard View. I sometimes call these conceptions doxastic conceptions because they restrict ignorance to doxastic components. I analyze the Standard View and the New View in turn.

Another brief preliminary note: Le Morvan argues for the Standard View and Peels argues for the New View, but they have coauthored an article that helpfully summarizes the arguments from their previous debate and in referring to formulations and claims made in that article about the Standard View and the New View, I will refer to and cite both authors, even though only one of them really is a proponent of the Standard View/New View.

3.1.1 The Standard View of Ignorance

The Standard View holds that ignorance is lack of knowledge. According to Le Morvan and Peels, this view goes together with the view that knowledge is justified true belief plus some Gettier condition. They briefly consider other accounts of knowledge (Le Morvan and Peels 2016, 20–21), but, ultimately, they presuppose a "justified true belief + Gettier condition" conception. On the basis of this assumption they distinguish doxastic ignorance, alethic ignorance, justificational ignorance, and Gettier-type ignorance:

i "*Doxastic ignorance* that *p* occurs when *p* is not believed" (Le Morvan and Peels 2016, 18).
ii "*Alethic ignorance* occurs when a proposition is not true" (Le Morvan and Peels 2016, 18f.).
iii "*Justificational ignorance* occurs when a proposition is believed without justification" (Le Morvan and Peels 2016, 19).
iv "*Gettier-type ignorance* occurs when a proposition is true and believed with justification, but is subject to Gettier-type counterexamples" (Le Morvan and Peels 2016, 19).

My first worry already appears at this juncture: it is not clear why an account of ignorance should go back to a conception of knowledge that is contested and not without competitors and alternatives. Le Morvan and Peels could have given an argument for starting with "justified true belief + Gettier condition" conception since one might be just as convinced that a capacity conception of knowledge is more appropriate to capture what it means to say that ignorance is lack of knowledge. There are clearly advantages in using the four components – belief, truth, justification and the relevant Gettier condition – to capture ignorance: They factor into forms of ignorance. But that by itself is not an argument for taking this approach since the costs for accepting it might be too high.

Some of the costs of the "justified true belief + Gettier condition" conception certainly lie in its simplistic assumptions about the epistemic subject, an anemic subject, one might say. The subject S at the heart of the conception is neither situated, nor social, nor does the conception adequately include epistemic attitudes of the subject. That also means that a conception of knowledge as situated knowledge (cf., e.g., Code 1991) may be more apt for spelling out ignorance as lack of knowledge. My criticism specifically concerns interpretations of the lack of knowledge claim that presuppose an anemic subject and simplistic conceptions of knowledge as mere justified true belief plus some Gettier condition since that is how the approach is spelled out by Le Morvan.

The Unified Account Argument

Defenders of the Standard View cannot reject this objection by saying that the epistemological discussion about which conception of knowledge is right is irrelevant to the project of defining ignorance because the Standard View holds that the nature of ignorance "is completely determined by its contrast with the nature of knowledge" (Le Morvan and Peels 2016, 17). They have to decide on a conception of knowledge because ignorance is determined by the negation of knowledge only, "being purely privative and negational" (Le Morvan and Peels 2016, 17). They even go so far as to suggest that "every theory or conception of knowledge automatically yields by negation a theory or conception of its complement ignorance, and theorizing about both is thereby unified" (Le Morvan and Peels 2016, 17). In fact, this observation is cited as an argument in favor of the Standard View: the Standard View unifies theory of knowledge and theory of ignorance. I call this the Unified Account Argument: We should go for the Standard View because it provides a unified theory of knowledge and ignorance.

To be precise, Le Morvan and Peels spell out this unification argument in two ways. They spell it out in terms of different types of knowledge and in terms of different types of ignorance. There is factual knowledge, objectual knowledge and procedural knowledge (aka know-how) and, corresponding to these types of knowledge, there are factual ignorance, objectual ignorance and procedural ignorance. In addition, for factual ignorance they distinguish the above kinds of ignorance, corresponding to the constituents of knowledge: doxastic, alethic, justificational and Gettier-type ignorance.

The argument, however, does not work. First and foremost, and as Peels and Le Morvan admit, if one is not interested in a unified account, the argument is simply irrelevant. And they do not say why one should aim for a unified account. Since my distinction between logical and the empirical conceptions of ignorance was partly motivated by the observation that such a unified account of knowledge and ignorance on which ignorance is a mere privation is inappropriate, I am not convinced of the need of a unified account. One express aim of this study is to show that we should *not* go for a unified account of knowledge and ignorance because ignorance is more than non-knowledge.

Second, it is also not clear what the supposed unification consists of. Is the account unified because it says that there are factual, objectual and procedural knowledge and, correspondingly, factual, objectual, and procedural ignorance, and because ignorance is determined by lack of constituents of knowledge (belief, truth, justification + x)? If so, how do the two claims contribute to a unified account? Is the factual, object and procedural knowledge-ignorance observations enough for grounding a unified account?

The most serious downside of the unified account argument is that it entails that ignorance does not have a "substantive and positive nature of its own" (Le Morvan and Peels 2016, 17). The different cases of ignorance that I have introduced in the Introduction and the discussion of conceptions of ignorance show that ignorance does have a "substantive and positive nature of its own." Ignorance might be *logically* determined as lack of knowledge, but ignorance as an empirical conception, as an empirical concept is not just lack of knowledge. Ignorance as a real-world phenomenon is integrated in society; it is manifest in human beings that are members of societies; it is reflected in people's belief sets and their behavior. Ignorance can be manifested as the mental state of a scientist conducting experiments to get clearer about a particular problem, but it can also be manifested as the mental state of a citizen who is uninformed about the situation of a minority group and therefore discriminates against members of this group.

The Standard View and the unified account argument do not capture ignorance adequately; they do not see ignorance as a state (or: disposition) in its own rights and thereby underestimate ignorance and its effects. Anyone who holds that ignorance is nothing but mere lack of knowledge and aims at a unified account, thus, trivializes ignorance.

Le Morvan might reply that the claims of the Standard View are only concerned with the epistemic side of ignorance (cf. Peels and Blaauw 2016, 9), and therefore any challenges about ignorance as a real-world phenomenon are unfounded. But this reply would clearly be *ad hoc* and inconsistent. Since Le Morvan and Peels cite common language use as a valid argument for the Standard View (see later), it would be inconsistent to limit ignorance to some epistemic variety. Their distinctions of varieties of ignorance also are clearly meant to model real-world phenomena. Moreover, in times of social epistemology, applied epistemology, non-ideal epistemology, etc., it is archaic to just insist on the distinction between epistemology and ethical, social, practical issues.

The Argument from Common Language

As I have just noted, another argument for the Standard View is common language usage and dictionary entries. Le Morvan and Peels invite us to

consider the Oxford English Dictionary's definition 1a of the word "ignorance": "The fact or condition of being ignorant; want of knowledge (general or special)." The current meaning of "ignorance" as an antonym of "knowledge" squares with its etymology since the English term "ignorance" comes from the Middle English "ignor-ance" or "ygnoraunce," from the Old French "ignorance," from the Latin "ignōrāntia," from the Latin "ignosco" derived from "in" (meaning: the opposite of) and "gnosco" (meaning: know).
(Le Morvan and Peels 2016, 15)

And they add that similar observations hold for other languages (see also Peels 2023, 54). Le Morvan and Peels admit that such an argument is not conclusive, but they still want to include it in the argumentation (Le Morvan and Peels 2016, 15).

There are several issues with this defense and the argument itself. First, it is not clear that the philosophical investigation of ignorance really "seeks to understand what is *ordinarily* meant by a term" (Le Morvan and Peels 2016, 15, my emphasis); philosophical investigation certainly aims to explicate a term, but it is controversial what role the ordinary understanding of a word should take in this project. Normative epistemology, for example, does take ordinary understanding into account but aims to improve the ordinary understanding (e.g., Haslanger 1999). So ordinary understanding is not allowed to lay any particular claims on the resultant conception.[1] If the Standard View is supposed to go with Ordinary Language Philosophy, which would make the common usage observation stronger, that is quite a commitment to take, and again, it would need additional argumentative support. Moreover, it is not obviously true that a dictionary is the best place to find the ordinary *understanding* of a term. Le Morvan and Peels might have to devise studies to examine the ordinary understanding and, thus, engage with experimental philosophy.

Second, I do not think that it is even substantially informative to look at a dictionary entry or ordinary understanding. To an epistemologist, "want of knowledge (general and special)" is not particularly informative because she will at once think of the debates surrounding the term *knowledge*. And so it is an open question whether "want of knowledge" means the same to a non-philosopher as to a philosopher and we might ask ourselves, why we should give any weight, even light weight, to this consideration? It is interesting to know but not decisive.

Finally, even if one accepts that referring to a dictionary entry and common usage is helpful, the common usage observation can be challenged easily. Le Morvan and Peels summarize the common usage insight as: " 'ignorance' as *an antonym* of 'knowledge' " (Le Morvan and Peels 2016, my emphasis). But as the indefinite article indicates, "knowledge" is but one antonym of "ignorance." *Roget's Thesaurus*, for example, has the following list of antonyms of ignorance: "Cognizance, Understanding, Competence, Cultivation, Education, Experience, Intelligence, Knowledge, Literacy, Talent, Wisdom" (Kirkpatrick and Roget 1998). Why is the Standard View allowed to ignore these nuances and focus only on knowledge?

To be clear, the common usage observations are not irrelevant to a study of ignorance, but they should not be counted as an argument or be treated as convincing. Note that the same objection applies to accounts that draw conclusions from the *etymology* of a term – in fact, the common usage argument also, in passing, relies on the etymology of *ignorance*. In many languages the word for *ignorance* does contain a *negation* and *knowledge* (cf. e.g., Peels 2023, 54), but this is not relevant for what the right account of the *phenomenon* ignorance is. The observation is a linguistic observation, not a philosophical argument for the *nature* of ignorance or the right conception of ignorance.

The Argument from Ignorance of Falsehoods

The third argument turns on the fact that the Standard View can include ignorance of falsehoods. The New View cannot include ignorance of falsehoods and so it is at a disadvantage in comparison with the Standard View. Again, this is strictly speaking not an argument. It is only an advantage of the Standard View that someone who thinks that there can be ignorance of falsehoods might deem relevant. But it is not independently decisive. – Admittedly, Peels and Le Morvan say that they are not after *decisive* arguments, but that does not mean they can just call advantages "arguments."

The Standard View explains the possibility of ignorance of falsehoods by way of examples. Take two propositions, one true, one false.

a "*The New Yorker* is sold in some book stores in Zurich." (true)
b "*The New Yorker* is not sold in some book stores in Zurich." (false)

Aristotle was ignorant of both propositions. He was *pre-conceptually ignorant* of the falsehood (and the true proposition) since he did not possess the concepts required to hold an attitude toward the falsehood, for example, "magazine," "book stores" (Le Morvan and Peels 2016, 23).[2] Another case of ignorance of falsehoods is *post-conceptual ignorance*: S possesses the conceptual framework, but does not have an attitude toward that falsehood, for example, you might have been post-conceptually ignorant of the falsehood "The New Yorker is not sold in some book stores in Zurich." before reading this paragraph because you possessed all relevant concepts but you did not know that the *New Yorker* is sold in some book stores in Zurich.

As I said, if you think one can be ignorant of falsehoods, this may be a consideration in favor of the Standard View, but, clearly, it cannot be decisive. Moreover, it is not clear how this advantage relates to arguments for the Standard View in general. Maybe one can really want to be able to say that one can be ignorant of a falsehood, but it is doubtful that this can force one to commit to the Standard View. It most certainly cannot lead one to accept the Standard View because Peels and Le Morvan do not give arguments for the Standard View. They just adduce considerations that speak for it.[3]

The three "arguments" might be assumptions in the background of the Standard View according to Le Morvan, but they are not arguments for the Standard View in the strict sense, and, thus, do not show why one should accept the Standard View of Ignorance as spelt out by Le Morvan. Moreover, the arguments are not convincing, they include desiderata about a theory of ignorance that can easily be rejected (the unification of knowledge and ignorance argument) and are based on bad arguments from common usage. On the basis of these considerations no one will be tempted to accept the Standard View who has not been holding it previously.

And the above issues with restricting ignorance to lack of knowledge, thereby, misconstruing ignorance are bound to impede the Standard View's bid for determining the first sentence. A view that misconstrues ignorance cannot be allowed to determine ignorance and what's most central about ignorance.

3.1.2 *The New View of Ignorance*

The situation is not much different for the arguments for the New View. The New View holds that ignorance is lack of true belief. On this picture there are three kinds of ignorance:

i   Disbelieving ignorance: one disbelieves that p while p is true.
ii Suspending ignorance: one suspends belief and disbelief on p while p is true.
iii Deep ignorance: one neither believes nor disbelieves nor suspends belief and disbelief on p while p is true.

(Le Morvan and Peels 2016, 26)

It is important to note that the New View is not set up as an independent position, rather it is developed in opposition to what Le Morvan has started out calling the "Standard View" (Le Morvan 2011b, 335). In

Peels' original paper the view is framed as a rejection of "what is widely assumed among philosopher" (Peels 2010, 59).[4] This is also reflected in the arguments for the New View. They are mainly arguments detailing why the New View is better than the Standard View, rather than independent arguments for the conception of ignorance as lack of true belief. We have seen a similar problem with the considerations that Peels and Le Morvan present as arguments for the Standard View. Peels gives three arguments for the New View, but, as we will see, they, too, are not decisive.

The Argument from Conflicting "Intuitions about Cases of True Belief That Fall Short of Knowledge"

The first argument notes that the Standard View cannot explain the intuition that instances of true belief that fall short of knowledge do not count as ignorance. The New View can explain this intuition. Peels gives two examples to illustrate the argument: Imagine Sam who walks into a room, looks at the clock and sees that it is set on 7 p.m. Sam knows that the clock is reliable, and he forms the belief that it is 7 p.m. But Sam does not know that the clock has stopped working 24 hours ago. So, the clock is unreliable, but it happens to show the right time to Sam. Sam, thus, has the true belief that it is 7 p.m., but he does not know that it is 7 p.m. On the Standard View Sam counts as ignorant as to the time, since he does not *know* that it is 7 p.m. The New View claims that this verdict conflicts with our intuitions; New View supporters hold that we are reluctant to say that Sam is ignorant. On the Standard View Sam counts as ignorant as to the time, since he does not *know* that it is 7 p.m. The New View claims that this verdict conflicts with our intuitions; New View supporters hold that we are reluctant to say that Sam is ignorant (Le Morvan and Peels 2016, 26–27).

Similarly, for a case of lucky true belief of Alfred which is constructed along the lines of the first Gettier example (Gettier 1963): Alfred believes that he will be the next president of the USA and that, thus, the next president of the USA currently lives in Columbia, Missouri. The latter belief is true because Ms. Howard who currently lives in Columbia, Missouri, will be the next president of the USA. So, Alfred has a true belief that is not justified. Is he ignorant or not? The New View holds that he is not ignorant. True belief that falls short of knowledge and merely true belief do not count as ignorance, and the New View concludes that this also means that cases between those poles also do not count as ignorance. Peels and Le Morvan note that accepting one of the examples is enough to defeat the Standard View, but you need to accept all three steps (true belief that falls short of knowledge, merely true belief, in-between cases) to produce support for the New View (Le Morvan and Peels 2016, 27).

How strong is this argument from "Intuitions About Cases of True Belief that Fall Short of Knowledge" (Le Morvan and Peels 2016, 26)? Obviously, it is not doubtful that an appeal to intuitions can constitute a strong argument. But this argument from intuition does not count as a convincing argument for a theory about the nature of ignorance. The argument is based on the set up that Le Morvan and Peels have chosen. Other views that have a different conception of knowledge than Le Morvan might be able to deal with intuition. They might be able to offer nuances for dealing with the cases of mere true belief. For example, a competence conception of knowledge (cf., e.g., Greco 2009) may be able to pull apart the mere true belief case (Sam's case) and the belief that falls short of knowledge case (Alfred's case), say, locating a mistake in Alfred's reasoning, whereas Sam did not make a mistake but was simply in unfavorable, non-standard circumstances.[5] Why should we choose the two examples as two poles?

In addition, Pritchard's Normative View shows that one may disagree with Peels' intuitions. Pritchard argues that the New View is unable to identify some cases of ignorance that we would want to call ignorance. On the New View a gullible person who just accepts a particular true belief would not count as ignorant, but on the Normative View that person would count as ignorant – since she did not meet the relevant duties of inquiry – which is presupposed by her gullibly accepting the belief (Pritchard 2021b). Peels argues against the Normative View (Peels 2023, 63–72), but he does not weaken that particular argument against the New View, and thus Pritchard's objection against the New View remains relevant.

The Argument That Ignorance Excuses

The second argument for the New View is supposed to be a "simple modus tollens" (Le Morvan and Peels 2016, 29). Blameless ignorance can be an excuse whereas "any kind of true belief that falls short of knowledge does not excuse" (Le Morvan and Peels 2016, 29, emphasis deleted, N.E.), and thus the defender of the New View concludes that ignorance cannot be lack of knowledge (Le Morvan and Peels 2016, 29, see also Peels 2023, 59f.).

At first glance, this might look like a promising argument for the New View, but again the argument only favors the New View relative to the Standard View and does not offer an independent argument. In their joint paper Le Morvan and Peels also note that the New View can give a *unified* account of excuse and that such an account is more attractive (Le Morvan and Peels 2016, 30). But again, it is questionable whether aiming to develop a unified account is a sufficient argument for a(ny) theory. Moreover, one may wonder why it's important to meet the intuitions about excusing powers of ignorance and not other intuitions.

Ignorance Comes in Degrees

Peels calls the third argument – Ignorance comes in degrees – "perhaps the strongest argument for the New View" (Peels 2023, 61). Ignorance comes in degrees (see also Brogaard 2016, 57) and the Standard View cannot account for this fact, since knowledge does not come in degrees – and the Standard View claims that ignorance simply is the antonym of knowledge. "To be ignorant of" is "moderately relatively gradable" (Peels 2023, 61). One needs the context to determine what "to be ignorant of" means (Peels 2023, 62). And finally, "is ignorant of" can produce sorites paradoxes and therefore is gradable (Peels 2023, 62). Again, this argument may speak against the Standard View – and indeed it looks promising –, but it is not an argument for the New View over other views that may also be able to account for the fact that ignorance comes in degrees nor is it an independent argument for the New View.[6]

Since the Standard View and the New View are entangled in these argumentative ways and since neither view can establish their argumentative superiority with independent arguments, I suggest we look at alternative conceptions that are not reductionist.

3.2 Agential Conceptions: Ignorance as Actively Upheld False Outlooks

I want to turn to a group of candidates from philosophy that include some components of the previous "ignorance is lack/absence of knowledge/true belief" suggestions, but at the same time are radically different because they focus on the cognizer as a subject in a normative or even sociopolitical context. Consequently, ignorance is not simply seen as a state, but as a state *of an epistemic agent*. There are two branches of agential conceptions. The first group of approaches to formulate agential conceptions was part of epistemologies of ignorance, theories that examine the social and political nature of ignorance. On these conceptions, the ignorant subject is regarded as a member of a hierarchically organized and unjust community. There is considerable overlap between epistemologies of ignorance and feminist philosophy and critical race theory. Some of the authors working with a feminist and critical race background distance themselves from more traditional epistemology of ignorance by using the plural of *epistemology* – epistemologies of ignorance – thereby noting that there is not just *one* epistemology (cf. Alcoff 2007). The second group of approaches focuses on the normative traits in ignorance, so-called Normative Views of ignorance. Pritchard has first put forward a normative conception of ignorance (2021). Anne Meylan also advances a normative account of ignorance, building on Pritchard but offering an adapted version of the position – for example, by introducing talk of "improper inquiry" – and an independent argument for this normative conception (2022). I'll start with normative conceptions of ignorance because they are closer to the traditional approaches to ignorance and then turn to epistemologies of ignorance.[7]

3.2.1 The Normative View of Ignorance (Pritchard and Meylan)

Duncan Pritchard has first introduced the notion of a Normative View of ignorance into the debate (2021). Pritchard holds that "to be ignorant is to be unaware of a fact that one ought to be aware of" (Pritchard 2021b, 226). This conception of ignorance is conjunctive since it combines the epistemic standing of a subject – "be[ing] unaware of a fact" (Pritchard 2021b, 226) – and the normative demands on the subject's belief. In other words, in order to be ignorant a person needs to lack awareness of a fact when she ought to have awareness of this fact (cf. Pritchard 2021b, 237). Mere lack of awareness is not enough, the ought-condition also has to be met. Pritchard's epistemic state in question is "awareness of a fact" (Pritchard 2021b, 240) rather than knowledge. Awareness amounts to direct or indirect epistemic access to a fact, access via perceptual experience or via testimony. According to Pritchard, awareness is more than true belief and less than knowledge, something in-between.

By introducing the ought-condition, Pritchard aims to distinguish cases in which we would not attribute ignorance to a subject from those cases in which we would attribute ignorance to a subject. The most pertinent case is not knowing pointless truths – for example, how many ships and boats are on Lake Lucerne while I am writing this sentence. I don't know that number, but, Pritchard claims, we would be reluctant to call me ignorant in such a case of pointless truths. Similarly for unknowable truths. We can't know them, but we still wouldn't call ourselves ignorant if we don't know unknowable truths. So there is an important difference between not knowing something (some proposition or a fact) and ignorance.

How does Pritchard determine what "one ought to be aware of" (Pritchard 2021b, 226)? One ought to be aware of those truths that are epistemically available (Pritchard 2021b, 229) or practically important (Pritchard 2021b, 229). Pritchard notes that a parent who could read the diary of their child but does not read the diary is not ignorant because they are not subject to an ought. He also refers to the Sentinelese to specify when someone counts as ignorant: they do not know about "modern science" because they shun any contact with the outside world, but we "will be reluctant to describe them" as ignorant because they have a "good rationale, by their own lights at least" (Pritchard 2021b, 234).

Pritchard's normative conception can be regarded as an advancement of philosophical debates about theories of ignorance because he avoids the derivative approach of the Standard View and the New View and includes normative considerations in the conception of ignorance itself.

The Normative View does not reduce individuals who are ignorant to epistemic subjects with doxastic states who are not embedded in an environment. It is a conjunctive conception on which someone is ignorant only when they lack awareness and ought to have this awareness because it is practically relevant or epistemically available. Individuals can assess practical relevance and live in groups and contexts in which there are oughts, for example, obligations and expectations (inter alia). And Pritchard's evaluation of whether an individual ought to have awareness takes into account the situation of the individual. For example, for the Sentinelese tribe not knowing about modern science is, as Pritchard puts it, rational "by their own lights at the least" (Pritchard 2021b, 234). And so Pritchard does include identities and situatedness and social contexts in the evaluation of ignorance. They are indirectly built into the definition of ignorance because they are necessary for explicating and determining whether the subject ought to have this awareness and what is practically relevant. They are not in the definition or conception of ignorance itself, but they come up when the conception is applied to the individual case. The crucial difference to the Standard View and the New View is that the Normative View opens up space for constitutive factors beyond the doxastic level, namely the normative realm of oughts. It acknowledges that oughts are central for determining ignorance.

Meylan aims to expand Pritchard's normative conception of ignorance by offering an independent argument for the normative conception. Since Meylan's reconstruction of the normative conception does not include the conjunctive setup of Pritchard, I discuss it separately. Meylan holds that "ignorance is the lack of a valuable cognitive state (knowledge/true beliefs) that is due to an improper inquiry" (2024, 210).

On her conception, ignorance is prima facie bad because it is a "disvaluable cognitive state," the absence of something valuable. Ignorance can be all things considered good, but it remains prima facie bad. That is also why Meylan claims that ignorance is "the fitting object of negative emotions" (2024, 214). She argues that if we "isolat[e] the instance of ignorance from the specific circumstances in which it takes place" (2024, 219) a negative emotion will always be correct or fitting. I will take issue with this claim later, but before that I want to unpack the account and add Meylan's independent argument for a normative conception. "Improper inquiry," the reason for ignorance, is improper because it is conducted too slowly or carelessly. And the term picks up on Pritchard's conception of an "intellectual failing that is concerned with a failing of good inquiry" (Pritchard 2021a, 115). Meylan endorses the Normative View of ignorance because it can account for the negativity of ignorance

50 *What Is Ignorance?*

and because it can explain the negativity of ignorance. Ignorance as the result of improper inquiry is bad because it is a "missed opportunity to know" (Meylan 2024, 213). We must not miss opportunities to know, Meylan holds.

In a way, Meylan's conception anticipates the Jamesian twin goals "Strive for truth, avoid falsehood" and assumes a rationalistic conception of the value of knowledge that is shared by an "economics of information perspective" (Hertwig and Engel 2021. 14) and "microeconomics" (Meylan 2024, fn. 15): If there's a cheap way to getting knowledge, one must take it. It would be irrational not to acquire this easy knowledge. On her conception, deliberate ignorance (cf. Hertwig and Engel 2021), cannot be rational or sensitive. I return to the Jamesian twin goals and whether they are good suggestion for dealing with ignorance in Chapter 8.

As I said earlier, I am not convinced that ignorance is always prima facie bad nor that it always elicits and warrants negative emotions. Meylan wants to focus on the reaction that ignorance gets when we "isolat[e] the instance of ignorance from the specific circumstances in which it takes place" (2022, 13) – but I do not understand what that would even mean, nor whether we can even get at such a reaction. What would we get if we isolate ignorance from the circumstances in which it takes place? What would such ignorance even be? And how would a reference to an emotion come in when one isolates from the circumstances of the case of ignorance? Moreover, Meylan's Normative Account of ignorance as the result of improper inquiry could not be understood or applied on this abstract idealizing model. We would certainly be unable to determine something as a case of ignorance that is the result of improper inquiry if we are to abstract away from the particular circumstances of that instance of ignorance. So the first issue is that we cannot adequately identify ignorance (as understood by Meylan's own conception). The second issue is that we cannot take this isolating stance toward ignorance and still take up an emotional or evaluative stance.[8]

I also do not think that one is required not to "miss [out on an] opportunity to know." We don't have to know everything that we can know. Think of knowledge that can lead to dangerous deadly development, for example, knowledge on how to make bacteria more heat resistant that would be conducive to biological weapons. Another argument is avoiding cluttering (cf. Harman 1986). Meylan might respond that her claim is just prima facie correct. But I do not think that this says much if the expectation that we must not miss out on an opportunity to know does not hold, as I'm sure many cases will show. And this also reflects back on Meylan's initial assumption that ignorance is prima facie disvaluable or bad. If we can come up with relevant examples of ignorance in which one is not faulted for remaining ignorant and if we can add cases ignorance is conducive to knowledge, for example, investigative ignorance that is not even epistemically bad, why hold on to the idea that ignorance is prima facie bad? The claim would be simply wrong.

3.2.2 Ignorance as Actively Upheld False Outlooks

The second branch of agential conceptions focuses on agents or cognizers, but they do not idealize agents, the environment or even ignorance itself. Instead, they are firmly rooted in and focused on human beings and the world as they really are.[9] And so they discuss ignorance as a facet of unjust oppressive communities, in particular in the shape of epistemic injustice, for example, pernicious ignorance as a feature in oppressive societies (e.g., Dotson 2011) or ignorance as actively brought about and maintained (e.g., Pohlhaus 2012, Medina 2013). Hence ignorance is mainly seen as a negative condition with detrimental effects on oppressed subjects in unjust societies.[10] I call the underlying conception of ignorance in this field "Ignorance as actively upheld false outlooks" (El Kassar 2018).

On these conceptions, ignorance is conceptualized as passive and active, as something that affects subjects, and also something that is constructed or produced by subjects. Charles Mills' conception of white ignorance and José Medina's conception of active ignorance may provide the blueprint for a conception of ignorance thus informed. Similar conclusions may be drawn from other authors in epistemology of ignorance, for example, Kristie Dotson's notion of reliable ignorance which "needs to be understood not as a simple lack of knowledge, but as an active practice of unknowing" (Dotson 2011, 243). Since Mills' work has been so groundbreaking and influences most authors – including Dotson's conception of ignorance – and since Medina's conception emphasizes the role of the epistemic subject in ignorance, I focus on Mills' and Medina's theories. I start with Mills' conception.

The term *white ignorance* is "meant to denote an ignorance among whites – an absence of belief, a false belief, a set of false beliefs, a pervasively deforming outlook – that [is] not contingent but causally linked to their whiteness" (Mills 2015, 217). While race plays a causal role in determining white ignorance, it is not restricted to white people but can be transmitted to nonwhites via unjust relations (Mills 2007, 22). White ignorance manifests itself paradigmatically in white people being unable to understand the world, make sense of other people's lives, question their own position in an unjust society. Such ignorance is "a cognitive tendency – an inclination, a doxastic disposition" (Mills 2007, 23).[11]

At first glance, Mills' white ignorance may seem restricted to propositional ignorance and doxastic attitudes.[12] But as becomes clear in Mills'

52 What Is Ignorance?

adapted description of *white ignorance* in his article on global white ignorance (2015), Mills' conception also takes the subject's motivation and her attitudes into account, thus going beyond a reductionist doxastic conception. The traces of this fundamental assumption are also in Mills' book *The Racial Contract* (1997) in which he develops "white ignorance" as a component of "an epistemology of ignorance, [as] a particular pattern of *localized and global cognitive dysfunctions*" (Mills 1997, 18, my emphasis). This kind of ignorance is manifest in people's outlook on the world and their actions, for example, in their avoiding evidence, their harboring false beliefs, in not listening to other people, etc. Their ignorance is an epistemic practice in which propositional ignorance is merely one of the contributing components.

As a representative of epistemologies of ignorance, Mills naturally transcends the propositional framework, for example, by going for a wide conception of knowledge on which it includes concept-possession, understanding and epistemic attitudes more broadly, because willful ignorance is not limited to the absence of true beliefs and the presence of false belief. Mills' view of ignorance as an epistemic practice that consists in a "pervasively deforming outlook" Mills 2015, 217 cannot be squared with any reductionist propositional approach.

Medina's concept of active ignorance also instantiates the agential conception of ignorance. Active ignorance is fed by epistemic vices – in particular, by arrogance, laziness and close-mindedness. More particularly, active ignorance is

> an ignorance that occurs with the active participation of the subject and with a battery of defense mechanisms, [it is] an ignorance that is not easy to undo and correct, for this requires retraining – the reconfiguration of epistemic attitudes and habits – as well as social change.
> (Medina 2013, 39)

For Medina's conception it is even more obvious that ignorance is not restricted to propositional ignorance. Active ignorance is constituted by the subject's "epistemic attitudes and habits," thus going significantly beyond ignorance as propositional ignorance. On these agential conceptions epistemologies of ignorance are social and political.

These agential conceptions of ignorance go beyond the reductionist propositional conception of ignorance in just the right way. They provide material for capturing ignorance more adequately. Think of the example of Hannah who does not know that the sulfur and carbon dioxide emissions of cruise ships are bad for the environment and also would not want to know that this is true of cruise ships. The agential conception can capture her close-mindedness.

What sort of conception for ignorance do these approaches lead to? On the basis of Mills' and Medina's considerations one might suggest the following statement:

> Ignorance is a cognitive dysfunction either passive or actively produced by the subject and it is realized in absence of knowledge, the presence false beliefs and "pervasively deforming outlooks" (Mills 2015, 217; see also Mills 2007, 16).

This conception fulfills some of my desiderata but also has some disadvantages. It includes the ignorant subject, but I am skeptical as to whether claims about the causes of ignorance – passive or active – should be included in the first sentence. In addition, talk of a dysfunction, albeit insightful, gets us on the wrong track because it suggests that ignorance is a process, when it seems more appropriately captured as a state, or a disposition. But the character of ignorance is not the only problem with this suggestion. There is a still more fundamental problem that is likely to affect any suggestion that comes from feminist and critical race epistemology of ignorance. As I have noted earlier, these conceptions regard ignorance as a negative condition, and in the case of oppressed subjects in unjust societies, ignorance has detrimental effects on these subjects. After all, ignorance is social and political. But ignorance is not always negative; the conception of ignorance should leave space for scientific ignorance and other conceivable cases of positive or beneficial ignorance (see Introduction). And so these observations about ignorance are crucial, but they are too specific as a general conception of ignorance. But as I will show in the Integrated Conception, we can disconnect the valuable insights about the role of the epistemic agent in ignorance from the claim that ignorance is bad and make sure that they are reflected in the first sentence.

3.3 The Structural Conception: Ignorance as a Substantive Epistemic Practice

Linda Alcoff's conception of ignorance is also representative of the approach in epistemologies of ignorance – in fact, Alcoff's 2007 article is titled "Epistemologies of Ignorance" and she argues for the plural formulation. The conception is related to the agential conception but goes one step further since Alcoff conceives of ignorance as a *"substantive* epistemic practice" (Alcoff 2007, 39, emphasis in original) including individual, social and *structural* belief-forming practices.

> Even in mainstream epistemology, the topic of ignorance as a species of bad epistemic practice is not new, but what is new is the idea of

explaining ignorance not as a feature of *neglectful* epistemic practice but as a *substantive* epistemic practice in itself. The idea of an epistemology of ignorance attempts to explain and account for the fact that such substantive practices of ignorance – willful ignorance, for example, and socially acceptable but faulty justificatory practices – are structural. This is to say that *there are identities and social locations and modes of belief formation, all produced by structural social conditions of a variety of sorts, that are in some cases epistemically disadvantaged or defective*.

(Alcoff 2007, 39–40, first emphases in original but last emphasis mine)

Her conception of ignorance, thus, is agential but also structural. Ignorance is a "bad epistemic practice" (Alcoff 2007, 39) that is also structurally manifested. Ignorance as a (bad) practice is not just rooted in the beliefs, epistemic vices, and the outlook of the individual but also manifest in and maintained by social and institutional structures and mechanisms. Let's call this the *structural conception of ignorance*.

Nancy Tuana also employs this conception when she shows how several kinds of ignorance "intersect with power" (Tuana 2006, 3). Despite appearances, this holds in particular for ignorance in science. Tuana also rejects the standard propositional conception of ignorance:

Ignorance in the realm of science is typically depicted as a gap in knowledge: something that we do not (yet) know. But the condition of not knowing is not (always) that simple. Just as any adequate account of knowledge must include far more than the truth of that piece of knowledge – including, for instance, an analysis of why those who are in a position of authority (which itself requires a genealogical analysis) have come to accept that belief as true – so too ignorance in the fields of knowledge production is far more complex an issue than something we simply do not yet know.

(Tuana 2006, 3)

We need to recognize that ignorance is situated, Tuana argues. She parallels this development in conceptualizing ignorance with the insight that knowledge is situated (Tuana 2006, 3), though, of course, the claim that knowledge is situated is still fairly contested in epistemology. This gives us an idea of how controversial Alcoff's and Tuana's conception of ignorance may sound to some.

Conceptualizing ignorance as an epistemic practice may seem equally controversial. But it is possible to spell out ignorance in terms of an epistemic practice. Including the claims about ignorance as structurally manifested or collective requires carefully integrating theories of social ignorance and institutions, and asking whether there is something like ignorance in social institutions. A role model for extending a somewhat individualist conception to a structural conception is Anderson's structural interpretation of epistemic injustice (Anderson 2012).

On the basis of Alcoffs' remarks we can formulate the following structural conception of ignorance:

> Ignorance is a practice that involves individual, social and institutional belief-forming practices that are biased, mal-informed or in other ways dysfunctional.

But this proposal has the same drawback as the second agential conception: it pictures ignorance as purely negative when ignorance may, in fact, be valuable in the sciences and in inquiry quite generally (e.g., Bromberger 1992, Firestein 2012).

Moreover, despite all the previous criticism of reductionist propositional conceptions, it would be a mistake not to explicitly mention the considerations about propositional ignorance, and the relations between knowledge/true belief and ignorance in the conception. The debate between the Standard View and the New View is misguided and works with a faulty dichotomy, but these propositional ignorance conceptions have still suggested valuable details about propositional ignorance that are also fruitful for more practice-oriented conceptions.

The Standard View and the New View cannot lay claim to being complete and definitive accounts of ignorance, but they do address central facets of ignorance. For example, the three-partite distinction of kinds of ignorance of the New View could be useful for distinguishing importantly different kinds of *propositional ignorance* in a person. It enables us to distinguish at some level Hannah who is *deeply ignorant* that cruise ships have high emissions of both carbon and sulfur dioxides and, therefore, are bad for the environment and Monika who is *suspendingly ignorant* that cruise ships have high emissions of both carbon and sulfur dioxides and, therefore, are bad for the environment. They are both ignorant but in importantly different ways. The practice conception itself does not include propositional ignorance and does not mention these details of the doxastic component of ignorance. It is, thus, also not sufficient for capturing ignorance.

I have now discussed the most salient options concerning ignorance currently on the market, but we have seen that every position is lacking is some or another aspect. At the same time, we have also seen that, in addition to their disadvantages, there are some advantages to all of the positions. It is just that all on their own and because of their individual limitations they are not fit to formulate the first sentence for an encyclopedia entry on ignorance, in other words: they cannot determine the core of ignorance. Consequently, the only promising positions are a disjunctive or a conjunctive conception of ignorance.

One might also take a Wittgensteinian route and reject the very possibility of finding a first sentence for ignorance, and of defining ignorance, but this is no option in this project. The definition does not have to capture all there is to ignorance, it should just be appropriate to the phenomenon and allow for a discussion of ways of dealing with ignorance. I endorse what I call an *Integrated Conception*, but before I turn to outlining this conception, I want to formulate adequacy conditions that a conception of ignorance that can determine the first sentence will have to meet.

3.4 Adequacy Conditions

These adequacy conditions are partly based on the discussion of the different candidates for the first sentence in the previous sections, but they are also developed from the demands of the second question of this study – how to rationally deal with ignorance.

3.4.1 Ignorance Is a Real-World Phenomenon

The conception must adequately capture ignorance as a real-world phenomenon that is multifaceted and differently instantiated, and not just as an abstract logical concept. We have seen in the logical approaches by van der Hoek and Lomuscio (2004) and in the semi-formal approach by Olsson and Proietti (2016) that such approaches have a restricted picture of ignorance that does not fit with the non-ideal, messy, real-world manifestations of ignorance that are the interest of my epistemological questions about ignorance and ways of dealing with ignorance. The conception should avoid abstractions that make ignorance unclear (e.g., as in Meylan's (2024) abstraction suggestion or in the Standard View and New View).

3.4.2 Ignorance Is a Self-Standing Phenomenon

The conception must approach ignorance as a self-standing phenomenon that is not just determined derivatively by its relation to knowledge and true belief. In the debate between the Standard View and the New View we have seen that ignorance is more than lack of knowledge/true belief, and instead is a state of an epistemic agent that needs to be examined as such. Of course, it is connected to knowledge and true belief in important ways, but this is just one facet of ignorance, as the agential conception and the structural conception have indicated. In addition, by choosing this approach we can also make sure that we do not forget that ignorance can also consist in error and false belief.

3.4.3 Avoid Narrow Conceptions of Knowledge

The conception has to avoid narrow conceptions of knowledge, for example, equating knowledge with justified true belief or presupposing a justified true belief + x conception of knowledge. Instead it should employ a wide conception of knowledge, on which knowledge is realized in concept-possession, understanding, justified true beliefs, interrelated networks of pieces of knowledge.

3.4.4 Avoid Mistakes and Embrace Advantages of Other Conceptions of Ignorance

We are looking for a conception that preserves the advantages of the other conceptions and avoids their mistakes. The advantage of propositional conceptions lies in the nuances in the doxastic structure that they provide. The advantages of the agential and structural conceptions lie in recognizing that ignorance is not limited to the doxastic level but is also manifest in the agent herself and in social structures. And, more particularly, they acknowledge that ignorance is manifest in the epistemic attitudes of an epistemic agent.

3.4.5 Ignorance as the State of an Agent

The conception must take seriously that ignorance is a state of an agent and that this agent is not some anemic abstract being but an epistemic agent that is modeled after real non-ideal human being.

3.4.6 A Neutral Conception of Ignorance

We are looking for a neutral conception of ignorance that is not limited to ignorance being dysfunctional or in other ways negative. Ignorance can be negative, for example, in close-mindedly not wanting to know about unjust conditions in one's community, or in a doctor not knowing about the standard treatment for the condition of one's patient. But ignorance can also be positive, for example, when one does not know how algae blooming is related to the water temperature as one just starts one's project to work on the relation between the water temperature and algae blooming, or in not knowing what one will receive as a birthday present from one's partner.

3.4.7 Connection to the Question "How Should We Rationally Deal with Ignorance?"

The conception should provide the material and grounds for answering the question "How should we rationally deal with ignorance?" We have seen that the Standard View and the New View do not provide sufficient material because they would tell us to focus on the doxastic level only, on getting knowledge or getting true belief. But there is more to dealing with ignorance because there is more to ignorance than the lack of knowledge or true belief.

3.5 The Integrated Conception of Ignorance

After this discussion of current conceptions of ignorance and after having formulated adequacy conditions for an apt conception of ignorance, I can turn to developing and explicating my conception of ignorance. I call it an *Integrated Conception of Ignorance* because it includes insights from the different conceptions of ignorance and at the same time aims to avoid their disadvantages.

One crucial disagreement between my Integrated Conception and reductionist conceptions of ignorance lies in the scope of ignorance that a conception should have. This is paradigmatically manifested in Peels' criticism of my previous formulation of an Integrated Conception (Peels 2023). I have previously argued that

> ignorance is a disposition of an epistemic agent that manifests itself in her beliefs – either she has no belief about *p* or a false belief – her epistemic attitudes (doxastic attitudes, epistemic virtues, epistemic vices).
>
> (El Kassar 2018)

Peels rejects this conception and holds that his New View of ignorance and this account of the nature of ignorance can do everything that my Integrated Conception claims to do. Parts of Peels' criticism of the above formulation of the Integrated Conception are correct, but I still hold on to the core of the Integrated Conception because – as will become clear in this section – Peels has not shown that we can remain on the doxastic level in determining ignorance (neither in his 2019 comment nor in the 2023 book).

Peels claims that the nature of ignorance should be determined as follows: "Ignorance is the lack of propositional knowledge/the lack of true belief, or the lack of objectual knowledge, or the lack of practical knowledge" (Peels 2023, 41). And propositional ignorance should be understood as "lacking a true belief that is of significance" (Peels 2023, 73).

The Integrated Conception is at fault because it "confuse[s] the nature of [ignorance] with the accidental features of it that we value or disvalue" (Peels 2023, 47, my additions). Note that there is an ambiguity in Peels' very setup: The nature of ignorance is being lack of propositional knowledge or lack of objectual knowledge or lack of practical knowledge, but it is also lack of "a true belief that is of significance." Which of the statements is more fundamental?

Peels argues that my initial definition is faulty: First, "doxastic attitudes" can be dropped from the addition in brackets because belief or disbelief are doxastic attitudes. Second, epistemic virtues and epistemic vices are dispositions so they cannot appear in a disposition. Third, open-mindedness, close-mindedness and other virtues and vices are contingent or accidental features of ignorance and thus not central to the nature of ignorance.

Let me address the objections in turn. I could make the case why we can leave doxastic attitudes in brackets and why they are more than belief and disbelief, but I'll hand this point to Peels without much discussion because I want to aim further than the doxastic attitudes. Similarly for the second objection. What's more important is that Peels confuses determinables and determinates with regard to virtues and vices in general and particular virtues and vices, such as open-mindedness and close-mindedness. Saying that ignorance is co-constituted by epistemic virtues and or vices does not mean that particular, determinate virtues always constitute ignorance. It means that virtues or vices as determinables co-constitute ignorance. Peels' objection against my first formulation of an Integrated Conception of Ignorance misconstrues the conception and thus does not affect the fundament of the actual conception.

As I said, I have modified my first formulation of an Integrated Conception because virtues or vices are not the only constituents that need to be considered for ignorance. But let me first take issue with Peels' idea of the nature of ignorance. His proposal that includes lack of propositional knowledge (true belief), objectual knowledge and practical knowledge is progressive because it goes beyond lack of propositional knowledge or lack of true belief in determining ignorance. But, nevertheless, it does not suffice for an adequate account of ignorance. If we try to explain ignorance and simply use Peels' claims about the nature of ignorance and his New View of propositional ignorance, we have not really explained what ignorance *is*. There are facets of ignorance – that all instances of ignorance have – that are not captured by his approach. For example, we cannot capture *white ignorance* with the New View or Peels' remarks on the three types of ignorance that constitute the nature of ignorance. Peels says that white ignorance "is the lack of belief, false belief, or various false beliefs (all captured by the conception of propositional ignorance), in certain cases brought about or caused by factors related to race, gender, and the like" (Peels 2023, 171). But this is a faulty and gappy reading of white ignorance – Peels does not see that it is *not* contingent that white ignorance is caused by "factors related to race, gender and the like" (Peels 2023, 171). That's a necessary feature of white ignorance. In addition, he does not recognize that white ignorance is not merely *caused* by these factors but *constituted* by them and by further psychological processes as well as perception, reasoning and memory. Mills himself describes white ignorance as an outlook on the world, not just a set of false beliefs (Mills 2007, 22f.).

I have noted that I do not subscribe to my original formulation of an Integrated Conception of Ignorance in El Kassar (2018) anymore. In the light of agential and structural conceptions of ignorance, one could go for a psychological conception that emphasizes psychological factors or ignorance or one could go for an Integrated Conception that also includes structural components. I put forward this (admittedly, more demanding) notion:

> Ignorance is a disposition of an epistemic agent that is constituted by (1) beliefs, (2) epistemic attitudes, (3) epistemic character traits, (4) conduct and (5) socio-political structures.

Let's look at the constituents in turn. (1) Beliefs are the primary constituents of ignorance, either lack of true belief or false belief. But ignorance can also be constituted by (2) epistemic attitudes, for example, asking questions, suspending belief, inquiry. Ignorance can also be co-constituted by the character traits (3) of the individual, for example, when they are arrogant and thus arrogantly ignorant, or when they are curious and thus curiously ignorant. Ignorance can also be co-constituted by the conduct (4) of an epistemic agent, for example, when they are dismissive or when they act encouragingly or inquisitively. Such ignorance can be manifested in silencing a subject that knows more about the topic at hand but is not allowed to speak because of identity prejudice. Finally, ignorance is not just constituted by traits or facets in an individual, but also co-constituted by structures – social structures and political structures. There is a large group of structures relevant for ignorance. And literature on epistemic injustices, in particular, can lead us to these structures. They can range from concepts or terminology (cf. hermeneutical injustice (Fricker 2007) or inaccessible technical language, etc.), listening practices (e.g., Habgood-Coote, Ashton and El Kassar 2024) or silencing practices (e.g., Dotson 2011) to laws (e.g., Bright and Kwak 2023). Medina's "battery of defense mechanisms" in active ignorance can also consist in such structures.

Peels would probably object that my list of co-constituting elements really is a list of contingent factors or causes of ignorance. But that impression may come up because I have not yet fully developed the position and its arguments. They follow now.

In order to understand the disagreement between Peels' view and my view it is instructive to look at the exchange between Sally Haslanger und Tommie Shelby regarding ideology. They include very similar dynamics with Shelby taking Peels' position and Haslanger taking my position. Shelby holds that "an ideology is a widely held set of loosely associated beliefs and implicit judgments that misrepresent significant social realities and that function, through this distortion, to bring about or perpetuate unjust social relations" (2014, 66, italics in original deleted). The view is cognitivist because it determines ideology in terms of "shared (false) beliefs and shared (invalid) patterns of thought" (Haslanger 2017, 7). Haslanger argues that this cognitivist account does not see that "belief and thought are themselves products of psychological processes involving perception, attention, memory and the like" (Haslanger 2017, 7). The account is too limited because it does not recognize that the false beliefs that constitute ideology are also shaped by ideology (Haslanger 2017, 8). Haslanger continues: "what we absorb through socialization is not just a set of beliefs, but a language, a set of concepts, a responsiveness to particular features of things (and not others), a set of social meanings" (Haslanger 2017, 9). In other words: Ideology is also constituted by "[problematic] attitudes and habits of the mind" (Haslanger 2017, 9). Ideology should be "[understood] in terms of the concepts, rules, norms, stereotypes, scripts and the likes that partly constitute a practice" (Haslanger 2017, 8). According to Haslanger, we need such a practice-first account of ideology to be able to deal with the challenges we face with respect to ideologies, in particular, to be able to efficiently critique and overcome ideology.

There are important differences between ideology and ignorance – first, ideology is almost always bad, ignorance is not necessarily bad – but the fault lines in the debates are the same. Cognitivist account vs. a Practice-first account. Reductionist account vs. Integrated account. My integrated account of ignorance can also be read as a practice-first account, or at least as a practice-oriented account. Ignorance is not merely cognitive. And the advantages of Haslanger practice-first account are also the advantages of my integrated account of ignorance: We are not limited to doxastic traits in saying what ignorance is and we can determine better ways of dealing with ignorance (whether valuable or pernicious ignorance).

In addition, white ignorance, in particular, seems to function rather like ideology: it consists in false beliefs or lack of true beliefs that are *constituted* by perception, memory, concepts, language, etc. Importantly, these beliefs are *not* simply caused by the practices (perception, memory, concepts, etc.) – *pace* Peels. Rather, they are *co-constituted* by the practices.

62 *What Is Ignorance?*

They are also constituted by institutions and norms that embody and sustain white ignorance.[13]

I don't want to overstretch the parallel and I think the general idea is clear. Now, Peels (and others) will probably respond that we can tell the whole story in terms of *causes* of ignorance (and ideology) and in terms of contingent features of ignorance. But again, the arguments I have given earlier kick in, and in addition, there is an additional argument against Peels' rejection of causes of ignorance and his claim that causes of ignorance don't belong in a conception of ignorance: the *Argument from Building Relations*. Causal relations can be building relations and, thus, something that we describe as a cause of O can be a constituent of O. Institutions and norms can stand in building relations to (mental, physical, bodily, etc.) states of individuals.

In order to develop this argument, I rely on Karen Bennett's account of building.[14] Bennett argues that one should not separate causation from building relations and spells out a diagonal relation (rather than separating vertical causation and horizontal causation). For example, a cake is made from eggs and so they "feature in a special way in the cake's causal history" (Bennett 2017, 89). They are not part of the cake *as* eggs, but "parts of the eggs became parts of the cake" (Bennett 2017, 89). A Lego castle that is built with Legos also has Legos in its causal history, but they are still included as Legos. It is made of Legos. In contrast, Bennett observes, a cake is *made from* or *made out of* eggs, flour, butter, etc. It is not made of eggs, flour, butter etc. Parts of these constituents make up parts of the cake.

The same applies to ignorance: Ignorance is *made from* doxastic components, agential components (e.g., virtues or vices, habits, perception, memory, behavior) and structural components (e.g., institutions, laws). They figure in a special way in the causal history of ignorance. Ignorance is built from these components and thus we need to also mention them in defining ignorance or developing a conception of ignorance. When Peels relegates these factors to causes, he does not succeed in excluding them from the conception.

Note that when Peels turns to more real-life instances of ignorance, such as group ignorance, he also seems to acknowledge that ignorance is determined by factors outside the purely cognitive and doxastic realm. For example, he puts forward the "dynamic account of group ignorance" on which

> a group G is ignorant of a true proposition *p* if and only if (i) either a significant number of G's operative members are ignorant of *p* or enough operative members of G know/truly believe that *p* but G as a group fails to know/truly believe that *p*, and (ii) this is the result of a

group dynamic, such as group agency, collective epistemic virtues or vices, external manipulation, lack of time, interest, concepts, resources, or information, or a combination of these.

(Peels 2023, 117)

In other words, group dynamics are required for a group to be ignorant. Why doesn't he see that similar dynamics are also involved in the individual case? Such dynamics could be psychological processes, structures, etc. Peels might reply that we need the dynamics to get *group* ignorance rather than distributed ignorance, but this reply seems *ad hoc*. Especially once we have Bennett's theoretical framework in shape to provide the philosophical background for the role of processes and influences that Peels reduces to mere causes and contingent features.

3.6 Two Objections against the Integrated Conception

Before I look at facets of ignorance that help shape the picture of ignorance, I want to discuss two objections against the Integrated Conception of Ignorance. The first objection holds that ignorance does not always contain structural components. There can be benign ignorance that is not structural. For example, there are no structural components in someone not knowing the birthday dates of their colleagues. The second objection accepts that all ignorance contains structural components, but notes that not all structures are as pernicious as, for example, in white ignorance.

First, ignorance that looks benign at first glance may reveal structural components at second glance. In addition, the term is ambiguous. "Benign ignorance" can refer to ignorance that is trivial and to ignorance that is not objectionable. And in both cases we can find structural components. In the example from the objection someone does not know the birthday dates of their colleagues. If this is trivial ignorance, there are still structural components in this ignorance and they contribute to making it benign or trivial. Such structures may be that in this society having knowledge about the birthday dates of one's colleagues is not particularly important, or that there is a strict distinction between private and work-related interactions. Those structures co-constitute the person's ignorance. The same holds for ignorance that is not objectionable. Objectionability only works against the background of norms, society and structures. The complex phenomenon "ignorance" can only be grasped with structures as co-constituents.

Second, ignorance that seems benign at first glance may in fact turn out to be problematic. And we can only understand these dynamics if we understand that ignorance is constituted by structures.[15] For example, some people construe white ignorance or ignorance about inclusive language as benign ignorance, and they can only do so because ignorance is co-constituted by structures. And someone's ignorance about their colleagues' birthday dates can also be problematic, for example, if they know the birthday dates of their peers but are ignorant about the birthday dates of the administrative staff because they believe that they are inferior. We cannot capture ignorance if we ignore these structural components.

In responding to the first objection I have already given the beginnings of a response to the second objection, too. I agree with the objection's observation that not all structures in ignorance are pernicious. Structures are also constitutive of benign or trivial ignorance. And not pursuing a particular research direction, say, because it would improve biological weapons is also structurally co-constituted ignorance since it does not simply amount to or reduce to "We do not know how these bacteria become heat resistant" nor "We do not want to know how these bacteria become heat resistant." And this ignorance about making bacteria heat resistant is not pernicious. So not all structures are constitutive of pernicious ignorance.

Now that the basic conception of ignorance is clear, I want to look at further facets of ignorance that help us get a clearer grasp of what ignorance is. These explorations are important because they keep us from being tempted to reduce ignorance to mere lack of knowledge or lack of true belief or a lack of awareness and reveal more about the nature of ignorance.

Notes

1 As I have noted in the Introduction (Chapter 1), revisionary epistemology makes similar claims (cf. Fassio and McKenna 2015).
2 I have changed the example; Le Morvan and Peels talk about King Herod I being ignorant about a falsehood about the most popular iOS app in 2014.
3 See also Peels (2023, 56) for further criticism of the Falsehood Argument.
4 Nottelmann (2016) observes that Goldman (1999), even before Peels, has claimed that ignorance is lack of true belief (1999, 5). For a discussion of some issues with Goldman's view, see Nottelmann (2016, 33).
5 Such an argumentation would work like Greco's competence and environment solution to Gettier cases and cases of environmental luck (cf. Greco 2009).
6 In their joint paper on the dispute, Peels and Le Morvan also introduce the following argument for the New View: If the Standard View were correct, we would have to find cases of factive ignorance, objectual ignorance and procedural ignorance – corresponding to the three different kinds of knowledge: factive knowledge, objectual knowledge and procedural knowledge (know-how) (Le Morvan and Peels 2016, 30f.). But there are no cases of objectual ignorance nor cases of procedural ignorance; thus, the Standard View is false. Le Morvan and Peels are open in admitting the limited scope of this argument:

> If certain cases of objectual knowledge do not have objectual ignorance as their contradictory or complement, the Standard View is in trouble, but it does not follow that the New View is correct; more work would be needed

for that, namely that every case of seemingly objectual or procedural ignorance is in fact a case of factive ignorance."

(Le Morvan and Peels 2016, 31)

But we do not need this explicit qualification to reject the argument. Again, it is not clear why the Standard View should come with the distinction of factive, objectual and procedural knowledge and ignorance, nor is it clear why the Standard View is committed to the claim of a unified account of knowledge and ignorance. As I have noted before, we see in Haas and Vogt (2015) that one can explicate knowledge in a different way. On their view, knowledge is not jtb + x but instead knowledge "includes elements of concept-possession, grasping, understanding, as well as a range of related cognitive achievements" (Haas and Vogt 2015, 19). This is a viable explication of ignorance as lack/absence of knowledge, and Le Morvan and Peels would have to show that their way of explicating knowledge is better or even best.

It is thus not clear that the argument shows that "the Standard View is in trouble." Maybe "Le Morvan's version of the Standard View" is in trouble, but this is not *the Standard View*. One can agree that ignorance is lack/absence of knowledge, a position that prima facie deserves being called "Standard View" – on the assumption that there is something like a Standard View – without accepting that one should go for a unified account of knowledge and ignorance, or that such an account is even appropriate to the phenomenon.

7 Another way to escape the "lack or absence of knowledge (true belief)" structure is to endorse Sylvain Bromberger's approach to ignorance. Bromberger is interested in determining how people decide which ignorance they want to alleviate and which they are going to ignore (Bromberger 1992, 128). Bromberger makes the following stipulations:

> Ignorance is the relationship between a person P and a set of questions Q, when P does not know the correct answer to any of the members of Q and has no strong views as to what the correct answer to any of them is.
> (Bromberger 1992, 128)

To some extent Bromberger's suggestion can be seen as a version of the suggestion that ignorance is the absence of "the answer to a question" (Haas and Vogt 2015, 18) that Haas and Vogt consider. Haas and Vogt reject the suggestion because it does not avoid the problem that is relevant in the context of their article, namely that ignorance is not lack of propositional knowledge.

But it is still possible that conceiving of ignorance as a relation between a person and questions is a good approach. It looks promising because it avoids using the contentious terms *knowledge*, *lack* and *absence*. Yet, there are other considerations that speak against this question-based conception. First, it is not clear that all ignorance indeed is related to an unanswered question. An ignorant subject might not even be able to formulate the relevant question to which she does not know the answer, for example, as in a case of deep ignorance (cf. Wilholt 2019). Bromberger could follow Goldman in rejecting this observation and note that the question does not have to be explicit but can simply be implicit (Goldman 1999, 89), but that seems *ad hoc*, and Bromberger's talk of a relationship between a person P and a set of questions seems to prohibit this move. Can there be a relationship between a person P and an implicit question? As a third-personal descriptive stance, this may be possible, but not for a first-personal ignorance ascription.

So Bromberger's stipulation seems to amount to a *description* of ignorance, not to a claim about what ignorance is. What is the use of the relationship between P and the set of questions Q? The relationship is a higher-level description that is not needed to capture manifestations of ignorance *simpliciter*. It might be relevant if one wants to capture ignorance in the context of investigation and sciences: it is a special instance of P not knowing the answer to any question from a set of questions, where P stands in a conscious relationship to those questions. But maybe Bromberger's statement should not be read in such a strict way since he later groups questions and, what he calls p-predicaments, as objects of *nescience* – countable objects of not knowing. P-predicaments are introduced as follows:

> A person is said to be in a p-predicament with regard to a question Q if, on that person's assumptions and knowledge, Q is sound and has a correct answer, yet that person can think of no answer, can conjure up no answer to which, on those assumptions, there are no decisive objections.
> (Bromberger 1992, 108)

But p-predicaments in effect are questions, too. So there is still the problem: Is ignorance a relation to a question?

I suggest that we should say that ignorance can be a relation to a question or a set of questions, but that there is *another* level in addition to this level on which ignorance does, after all, consist in something else, including absence of knowledge, in the sense of not knowing what the answer to the question is. In the context of a scientist's investigation, one may want to emphasize that they are ignorant with an investigative attitude toward their ignorance, and, thus, that they stand in a relation to the set of questions Q for which they do not know the answer. The question-based approach thus has general limitations and is not enough. Ignorance may consist in a relation between a person and a set of questions, but that is just *one* variety of ignorance that can be traced back to other elements of ignorance, and thus it is not suitable to be a first sentence that captures manifestations of ignorance generally.

8 Note that these abstractions also locate Meylan's approach in the camp of ideal theories (cf. Mills 2017, McKenna 2023, El Kassar fthc).
9 Cf. McKenna (2023).
10 But see also (Bailey 2007) for the strategic usefulness of ignorance for oppressed groups.
11 Note that I read Mills' remarks about white ignorance as making claims about the nature of ignorance that hold for other kinds of ignorance, too.

12 Philosophers who are critical of Mills' cognitivist take on ignorance, for example, Bailey (2007), might reject this extension, but I think that Mills' later notion of white ignorance as a "pervasively deforming outlook" (Mills 2015, 217) suggests that he could go beyond the notion of ignorance as false belief.
13 Think of discriminatory housing policies, the effects of inheritance on continuing financial injustice, or also of unjust legal conditions, as outlined by Bright and Kwak (2023).
14 Thanks to Martin Kusch for introducing the account at a workshop at the University of Freiburg.
15 Cf., e.g., Wekker (2016).

4 Facets of Ignorance

The aim of this chapter is to review different typical facets of ignorance and on that basis develop a systematic picture of the symptoms of ignorance. This review is informed by current philosophical literature on ignorance but also adds symptoms that are not mentioned in the philosophical literature, but are still highly relevant for ignorance. By collecting various symptoms, I will home in on cardinal signs of ignorance and present paradigms of ignorance with which I can examine the different proposals for dealing with ignorance.

Most of today's philosophical taxonomies of ignorance (Le Morvan and Peels 2016, Nottelmann 2016, van Woudenberg 2009) presuppose a propositional or doxastic conception of ignorance and are, therefore, inadequate for getting a full overview of symptoms of ignorance. They offer plausible distinctions, for example, doxastic ignorance, alethic ignorance, justificational ignorance and Gettier-type ignorance (Le Morvan and Peels 2016), but because of their propositional approach they are restricted to symptoms in the subject's belief set. Yet, as I have argued, ignorance can also be manifest in the subject's attitudes. I, therefore, do not introduce their taxonomies in detail and only refer to the labels when they are relevant for discussing symptoms in the belief set.

In contrast, Haas and Vogt (2015) put forward a taxonomy that also includes the subject's attitudes and motivation. Their approach is, thus, much more appropriate for ignorance as a real-world phenomenon and respects the role of epistemic subjects in instances of ignorance. Ignorance is always someone's ignorance and a taxonomy of ignorance as a real-world manifestation must include whatever components constitute the different instances of ignorance.[1]

As I show in this chapter, Haas and Vogt's taxonomy distinguishes important forms of ignorance, but it is not complete as a list of symptoms of ignorance – admittedly, they do not claim that the list is exhaustive. Haas and Vogt's taxonomy focuses mainly on reflective forms of ignorance,

DOI: 10.4324/9781003375500-5

instances in which a subject has some doxastic attitude toward her ignorance, but there are, crucially, also non-reflective forms of ignorance. My study of the symptoms of ignorance further examines these non-reflective forms of ignorance, and their relation to reflective forms of ignorance and, thereby, enhances Haas and Vogt's taxonomy. In order to reach this result, I first introduce Haas and Vogt's taxonomy and then go through symptoms of ignorance in the belief set, the epistemic attitudes and a subject's affects to develop a more complete picture.

Haas and Vogt's (2015) taxonomy of ignorance is amenable to the Integrated Conception of Ignorance because, unlike the taxonomies of propositional conceptions of ignorance, it focuses on the subject's attitudes and motivations. Haas and Vogt distinguish Preferred Ignorance, Investigative Ignorance, Complete Ignorance, Presumed Knowledge.

In a case of preferred ignorance a subject does not know something and prefers not knowing. Haas and Vogt's example is of Socrates who does not know about fashion, and, in addition, Socrates does not care about not knowing about fashion. He prefers ignorance. Preferred ignorance itself can be blameworthy or "unobjectionable" (Haas and Vogt 2015, 20). In order to evaluate an instance of preferred ignorance, one needs to look at the particular circumstances.

Investigative ignorance consists in "attitudes" (Haas and Vogt 2015, 20) which a subject that is involved in inquiry takes up. The subject does not know something but wants to find out about it. For example, Socrates does not know what the good is, but attempts to find out and engages in investigation (Haas and Vogt 2015, 17).

Complete Ignorance is different from investigative and preferred ignorance because the subject does not hold a doxastic attitude toward her ignorance. Haas and Vogt distinguish

a ignorance of something of which the subject has never heard – this could be deep ignorance as on the propositional conception (cf. Haas and Vogt 2015, 21);
b ignorance because the object about which the subject has beliefs does not exist (cf. Haas and Vogt 2015, 21);
c incomplete complete ignorance in which the subject has some beliefs about some state of nature/fact but her beliefs are hazy, not complete, for example, inchoate beliefs about evolutionary biology (cf. Haas and Vogt 2015, 22).

Such incomplete complete ignorance amounts to a "mental blank" (Haas and Vogt 2015, 21) of which the subject is aware. It consists in "attitudes that delineate the domain where a reflective cognizer perceives gaps" (Haas and Vogt 2015, 22). The German expression *Halbwissen* (literally translated: Half-Knowledge) might capture this variety of ignorance. The subject knows some things but does not possess the relevant background knowledge and interconnected knowledge to really understand the topic or the fact.

The term *Halbwissen* can be neutral, but it can also have a marked negative connotation when the half-knowing subject presumes that she has the same entitlements as a full knower and underrates her own ignorance – I return to a more detailed discussion of *Halbwissen* in Section 4.5. In these cases *Halbwissen* is also closely related to what Haas and Vogt call presumed knowledge. In addition to some true beliefs about a subject matter, the subject also holds a false belief (or several false beliefs) to be true, but she does not know that she is wrong, she thinks that she is right, that she knows that *p*. The term *presumed knowledge* fits this type of ignorance very well because "from the inside, this kind of ignorance feels like knowledge" (Haas and Vogt 2015, 19). In cases of presumed knowledge, the subject is "not motivated to inquire, qualify her views as tentative, or anything of that sort" (Haas and Vogt 2015, 19).

I will employ the terminology and distinctions that Haas and Vogt have introduced to illuminate the nature of ignorance, looking at symptoms of ignorance and at various manifestations of ignorance. These manifestations may sometimes appear too complicated or too fine-grained, but they are necessary for really getting at ignorance as real-world phenomenon that is not too idealized to be relevant for human epistemic lives. On the basis of these manifestations, I paint a richer picture of types and kinds of ignorance at the end of this chapter.

4.1 How Widespread Is Ignorance?

An encyclopedia article on a syndrome contains a section on how prevalent and how frequent the syndrome is – its epidemiology. So: how widespread is ignorance? This includes questions such as: who is affected by ignorance? Who is ignorant? Who can be ignorant? To some extent the answer is very easy: ignorance is widespread among all human beings. Every human being can be ignorant and, in fact, every human being *is* ignorant. Ignorance, according to St. Augustine, is one of the *primordia naturalia*, all human beings are born with it (Fuhrer 2010).[2] That is what I call the "trivial answer" to how widespread ignorance is – even though, of course, St Augustine's view is far from trivial. The main claim is simply trivial because it says that every human being is ignorant.

But there are more nuanced answers. Even though ignorance is a normal state for human beings, one can specify particular kinds of ignorance that are somehow more relevant or pertinent than others. And second, when people say that all human beings are ignorant, that ignorance is widespread, the claim can be critical of humanity at large or a mere description without a judgmental undertone. We find the later, for example, in medicine, there are areas like genetics, in which there is also widespread ignorance because researchers and practitioners do not know enough about the exact working and effects of manipulations of genes (cf. Doudna 2015 on CRISPR CAS-9) or how the brain and the intestines affect each other (cf. Carabotti et al. 2015). Or there is ignorance about the origins of the earth in physics that does not come with a judgmental undertone. There are models and possible explanations, but no one knows for sure. Let's look at the different facets of the epidemiology of ignorance.

4.1.1 *The Trivial Answer*

The trivial answer is: All human beings are ignorant and so ignorance is universal. There are three routes to the trivial conclusion that all human beings are ignorant. First, an Argument via Non-omniscience. Second, an Argument via Ignorance of the Humanly Knowable. Third, an Argument via Fallibility and Limited Cognitive Capacities of Human Beings.

The first suggestion is that every human being is ignorant because no living human being is omniscient. I presuppose this definition of omniscience: "S is omniscient = Df for every proposition p, if p is true then S knows p" (Wierenga 2018).[3] But we can be more precise regarding who is ignorant and why. What I have just said is trivially true. No human being is omniscient so all human beings are ignorant. Since this claim is trivial, it is doubtful whether much is gained by saying that subjects are ignorant in this respect. Human beings cannot attain omniscience and so it does not seem helpful to say that human beings are ignorant in the sense of not being omniscient.[4] The statement is informative only under certain conditions.

But epistemic subjects are not just ignorant relative to all possible knowledge (omniscience), they are also ignorant relative to what human beings in general can know, and ignorant relative to what they individually can know. "What human beings in general can know" is ambiguous between "what is knowable and is known by at least one subject" and "what is knowable." And in the individual case there would also be conditions of the individual's context that might make something unknowable to her and, thus, make her ignorant.

Kant's observations published in the *Jäsche Logic* provide a helpful framework for setting out the different routes to determining ignorance of what is knowable.[5] I return to Kant on error and ignorance in more detail in Section 9.5 and Chapter 10; here I just want to introduce Kant's notion of a horizon and the related distinctions between an absolute/universal horizon and particular/conditioned horizon to understand the different levels of "what is knowable." Kant develops the notion *horizon* on the basis of Georg Friedrich Meier's notion of the concept, as developed in Meier's *Doctrine of Reason* (Meier 1752/2015).[6] A horizon relates all *Erkenntnis* with the "capabilities and ends of the subject" (Kant, JL, AA IX, 40).

The horizon determines and judges (evaluates, we may say) *what man can know*, *what man is permitted to know* and *what man ought to know*.[7] And so ignorance is determined in relation to the horizon. There are three ways of determining the horizon. The horizon is logically determined if it is related to the "interest of the understanding" (Kant, JL, AA IX, 40). The relevant questions for this approach are: How can far we go in our *Erkenntnis*? How far do we have to go in our *Erkenntnis*? How can certain cognitions be logical means for our more general principles of cognition? The horizon is aesthetically determined if the cognition are related to taste, and if one looks at the "interests of feeling" (Kant, JL, AA IX, 40). On this approach, science is put in relation to the taste of the public, and to the unlearned. This approach determines what man is permitted to know. And, finally, the horizon is practically determined if it is related to the "interest of the will" (Kant, JL, AA IX 40–41). In the practical determination, cognition captures what effect "a cognition has on our morality" (Kant, JL, AA IX, 41). This approach determines what man ought to know.

In addition, there are two ways for logically determining a horizon: *determination from the object's perspective*, *determination from the subject's perspective*. If the horizon is determined from the object, there is a historical horizon and a rational horizon. Kant notes that the historical horizon is infinite because our historical cognition is unlimited. The rational limit is determined by the limits of the objects of cognition of reason, or mathematical cognition.

If the horizon is determined from the subject's perspective, there is the absolute/universal horizon and the particular/conditioned horizon. The absolute/universal horizon is determined by the limits of human cognition in general. The particular/conditioned horizon is what Kant calls the private horizon, and this horizon is determined by an individual's gender, class, standing, etc. The private horizon can also be generalized to a horizon of science and a "horizon of healthy reason" (Kant, JL, AA IX, 41).

We can use these distinctions to rephrase my above claims about the different ways of being ignorant: A subject can be ignorant relative to the absolute horizon, or she can be ignorant relative to the private horizon. And she does not know what is knowable to human beings (in general) because of her private horizon, or she does not know because human beings have limited cognitive capacities. Psychological research provides another route to these human limitations. Issues of necessary unknowability concern the rational horizon that is determined from the object's perspective.

Kant summarizes his insights as follows: "What we cannot know is beyond our horizon, what we do not need to know is outside our horizon" (JL, AA IX, 42). And what we ought not know because it would be harmful is *beneath our horizon*.[8] The two latter differentiations are always relative to the individual.

Kant's observations about the absolute and the private horizon lead us to the *third* way of supporting the claim that all human beings are ignorant: Human beings have limited cognitive capacities and therefore they are bound to be ignorant (relative to the absolute horizon). These limitations affect the scope and the performance of the subject. A subject's knowledge and ignorance are determined by what is relevant for her and what she can remember given her situation (private horizon) and they are determined by how much a human mind can store, process, remember etc.

Imagine Tina who has lived in Switzerland all her life, she has never heard of the 17th-century feminist intellectual Sor Juana Inés de la Cruz, and inter alia she does not know that de la Cruz wrote poems. But we can explain this by Tina's circumstances and conditions. Tina is well read in European literature, but she is a physicist by training and not a literary scholar, she has a full workday and rich social life and she does not have time to read and study literary works from other continents. That is just a natural restraint: there is only so much time in a day, and there are infinitely more things to know than an individual can possibly take time to know (cf., e.g., Innerarity 2013). This natural time constraint is related to a cognitive restraint: there is only so much that a human mind can store and consider and this is a natural limitation to knowledge that leads to ignorance. Human beings are necessarily ignorant.

Note that the constraints on cognitive capacities only entail necessary ignorance, but do not entail claims about necessary unknowability. They only entail that a human being is necessarily ignorant, even if one does not take omniscience to be the standard. Irrespective of the possibility of omniscience, human beings are ignorant because their capacities are limited.

Necessary unknowability introduces another way of determining ignorance that does not relativize ignorance to knowledge. Instead, ignorance in the sense of necessary unknowability is explained and determined by necessary limitations of human cognitive capacities and the objects of cognition – this approach is reminiscent of what Kant calls the rational determination of the horizon by looking at the object of cognition (JL, AA IX, 41). Nicholas Rescher studies this kind of ignorance, "those aspects of ignorance that betoken inherent limits to human knowledge" (Rescher 2009, 3). The necessarily unknown is "that which cannot be known at all" (Rescher 2009, 4). Knowledge about past events that one did not attend, for example, is necessarily unknowable. The important difference to the other approaches to determining ignorance is that ignorance is determined by saying what cannot be known, not by saying what can be known but is in fact not known or unknown. Necessary ignorance and necessary unknowability must be kept separate: the one is a statement about epistemic subjects, the other is a claim about epistemic subjects and objects.

Observing that all human beings are *fallible* – they all make mistakes and errors, some conscious, some not conscious – is a related route to saying that all human beings are subject to ignorance, and this route, too, leads to a trivial ascription of ignorance that must be distinguished from particular instances of ignorance that can be examined in more detail.

I restrict fallibility to cognitive and epistemic fallibility, but, of course, it may be extended to practical cases, too. Like in the case of deducing ignorance from non-omniscience, the claim at first glance looks trivial. Humans are not infallible, so they are necessarily bound to be ignorant – in some sense. But again, if we look at the explanations of the fallibility, such as that human beings are prone to systematic error in judgment (Kahneman and Tversky 1974), or that the judgments and beliefs of human beings are influenced by surrounding conditions (Gigerenzer 2002), we see that the observations about human fallibility are by no means trivial, nor are they self-evident.

Before I turn to introducing evidence from psychology on human fallibility into the picture, let me emphasize with a view to the question of how one should deal with ignorance, that in all four versions of the trivial ignorance claims the *details* of an instance of a mistake or an error, or types of mistakes and errors, matter for determining the reaction to the particular instance of ignorance or kinds of ignorance. A false belief based on a prejudiced judgment calls for another assessment and another remedy than a false belief based on an honest mistake.

4.1.2 Psychological Research on Human Limitations and Fallibility

Research on ignorance in psychology undergirds and elaborates the trivial ignorance claims. They study ignorance by studying human cognitive limitations and fallibility. In this section I introduce work on meta-ignorance, on human irrationality, self-evaluation biases and studies on deliberate ignorance. I also return to this topic in Chapter 5 on causes of ignorance.

The Dunning–Kruger effect refers to a form of meta-ignorance (cf. Fine's second-order ignorance, Fine 2018) which affects incompetent subjects:

In short, those who are incompetent, for lack of a better term, should have little insight into their incompetence – an assertion that has come to be known as the Dunning–Kruger effect.

(Dunning 2011, 260)

Dunning and Kruger, in a number of studies, asked participants who had just completed a test of "intellectual expertise" (Dunning 2011, 260) to assess how they had performed on the test. Participants whose results were in the lowest quarter of performance overestimated their results by up to 45 percent – over the years they have conducted these studies with relative and absolute scales. Their explanation for this radically mistaken evaluation is that someone who is incompetent faces a "double burden" (Dunning 2011, 260): they do not know the answers to the questions and they lack the expertise to determine whether they gave the right answers to the questions on the test (Dunning 2011, 260f.).[9]

Research on human irrationality by Tversky and Kahneman may be cited as further evidence against the reliability of human cognitive capacities and their problems with ignorance: human beings use cognitive heuristics to draw conclusions and answer questions. But they frequently use faulty heuristics, that is, most famously they resort to beliefs that are easily available (availability heuristic), they use features that they take to be representative of categories (representativeness heuristic), and they use arbitrary numbers that they have just encountered as anchors when making estimates (anchoring and adjustment heuristic) (Tversky and Kahneman 1974, Kahneman 2013). Human beings are prone to making these mistakes, they are prone to be irrational.

The interpretation of these results has been challenged by Gerd Gigerenzer. He notes that most remarks about heuristics are set within a particular theoretical framework that presupposes a Bayesian rationalist model of inferences and starts with an ideal omniscient rational agent and aims to account for the rationality of finite non-omniscient human beings via "optimization under constraints" (Gigerenzer 2008a). On this setup, human beings systematically deviate from laws of logic and optimization and therefore are irrational. Against this, Gigerenzer argues that human beings are finite limited thinkers and, therefore, we should not use a Bayesian rationalist model of inferences nor try to study or understand their actions and behavior starting from an ideal omniscient rational agent, and laws of logic and optimization. We should work with "ecological rationality" that acknowledges the limited capacities of human beings and use standards that are relevant, that is, attainable, for human beings, starting with "mind and environment" (Gigerenzer 2002, 57). Then one understands that it is not at all irrational how human beings are influenced by ecological circumstances.

Further psychological findings that are relevant in this foundational project concern self-evaluation bias. Participants in various studies tended to overestimate their prospects, their control over their own actions, their own performance or qualities in various fields, such as intelligence, character traits, abilities. For example, Dunning et al. found that all participants tend to judge their own performance as "above average," the so-called above-average effect. There are several other varieties of self-evaluation bias, for example, "self-serving causal attributions" in which one accepts responsibility for successes and rejecting responsibility for failures (cf. Brown and Rogers 1991, Hazlett 2013, 45, Fiske and Taylor 2013), "selective inquiry" (Hazlett 2013, 46, Dunning 2012), avoiding negative information about oneself, or "biased social comparisons" (Hazlett 2013, 47).[10]

The omnipresence of such self-evaluation biases, in effect, means that human beings have all these false beliefs about themselves: they are ignorant about the reality of their abilities, traits etc. The tough call though is between the Dunning–Kruger effect and the benefits of self-enhancing biases. How is one to determine whether one is affected by a beneficial variety of ignorance, rather than in a state of delusion as in the Dunning–Kruger effect? The results of the psychological studies and the perceived worry may lead one to self-doubt or certainly into realizing a tension that Adam Elga expresses well when he notes that we are left "with an uncomfortable tension in our beliefs: we knowingly allow our beliefs to differ from the ones that we think are supported by our evidence" (Elga 2005, 115).

There is another sense in which psychological research complicates things for epistemologists looking to discuss ignorance as a real-world phenomenon: There is (empirical) evidence that false beliefs (and thus, ignorance) may have beneficial effects on the subjects that hold those false beliefs, and that they are not detrimental for them (Taylor and Brown 1988, McKay and Dennett 2009) – thus messing up the view that ignorance is always bad. The most well-known example are "positive illusions," for example, patients who have a negative prognosis for recovery but believe that they will recover are more likely to recover. Psychological research may thus provide motivation for the view that ignorance is not all bad after all; it may in fact even be healthy.

Another particularly striking kind of ignorance studied in psychology is so-called "deliberate ignorance". Hertwig and Engel define deliberate ignorance "as the conscious individual or collective choice not to seek or use information (or knowledge; we [Hertwig and Engel, N.E.] use the terms interchangeably)" (Hertwig and Engel 2021, 5). They emphasize that they "are particularly interested in situations where the marginal acquisition costs are negligible and the potential benefits potentially large, such that – from the perspective of the economics of information ... – acquiring information would seem to be rational" (Hertwig and Engel 2021, 5). Deliberate ignorance can be chosen for several reasons, for example, as a "emotion-regulation and regret-avoidance device" (Hertwig and Engel 2021, 6) – choosing not to know to avoid particular emotions – or as a "suspense- and surprise-maximization device" (Hertwig and Engel 2021, 6) – choosing not know in order to keep up the suspense, for example, when reading a crime story – or as a "strategic device" (Hertwig and Engel 2021, 6) – choosing not to know in order to avoid responsibility – or as a "cognitive sustainability and information-management device" (Hertwig and Engel 2021, 6) in order to avoid cognitive overload in the face of too much information and limited human mental capacities.[11] In these contexts deliberate ignorance is valuable – but Hertwig and Engel also emphasize that these studies are undecided on the dimensions in which the value of ignorance is determined (Hertwig and Engel 2021, 11f.). Is it valuable with regard to the individual's well-being or with regard to epistemic standards? What does it even mean that ignorance is disvaluable or vicious?

4.1.3 Widespread Vicious Ignorance

When people say that ignorance is widespread, they often do not mean the trivial sense of that statement that I have discussed so far, but instead express concern about some problematic dimension of ignorance: there are epistemic agents who do not know something or have false beliefs, and their epistemic situation has bad effects for the agents, their environment, their community, the world, etc. The statements about widespread ignorance in other individuals or groups often implicitly judge those people who are said to be ignorant. Their ignorance is evaluated negatively. – There are also cases of widespread ignorance in areas where this ignorance does not reflect badly on the ignorant subjects. But I first start with the variety that comes to mind more easily, especially in current times, where this non-trivial ignorance claim has turned into a complaint that also express profound worries.

Of course, in a sense, these cases of ignorance are also covered by the trivial ignorance claims, but the trivial claim is trumped by the negative evaluation and related worries. The underlying claim is that there is widespread ignorance that is not necessary and that things should be different. I call this "widespread vicious ignorance." People do not know, but they should know. Unlike in the trivial ignorance claims, the statements are complaints or laments that concern particular topics or subject matters, for example, climate change, politics, economy.

78 What Is Ignorance?

Instances of the widespread vicious ignorance claims are legion. One important and complex case of non-trivial ignorance claims is the claim that a large number of people – worldwide – are ignorant about climate change, very generally speaking.[12] And studies on voter ignorance in politics reveal that citizens lack the requisite political knowledge, that is, they do not know fundamental facts about politics in their country, their state or worldwide (e.g., Weinshall 2003, 42, Brennan 2016, 25f. for overviews). They are ignorant about political issues, players, and what Delli Carpini and Kelter call "rules of the game" (Delli Carpini and Keeter 1996, 65).

But so far these claims about trivial and vicious widespread ignorance have only addressed the doxastic level of ignorance and neglected the agential and structural components. How does the agential and structural components feature in the epidemiology of ignorance? We need to say more about how widespread close-minded ignorance, open-minded ignorance, humble ignorance, curious ignorance, etc. are. And there are some such considerations, e.g. in studies on politics and climate change.

And research on biases that I have just cited in discussing psychological research on limitations in human cognitive capacities and their fallibility may claim to provide evidence that close-mindedness based on faulty reasoning and heuristics, such as motivated reasoning (e.g., Kunda 1990) and intergroup bias (e.g., Hewstone et al. 2002, Dovidio et al. 2017), is widespread, thus bringing agential components into the picture.

Taber and Lodge (2006) observe that people with strong views on particular issues – they examined affirmative action and gun control – treat arguments for and against, say, affirmative action differently, depending on their own previously held view. They are "are biased-information processors" (Taber and Lodge 2006, 755). For example, they rate arguments that confirm their own view stronger than opposing arguments (*prior-attitude effect*), they think more about arguments from the opposing side (*disconfirmation bias*), they choose more arguments from their own side (*confirmation bias*), their attitudes become more extreme after reading pro and con arguments (*polarization effects*).[13]

The "nature of times" heuristic identified by Philip Converse (Converse 2006[1964], 16, cited in Weinshall 2003, 38) as well as the "issue public" heuristic might also evince widespread instances of ignorance that explicitly includes both the doxastic and the attitudinal component. In the "nature of the times" heuristic

> [the subject] bases his voting decision on a candidate's "temporal association in the past with broad societal states of war or peace, prosperity or depression." Thus if the economy is performing well or the

country has been successful in a war, then this type of voter will typically support the incumbent.

(Weinshall 2003, 3, my addition)

The "issue public" heuristic finds that people vote on the basis of just one issue of concern to them, disregarding any connections to other issues and not building up a "global perspective on politics" (Weinshall 2003, 3).

Finally, Kruglanski's work on the extrinsic need for nonspecific closure – "a desire for an assured opinion on a topic, as opposed to uncertainty and ambiguity" (Kruglanski and Boyatzi 2012, 220), in addition to an intrinsic goal of believing what is true, may also be cited as evidence in trying to answer the question of how widespread ignorance as a multi-component state is. These needs translate into varying degrees of open-mindedness or close-mindedness, depending on whether the information is conducive to closure or not.[14] This need for closure might be seen to lead people to precipitate conclusions that include false beliefs and are lacking in detail, and thus increase the likelihood and presence of ignorance. This holds both for the doxastic and the attitudinal level.

4.2 Ignorance as Absence of Belief

The most obvious symptom of ignorance in the belief set is the absence[15] of a true belief, or of a set of true beliefs.[16] Rachel does not know that there are sand beaches in Japan. Sam does not know what the functions of the diaphragm are. Tom does not know how algorithms work. If the three of them are aware of their own ignorance, they are reflectively ignorant; they have some beliefs about the relevant topic, but they lack particular true propositions, for example, that there are sand beaches in Japan. Note that workarounds, as they are used in sciences, for example, proxies developed in paleoclimatology, are also symptoms of ignorance that are connected to being reflectively ignorant – knowing that one does not know some fact to the matter. Most absence of a true belief (or true beliefs) is not reflective but non-reflective.

Ignorance as absence may also consist in the absence of a false belief, since one can be ignorant of falsehoods, for example, if one does not know what conspiracy theories about 9/11 claim. Critics of this view, for example, defenders of the New View like Peels, hold that one can only be ignorant of truths, and that ignorance of falsehoods really amounts to lack of awareness of false claims. But it is conceivable that ignorance of a false belief also amounts to lack of awareness of the relevant true belief, so this objection is not decisive. The critics' position might be shaped by the strange ring to sentences like "Aristotle did not know that the University of Lucerne is located in Zurich." (which is a falsehood). But if we said,

Aristotle was ignorant of the falsehood that the University of Lucerne is located in Zurich, or Aristotle was ignorant of the false belief that the University of Lucerne is located in Zurich, the strangeness vanishes.[17]

So, I take it that ignorance can also have absence of false belief as one of its symptoms. Epistemically, it is valuable to *know of* false beliefs, both of my own false beliefs and of other people's false beliefs, for example, in order to be able to work against these false beliefs, to avoid any disadvantages because of those false beliefs, to convince other people that these beliefs are false, or to acquire true beliefs instead. We find evidence for the epistemic value of knowing about (or: of) false beliefs in discussions of error in history of science. Jutta Schickore has shown that scientific researchers examine errors in order to avoid errors and to understand "potential sources of error" (Schickore 2005, 552). Her analysis of a dispute between microscopists in the 1830s shows that the participants discuss "arguments about error," the epistemological and methodological effects of errors, as well as "arguments from error … to indicate that their research took the potential sources of error into account" (Schickore 2005, 554).

Simple Propositional Ignorance

The idea of ignorance as the absence of a (true or false) belief – simple propositional ignorance – seems to fit with Peels' *disbelieving ignorance* and also with *deep ignorance*, but as we will see, there is much more to say about this seemingly simple absence of belief.

Picture this case. Rachel is disbelievingly ignorant if she does not believe that Fanny Hensel and Felix Mendelssohn Bartholdy were siblings. But if she was told that Fanny Hensel's maiden name was Mendelssohn Bartholdy and that they were in fact siblings, she would understand the statements and grasp the evidence and would then believe, and even know that Fanny Hensel and Felix Mendelssohn Bartholdy were siblings.

Since the focus on propositional knowledge and propositional ignorance is too limited to capture ignorance, simple propositional ignorance is but *one* facet of being ignorant about a fact. Such cases of *purely simple propositional ignorance* are rare on the Integrated Conception because agential and structural components also contribute to ignorance – and that includes Rachel's ignorance. But in discussing the symptoms of ignorance on the level of the subject's belief, it is useful to look at the doxastic component in more detail and learn more about the background conditions of ignorance at the level of the subject's beliefs. The Integrated Conception must not neglect the doxastic level. Moreover, in the case I have sketched, the doxastic level is primary and most relevant.

If someone is simply ignorant about some fact, or some proposition, or some phenomenon or some concept, she can know it, if she learns of it, as in the above case of Rachel. Ascribing *simple propositional ignorance* to Rachel presupposes that Rachel has some knowledge of Fanny Hensel and Felix Mendelssohn Bartholdy. She has heard of Fanny Hensel and Felix Mendelssohn Bartholdy, she might know that they were composers who lived in the 19th century, who composed classical music, she might have played pieces composed by the two when she was taking piano lessons. She knows that female composers were often underestimated and continue to be lesser known and underrepresented. She knows about structural constituents to ignorance about female composers, we might say. But this knowledge is not relevant for this case, because this is just about not knowing about the personal relation between these two individuals. Her ignorance can be alleviated by being told that they were siblings. And if she possesses a conceptual framework in which she can first disbelieve that Fanny Hensel and Felix Mendelssohn Bartholdy were siblings or related, she can understand and incorporate the correcting information that they were siblings. This is simple propositional ignorance.

Deep Ignorance and Cluelessness

If Rachel had never heard of Fanny Hensel and Felix Mendelssohn Bartholdy, did not know that they were composers, when they lived, had never even heard the names, had no beliefs about them, she would be *completely ignorant* (Haas and Vogt 2015) or *deeply ignorant* (van Woudenberg 2009, Le Morvan and Peels 2016) about the fact that Fanny Hensel and Felix Mendelssohn Bartholdy were siblings.[18] If, under these conditions, Rachel was told that Fanny Hensel and Felix Mendelssohn Bartholdy were siblings, she would not know what to make of this piece of information. She might guess that this is a statement about a man and about a woman, and about their status as siblings, but she would not understand any of the implications, or why this fact is relevant or interesting. Thus, upon receiving this one piece of information, she would not anymore be deeply ignorant but *clueless*.

Let's focus on the symptom *cluelessness*. We would not understand cluelessness appropriately if we only focus on the doxastic component of ignorance, and, thus, I now also include epistemic attitudes to describe the symptom *cluelessness*. The crucial characteristics of cluelessness come out more clearly in another example: Picture Rachel talking to Tom about her field of research and she says "I'm working on the NAO." Tom has never heard of NAO, he does not know what the abbreviation stands for, he has no idea what Rachel is talking about, he is clueless. If Rachel started to explain what the NAO is, initially, Tom might have trouble understanding what she is talking about, if he does not possess the conceptual framework to be able to understand NAO and related concepts such as *atmospheric pressure at sea level.* He would not just be ignorant, but clueless. This is more consequential than simple propositional ignorance because simple propositional ignorance is an issue of not being aware of some piece of knowledge that one would be able to understand quite early if one learned of it. With cluelessness there is a gulf between the subject and the knowledge that would replace her ignorance.

The idea of ignorance as a relation to a question (cf. Bromberger 1992) is helpful for capturing cluelessness. Before talking to Rachel, Tom does not know that there is a question "What is the NAO?" to which he does not know the answer. He is deeply ignorant (van Woudenberg 2009, 374). And when he has heard of the NAO and therefore is able to formulate the clarificatory question "What is the NAO?" he has no idea, what the answer might be. If he knows that Rachel is a meteorologist, he might guess that it is some weather phenomenon, so he has some leads, but as to the NAO itself, he has no ideas. A patient who is told that they suffer from aortic stenosis might also, at least initially, be cluelessly ignorant, for example, if the disease was found in a routine checkup and they did not experience any bodily signs of being sick. Like Tom they would only be able to ask "What is an aortic stenosis?"

Cluelessness can manifest itself in different ways, for example, the subject may be confused when faced with a knowledge claim that someone utters or with true sentences about the topic that she is clueless about, or she may be caught unawares, she may be genuinely surprised. Tara Westover in her autobiographical memory vividly captures her reaction when she hears of Martin Luther King Jr. for the first time and hears, for the first time, that he was killed. She writes, "I was still ignorant enough to be surprised" (Westover 2018, 179). *Confusion* and *surprise*, thus, are further possible symptoms of ignorance. They may appear together with cluelessness but do not necessarily co-occur. I return to "surprise" later.

Paradigmatically, cluelessness is *non-reflective*: the clueless subject is often unaware of her ignorance, and, in addition, would be unable to frame any questions regarding the fact that she is ignorant of because she lacks the requisite conceptual framework and background knowledge. The relevant topic is remote to her. Admittedly, cluelessness may also be somewhat reflective, namely, once one has become aware of an instance encompassing, broad ignorance on one's part. Think of Tom when he realizes he has no idea what NAO is and does not understand Rachel's attempts at explaining the North Atlantic Oscillation. One would not *ad hoc* understand any explanation into the details of what one is ignorant of but one is aware that there is this topic that one is clueless about. As you might expect, there are degrees of cluelessness and thresholds at which cluelessness turns into another form of ignorance. And reflective cluelessness may develop in various ways. It may lead to investigative ignorance, but it may also turn into preferred ignorance.

Cluelessness appears to be related to *Halbwissen*, but cluelessness is less concrete and more fuzzy and blurred than *Halbwissen*. With *Halbwissen* there are more building blocks for understanding and the subject does know some facts and propositions about the relevant topic but does not have substantial knowledge or comprehensive knowledge.

4.3 Ignorance as Suspending Belief

Le Morvan and Peels describe suspending ignorance as "one suspend[ing] belief and disbelief on *p* while *p* is true" (Le Morvan and Peels 2016, 26). One example for this doxastic attitude is found in Descartes' *Meditations* when he suggests that one should suspend judgment if one does not know whether the statement is true. In doing so one can avoid error.

> What is more, even if I have no power to avoid error in the first way just mentioned, which requires a clear perception of everything I have to deliberate on, I can avoid error in the second way, which depends merely on my remembering to withhold judgement on any occasion when the truth of the matter is not clear. Admittedly, I am aware of a certain weakness in me, in that I am unable to keep my attention fixed on one and the same item of knowledge at all times; but by attentive and repeated meditation I am nevertheless able to make myself remember it as often as the need arises, and thus get into the habit of avoiding error.
> (Descartes 2017, 49, AT 61-62)

Descartes himself notes that this suggestion is not practicable: one mostly cannot stop and examine whether one's belief is true or not because "the pressure of things to be done does not always allow us to stop and make such a meticulous check" (Descartes 2017, 71, AT 116). And the stance is not just not practicable, it is also not a stable state located between belief and disbelief.

Friedman proposes an alternative conception of suspension: We are suspending on a question, not suspending belief (2013). Suspending, thus, is an *interrogative attitude* and presupposes that the subject does not know the answer to a question. Friedman notes the following "Ignorance Norm": "Necessarily, if one knows Q at t, then one ought not have an IA [interrogative attitude, N.E.] towards Q at t" (Friedman 2013, 10). Thus, an interrogative attitude requires not knowing Q at t, it requires being ignorant. And so suspending as an interrogative attitude is a symptom of ignorance.[19]

84 What Is Ignorance?

On Friedman's reconstruction we can see that suspending is not the result of a deficient epistemic standing, because if a subject had deficient epistemic standing, she would not form or hold a belief, whereas suspending is an attitude toward a belief. Someone who suspends on a question is also an inquirer. Suspending on a question as a symptom of ignorance thus leads us back to investigative ignorance.

Suspending ignorance on this construal would also go together well with open-mindedness and curiosity as additional symptoms of ignorance. If one is able to formulate a genuine question in a certain domain, one is ignorant, but one has a reflective attitude toward the ignorance, and such reflective ignorance – awareness of one's ignorance – often comes hand in hand, maybe even presupposes, open-mindedness, curiosity, investigation and an inquiring stance.[20]

4.4 Questions as a Symptom of Ignorance

We can generalize the insights about questions as symptoms of ignorance in suspension and cluelessness. If someone does not know something, they may ask about it – if they are aware of their own ignorance and sometimes also if they are not aware of their own ignorance. Scientists also formulate questions to address their own ignorance in their research (cf. Bromberger 1992, Firestein 2012). For those in the know, questions can also be a sign of the degree and depth of someone's ignorance. I might go to a bike mechanic and pretend to be knowledgeable about bikes, but the way that I am formulating my questions gives me away as a novice. But in other cases, questions may also implicitly show the inquirer's expertise in the field.

Questions as symptoms of ignorance are also compatible with the Integrated Conception of Ignorance because they bring together the different components. They may be indicative of the details of the state of ignorance. Hence, a particular question may indicate that one is ignorant but in an open-minded way. And a question can also indicate that one is ignorant in a close-minded way. The following scene that Cassandra Byers Harvin describes in her article "Conversations I Can't Have" (1996) is an example for a question as a symptom of close-minded, vicious ignorance.

> In front of a computer in the public library, I try mightily to meet a writing deadline. But being incurably gregarious, I stop to listen to a white woman, early-50s-looking, introduce herself as a writer and ask what I am working on. Putting it simply, I say, "Raising black sons in this society." "How is that any different from raising white sons?" she replies without taking time to blink, her tone making clear that she just knows I am making something out of nothing. I politely make clear that

we are not going to have that conversation. I can say it is because I am running out of time. The truth is that I am out of patience.

(Harvin 1996, 16)

The woman who asks this question, in asking that question reveals her own ignorance, but it is a vicious variety of ignorance.[21] In the USA in 1996, this woman should and could be clear that the lives of Black children, teenagers, especially boys and adults are difficult. And even if she was indeed ignorant of what raising Black sons in the USA in 1996 is like, there would have been a more open-minded versions of her question, for example, "Oh, that's interesting. What's the focus of your research?" Clearly, her question as a symptom of her ignorance is also influenced by structural components, whether the public discourses address the experiences of Black boys, teenagers, adults or not, whether, for example, books like Ta-Nehisi Coates' *Between the World and Me* (2017) are available or not. There is much more to the structural constituents of individual and collective ignorance, but I cannot address them in this context.

For questions as symptoms of ignorance we can see that the context and the formulation of a question are indicative of the state of ignorance that the person who asks the question is in. "Is the question appropriate to ask?" "Is the formulation charitable?"[22] – these questions are good indicators for whether it is an instance of open-minded ignorance or close-minded ignorance.[23]

If a particular question presupposes the right conceptual framework for the topic, the person is most certainly not cluelessly ignorant, and probably not deeply ignorant. And if the person asks a (clarificatory) question about some topic, she is most probably aware of her own ignorance. Note that you might be aware of your ignorance and still be cluelessly ignorant. However, awareness of one's ignorance and deep ignorance are not compatible in the same way; by definition, in being deeply ignorant you are totally unaware of some fact and the background assumptions of this fact.[24]

4.5 Holding a False Belief as a Symptom of Ignorance

The other facet of ignorance that we may encounter in a belief set is the presence of a false belief or of a set of false beliefs. In other words: a false belief in a belief set is a symptom of ignorance. In addition to itself being a symptom of ignorance, a false belief is indicative of other symptoms of ignorance. In some cases, a false belief may indicate the absence of the corresponding true belief. But not all false beliefs have one particular corresponding true belief, and so a false belief might be related to a cluster of incomplete belief sets or of other false beliefs. For example, the belief that parallels do not meet does not simply correspond to the belief that parallels do meet because one needs to modulate the beliefs and their truth value relative to the space in which the parallels are set (Euclidean or non-Euclidean).

Or take this example: Rachel might believe that Japan does not have any sand beaches. That is a false belief, but this false belief is also indicative of a wider gap in her belief set: she has no idea that Japan has sand beaches, and she has no idea of Japan's landscapes. She is deeply ignorant, but she is not clueless. When Rachel goes to Japan and sees the beaches in Okinawa she is surprised – but unlike in a case of cluelessness she is not confused, or cannot understand what it is that she sees. Rachel's false belief may be similar to Haas and Vogt's *incomplete complete ignorance*: Rachel has some inchoate ideas about Japan's landscape, but that's at most just *Halbwissen*.

At the same time, she is not *simply propositionally ignorant*. Rather, since she holds a false belief to be true, she is also misinformed. Being misinformed is different from being merely ignorant because there is a presence rather than an absence – there is a false belief present in her belief set rather than a true belief absent. Of course, holding a false belief to be true and having it in one's belief set is more likely than not to go together with lacking a related true belief. In these examples we find old and new symptoms of ignorance: Possessing *Halbwissen*, being misinformed and being surprised upon learning something new or being corrected.

Error as a Symptom of Ignorance

But false belief can also indicate more: an error in reasoning, for example, drawing a wrong conclusion, or an error in the process of belief acquisition; for example, basing one's belief on misleading or false evidence. A false belief is the result of a flawed epistemic process, and an error occurs within the epistemic process. Someone who commits an error in her reasoning process but accidentally reaches a true belief may also be manifesting ignorance. For example, the Ptolemaic geocentric system did lead to some correct predictions of the movements of planets and astronomical observations although it is overall a false model of the universe.[25]

Peels and Le Morvan's example of Alfred who thinks that he will be the next president of the USA and, on the basis of this false belief, deduces the true belief that the next president of the USA currently lives in Columbia, Missouri (Le Morvan and Peels 2016, 27), demonstrates how both an error in belief acquisition and starting one's reasoning from a wildly false belief are symptoms of ignorance.[26] Alfred might end up with a true belief, but we still call him ignorant because he has acquired the belief that he will be the next president of the USA, and he maintains this belief, even though this belief is neither supported nor substantiated nor confirmed by further evidence or other relevant beliefs.

There is not much work on error in philosophy – a situation very similar to ignorance. And even if authors talk about error, they do not define error, as Giora Hon, one of the few philosophers studying error, notes (Hon 2009).[27] Hon makes a similar claim about studying error as I have made about ignorance in general – we cannot understand error if we simply regard it as the privation of knowledge.

> [The] implied view that the problem of error is some sort of a mirror image of the problem of knowledge is misleading if not mistaken. To be sure, error is an epistemological phenomenon that in the final analysis has to be analyzed with the tools of a theory of knowledge. However, nothing in such a theory reflects directly the phenomenon of error and it is clear that a special inquiry has to be undertaken.
> (Hon 2009, 13)

I suggest that in Kant's *Jäsche Logic* error is discussed as a phenomenon in its own right. And we find a definition of error that serves as an entry point for this section on why error is a form of ignorance. Kant explains that error (*Irrtum*) is "falsehood, which ... is taken for truth" (Kant, JL, AA IX, 53, emphasis deleted). An error includes a falsehood, that is, a false belief, that is taken to be a truth, and every error necessarily includes these two elements that can be separated into an objective and a subjective element.[28]

Michael Gamper also emphasizes the objective/subjective double-structure that any conception of error that is similar to Kant's identifies:

> Error is an objectively false sentence that is subjectively held to be true by the originator or an adherent. We can talk of error when the identifiable falsity of a sentence and the belief of a speaker that the sentence is true co-occur.
> (Gamper 2010, 93, my translation)

But both Gamper's and Kant's conceptions do not pick up on an ambiguity in the term *error*: error can be taken in the procedural sense and denote some flaw in a process, or it can be understood in the product sense and denote the result of an epistemic process that is in some way flawed, where the issue can be either in the process or in the circumstances. The latter sense of error may be captured by talking of false belief. In the case of epistemological error, the object of an error is standardly taken to be a statement, a belief, or a proposition (cf. Gamper 2010, 93, Schwarz

1976, Schwarz 2009, Schüling 2009) since error is in a judgment or is at least based on a judgment. Most authors agree that error includes a judgment, for example, Kant in the *Jäsche Logic* statement that I have given above, or also in *The Critique of Pure Reason* (Kant, KrV, AA III, 234–235, A293–A295).

And Kant also offers an explanation for error: sensibility influences us so that we conflate subjective and objective reasons (cf. also Kant, JL, AA IX, 53–54). In the *Jäsche Logic*, Kant explains that it is *illusion* that causes the confusion between subjective and objective judgment: "What makes error possible, then, is illusion, in accordance with which the merely subjective is confused in judgment with the objective" (Kant, JL, AA IX, 54).

I suggest that we should explicitly distinguish the process-sense of error and the product-sense of error because each has a different focus – process vs. a false belief – and each calls for a different remedy. Therefore, I use "error" to refer to the procedural sense, and "false belief" for the product of error.[29]

Halbwissen as Symptom of Ignorance

Halbwissen also qualifies as a symptom of ignorance. And it comes with a combination of true belief and false belief – like error. Since there is no adequate English translation of this telling label for this special combination of true and false beliefs, I continue using the German term. The literal translation would be "half-knowledge." The German dictionary *Duden* defines *Halbwissen* as "deficient, superficial knowledge" (Dudenredaktion n.d., my translation). As I have noted earlier, such *Halbwissen* is closely related to presumed knowledge.[30] But *Halbwissen* is not always (epistemically or morally) negative. First of all, it can take different forms, (a) it can come with incomplete knowledge of a phenomenon, (b) it can be manifest in true belief without justification, or (c) it can be true belief without what one may call *background knowledge*, knowledge that allows one to weight, structure, organize and order one's beliefs.

Remember the NAO example: Tom might know that the NAO is a weather phenomenon and that it is related to El Niño. But he does not know much more. That is *Halbwissen* because it includes true beliefs, and relevant concepts, but it is not proper knowledge because it is neither well justified, nor extensive. Tom knows that there is a relation between El Niño and NAO, and he knows he has learnt about it in school and at university, but he cannot recall the relation, nor explain it. He cannot say what the relation between El Niño and NAO is.

But, again, *Halbwissen* is not enough to fully determine a subject's ignorance: first, it is but one of the symptoms in a cluster of symptoms of ignorance, and second, it is also further influenced by doxastic attitudes of the subject. That is also why the term *Halbwissen* itself does not automatically yield a negative evaluation. We evaluate Tom's epistemic state – he believes that the NAO is a weather phenomenon and that it is related to El Niño – very differently, depending on whether Tom is just about to start reading scientific articles about the NAO, or whether he has, say, watched a 10-minute documentary about the effects of El Niño and boasts that he is well informed about El Niño. Both cases of ignorance are instances of *Halbwissen*, but it is central whether, for example, Tom humbly admits to his ignorance or whether he arrogantly claims that he is well informed despite being largely uninformed. In other words, Tom's attitudes toward his beliefs are crucial for determining his ignorance. Depending on Tom's attitudes and epistemic behavior, his *Halbwissen* can be a case of *presumed knowledge* or it can be a case of what Haas and Vogt call *investigative ignorance*.

In differentiating kinds of ignorance in this section, I have frequently used virtues and vices, such as humility or close-mindedness. The framework of epistemic virtues and vices is clearly helpful for understanding ignorance better and it also provides further symptoms of ignorance.

4.6 Virtuous and Vicious Ignorance

4.6.1 Being Open-Mindedly Ignorant

Picture Rachel – she was misinformed about Japan having sand beaches – and Kim – they do not hold any beliefs about sand beaches in Japan. Both are ignorant about sand beaches in Japan. But that is not all there is to their ignorance. Let's assume that they are ignorant and open-minded. When they are open-mindedly ignorant, they are able to accept new evidence, or choose situations in which they acquire knowledge. For example, we can imagine either choosing to go to Japan for their holidays and learning about the sand beaches in Japan while planning their vacation. Or they can learn about it by reading a book about Japan or watching a documentary. They are ignorant and open-minded.

Upon learning a new fact about Japan, Kim, who did not hold a belief about sand beaches in Japan, could take up the attitude of investigative ignorance toward Japan's landscape. They have realized that there is a gap in their belief set that they want to fill. They take up a complex epistemic attitude toward their own ignorance: they know that they are ignorant about Japan's landscape, they are *reflectively ignorant*, and they want to learn more about the landscape, so they are also *investigatively ignorant*. Both attitudes go together with Kim being open-minded. Open-mindedness and investigative ignorance are most obviously manifested by asking questions concerning the topic one is ignorant about, so here we, again, encounter asking questions as a symptom of ignorance and as a means to identifying ignorance.[31]

Asking questions also directs us to the different facets of investigative ignorance. Investigative ignorance is not restricted to something like a *scientist's approach to ignorance*, carefully and in an organized way scrutinizing the topic of one's ignorance. Nor is it restricted to what one might call a *private detective approach* to ignorance. The investigatively ignorant subject may take simpler and less systematic approaches. Everybody can be investigatively ignorant as long as they are aware of their ignorance and want to know more about the field. What unites systematic approaches to ignorance, as the scientist's approach and the private detective approach, with an everyday approach to conscious ignorance is the subject wanting to find out about what it does not know, wanting to know.

What does the virtue *open-mindedness* entail? Wayne Riggs describes open-mindedness as follows:

> Being open-minded is popularly associated with many other positive qualities like curiosity, fairness, and thoughtfulness. An open-minded person doesn't jump to conclusions, but considers alternatives carefully. An open-minded person is interested in learning new things; willing to cast aside cherished beliefs if new and better possibilities are on offer. An open-minded person doesn't discredit an opinion because of whom it comes from, but rather judges it on its merits.
>
> (Riggs 2018, 141)

There are further complications in relation to open-mindedness and ignorance that make the picture more complicated. First, note that open-minded ignorance is not necessarily reflective ignorance and investigative ignorance, that is, a form of conscious ignorance. This is because open-mindedness as an epistemic virtue is both an underlying trait – a disposition – that may (or may not) be actualized in the right contexts *and* an attitude that is actualized in particular contexts.[32] So one may be open-mindedly ignorant before one knows that one is ignorant whether *p*, but also when one is actually aware that one is ignorant whether *p*. I call such non-reflective open-minded ignorance *Open-minded Ignorance Simpliciter*, in contrast to investigative ignorance and Socratic ignorance.

Second, note that these virtues are contextual and domain-sensitive in the sense that someone who is open-mindedly ignorant regarding one field, may not display this open-mindedness in other fields. Rachel might be open-mindedly ignorant with respect to her ignorance about sand beaches in Japan, but she may be close-mindedly ignorant with respect to the reality of climate change.

That is also one explanation for why open-mindedness is primarily inherently good or epistemically virtuous. Critics of open-mindedness will remind us that open-mindedness is often accompanied by a gullible and naïve attitude, and that one may be open-minded toward faulty information (e.g., Kruglanski and Boyatzi 2012). Despite these complications, I think that, ultimately, virtuous (good) open-minded ignorance is *primary* because instances in which open-minded ignorance is gullible or naïve are most likely cases in which we can broadly say that externally something goes wrong with open-minded ignorance. For example, one may be open-minded toward inaccurate information, or more generally open-minded ignorance is perturbed by other factors and motivations. This possibility does not impugn open-mindedness and open-minded ignorance itself, it just shows that open-mindedness can lead to bad epistemic results if it works with faulty material or is actualized in pernicious circumstances or co-constituted by bad structures. And conversely, as we will see, close-mindedness may lead to good epistemic results and also to good moral results. Incidentally, that is also why merely looking at the consequences of one's beliefs (and epistemic conduct) is not enough for rationally dealing with ignorance, a problem for the consequentialist approach.

Another independent reason for why open-mindedness is inherently epistemically virtuous is that open-mindedness goes together with accepting that human knowledge is limited, that is, that there is more to know, as well as human fallibility and one's own fallibility. Someone who is open-minded may simply allow that one is factually ignorant or that one holds a false belief to be true, and attend to new or contrary evidence.

4.6.2 Being Close-Mindedly Ignorant

We could just as well attribute other epistemic attitudes to Rachel and Kim and thus have them react in a different way. They are both ignorant about the landscape of Japan, they learn that Japan has sand beaches, but Rachel holds on to her belief that Japan does not have sand beaches, and Kim is not interested in Japan's landscape and so they do not go on to investigate Japan's landscape – not so much in the private detective sense, just in the sense of searching out more information. Rachel and Kim would be ignorant and close-minded. Theirs would be cases of preferred ignorance (Haas and Vogt 2015). Their preferred ignorance may be either conscious or unconscious, reflective or non-reflective.

Evaluating close-minded ignorance is more difficult than it seems, just as we saw in the case of open-mindedness. In philosophical discussions of epistemic virtues and vices, close-mindedness is standardly regarded as a vice. On this standard reading, close-minded ignorance can go together

92 What Is Ignorance?

with various forms of (vicious) epistemic conduct, broadly construed, that will also constitute symptoms of ignorance. For example, ignoring valid evidence, shying away from searching out situations in which one learns new facts, in which one is able to acquire knowledge, shying away from talking to people with another background, not reading newspapers, reading books, watching documentaries,[33] etc. These symptoms belong with preferred ignorance.

Nancy Tuana's taxonomy of ignorance highlights that preferred ignorance may also refer to wanting others not to know: "They do not want us to know – the ignorance of certain groups is systematically cultivated" (Tuana 2006, 9), in addition to typical self-directed preferred ignorance in the shape of *willful ignorance*: "they do not know and they do not want to know" (Tuana 2006, 10).[34]

Such vicious epistemic conduct, and preferred ignorance, in general, can be reflective or non-reflective and conscious or non-conscious. And it may seem that in either variant close-minded ignorance entails dogmatism – stubbornly and inflexibly holding on to one's beliefs and views. Moreover, in avoiding new facts, additional evidence, opposing views, one implicitly claims that one's own epistemic position is sufficient, if not superior.

Non-reflective close-minded ignorance leads to a special form of ignorance that does not feel (appear) like ignorance from the first-person perspective; it is what Haas and Vogt call *Presumed Knowledge*. The subject disbelieves that p – she believes that p when p is false – she holds a false belief to be true, but she believes that she knows, and, therefore, presumes that she is a knower. In cases of presumed knowledge the subject is "not motivated to inquire, qualify her views as tentative, or anything of that sort" (Haas and Vogt 2015, 19). Her assumption that she knows justifies her not inquiring, not viewing her views as tentative. In contrast to non-reflective *open-minded* ignorance the subject believes that she knows and does not consider the possibility that her beliefs are false. As I said earlier, open-minded ignorance comes with accepting the fallibility of human cognitive capacities. Open-mindedness (as a state, not as a trait) and presumed knowledge in one domain are, thus, most probably incompatible.

But the term *dogmatism* that I have used for preferred ignorance comes with a negative connotation that is not appropriate for all preferred ignorance. There is a variety of preferred ignorance that I call *Well-Informed Preferred Ignorance* and which does not entail dogmatism. For example, a scientist may choose to be ignorant about racist anthropology because she finds the consequences of the theories dangerous, and because she rejects the fundamental premises of this research. Biologists may not want to investigate into the mechanism of how bacteria become more resistant to heat because they want to avoid providing results that could be used to improve biological weapons. They could close this field of research because the potential consequences conflicted with their practical values.[35] A related form of preferred ignorance is *cognitively preferred ignorance* where one does not want to know irrelevant true beliefs because knowing them would clutter one's mind with irrelevant material and detracting energy from valuable epistemic endeavors (Cf. Harman 1986, 15).[36]

Critics might object that well-informed preferred ignorance does not belong with close-minded ignorance because the subject did inquire into facts, circumstances, consequences of the topic in question before becoming close-minded, so she was open-minded, and there is reason to suggest that dispositionally she is still open-minded.[37] Nevertheless, I think we need to group well-informed preferred ignorance with close-minded ignorance because close-minded ignorance, even if well argued for, is close-mindedness toward possible evidence and arguments from opponents. The subject may also avoid encounters with opponents because she does not want to know more about that topic. Of course, there will be different degrees of open-mindedness and close-mindedness in well-informed preferred ignorance, but for the sake of simplicity I ignore those.[38]

I propose to add another type of ignorance in addition to close-minded and open-minded ignorance since there are cases of ignorance that look like close-minded ignorance – not wanting to know –, for example, I do not want to know how many buildings are on Clausiusstrasse in Zurich, I do not want to know what my colleagues had for lunch on each day of their lives, I do not want to know where the other people who are boarding the same train as I am are going. I am not going after evidence on these questions to overcome my ignorance. But, unlike in the case of close-minded ignorance, I do not necessarily reject hearing anything about these and similar facts – I just do not care and therefore do not investigate into the topic. *Moreover* – and this is also different to close-minded ignorance – I do not actively avoid any evidence that I stumble upon. These are cases of what I call *Indifferent Ignorance*. Just as in Tuana's category of "Knowing that we do not know, but not caring to know – [because it is] not linked to present interests" (Tuana 2006, 4).

Not going after evidence might suggest that I am close-mindedly ignorant, but it would be an exaggeration to call me close-mindedly ignorant when my ignorance concerns these facts that are irrelevant to me – and to most other people, too. In cases of close-minded ignorance, the topic is in some way or other relevant, with indifferent ignorance it is not. Unless some change of circumstances and facts makes the topic relevant. If the agent is aware of her own ignorance and she judges that ignorance to be irrelevant for herself, then she is indifferently ignorant. She does not care about her own ignorance, she is indifferent. Indifferent ignorance is not the same as preferred ignorance because there is less of a motivation in indifferent ignorance. Preferred ignorance translates into

Bartleby's "I would prefer not to" (cf. Melville 1985) and Indifferent Ignorance translates into "I don't care."[39] Indifferent ignorance refers to facts and topics that are simply not relevant and not interesting. They are like the so-called fun facts that scientists, experts and enthusiasts will blurt out upon on cue.

Of course, a subject's ignorance is not solely determined by *one* epistemic attitude. Other epistemic virtues are more likely to appear together with open-mindedness than others. Promising candidates are, for example, humility and curiosity, the other two virtues that Medina refers to as being central for epistemic resistance (Medina 2013). These candidate virtues are also discussed in relation with the topic "virtues and education" (e.g., Baehr 2016).

Close-mindedness, too, has like-minded vices that are likely to appear in unison with it. Again, Medina's list is helpful: epistemic arrogance and epistemic laziness are promising candidates, and as my examples of epistemically vicious, ignorant conduct indicate, they are well suited for complementing close-mindedness. Let's look at these other virtues and vices and their relation to ignorance in more detail.

4.6.3 Curiosity and Laziness, Humility and Arrogance

We find the same opposite structure as with open-mindedness and close-mindedness in these two other sets of epistemic attitudes: curiosity v. laziness, and humility v. arrogance. But it is less obvious that laziness and arrogance can also have positive sides to them than it was for close-mindedness. Let's work again with Rachel and Kim and their ignorance regarding Japan having sand beaches. As I've said earlier for open-mindedness and close-mindedness, each attitude can be manifested before they learn that Japan has sand beaches, when they learn that Japan has sand beaches, and after they have learnt that Japan has sand beaches.

Curiosity and humility – two attitudes that are also generally taken to be epistemic virtues in the current epistemological literature – can come in exaggerated forms and in appropriate forms.[40] One can be extremely curious, in the sense of nosy, for example, if one wants to know the details of another person's private life and is obsessed with this interest. Or one can be too humble, self-deprecating when making exaggerated claims about one's ignorance.

I focus on Rachel and Kim after they have learnt that Japan has sand beaches. Curious Rachel and Kim will want to know more, after having experienced their ignorance about Japan's landscape. Whitcomb argues that "curiosity is a desire at questions for knowledge" (Whitcomb 2010, 673). Their curiosity is a desire that consists in questions about Japan's landscape, and this desire will be sated by knowledge about Japan's landscape. Note that Whitcomb's definition of curiosity refers to a particular desire to know something, but as he notes, it also fits for curiosity as a character trait (Whitcomb 2010, 672).

Lazy Rachel and Kim might not even be interested in the new piece of information about Japan, they might be not interested in Japan, or any foreign country – What's this distant country to me? And even if they were interested in Japan or foreign countries, they would be too lazy or maybe otherwise distracted to focus their epistemic capacities to follow up on the new information. They would be ignorant about knowledge (topics) that they might learn about and lazy in not striving for this new knowledge. This description might also fit for Rachel and Kim before they learn about Japan's sand beaches. In their lazy personas the two would not seek out information about a distant country that they have not been to.

Laziness can go together with the kind of ignorance that Haas and Vogt have called *presumed knowledge*: the subject holds a false belief, but she believes that her belief is true. A lazy subject will not inquire into the credentials of her belief. And *presumed knowledge* also goes well with close-mindedness and arrogance – if Rachel believes that she knows that Japan does not have any sand beaches, and if she takes herself to be well informed, she might also avoid and ignore other evidence.

But note that presumed knowledge does not *have* to go together with laziness, close-mindedness or arrogance. It is conceivable that Rachel has made an honest mistake in acquiring the belief that Japan does not have any sand beaches, and that she is actively going for new information and experiences – open-minded, curious, inquiring – but accidentally does not get to the right information and does not learn that Japan has sand beaches. Again, we find that ignorance is compatible with *very* different attitudes.

Humility and arrogance seem more prevalent in the subject's reaction to being confronted with her own ignorance or to new information. A humble subject might know about the limits of her knowledge, she is aware of shortcomings in everybody's belief set, of systematic error in reasoning, and of the fact that we all have false beliefs in our belief set, or misuse concepts etc. When faced with her own ignorance, she accepts it, or aims to overcome it, or work around it, and when faced with new evidence (etc.) she might check it, and take it up, when it is convincing. Humility, thus, is also a possible symptom of ignorance. A being who is omniscient would probably not (have to be) humble.

Someone who is ignorant and epistemically arrogant (cf. Medina 2013, 43f.) rejects new evidence, or new information, challenges the authority of her interlocutor who gives her new information, avoids encountering interlocutors who would be able to tell her something that she does not know, either filling a gap, informing her about a new concept, or correcting a false belief. She does all of that because she thinks that her epistemic status is superior to that of other epistemic subjects. Other symptoms of ignorance might, thus, be rejecting new evidence, flat-out questioning of authorities or expertise, avoiding new evidence, not listening to testimony by other epistemic subjects, silencing other epistemic subjects.[41]

4.7 Psychological States That Occur with Ignorance

When we look at symptoms of ignorance, we must not overlook that some psychological states require ignorance. For example, as Cynthia Townley has argued, trust requires some ignorance, understood as the absence of a true belief. If you trust me that my testimony about the result of yesterday's football game is correct, that also requires you to not double check, and set out for further information to back up my testimony (cf. Townley 2011, 27). In addition, Smithson notes that "hope, aspiration, curiosity, suspense, thrill" (Smithson 2015, 398) all require ignorance. Surprise also requires ignorance. A surprise birthday party for my partner is only a surprise if my partner does not know that the party will take place and does not know of my plans for the party. Remember also Tara Westover's observation that she "was still ignorant enough to be surprised" (Westover 2018, 179).

These states involve ignorance about some future state or event. Hope is only appropriate if one does *not know* whether some desired future state will obtain, or an event will occur. Curiosity also clearly involves ignorance; there is some *p* (or some facts) that one does not know and one wants to know, and goes after the information. Suspense is created if one does not know something, say, who the murderer is, who is going to win the game, how the committee is going to decide. Similarly for thrill. The difference between suspense and thrill seems to be a matter of degree, with thrill involving more intense happy excitement than suspense.

Trust, hope, etc. requiring or involving ignorance is ambiguous between ignorance being causally related to these states and ignorance being constitutive of these states. I submit that ignorance is not just causally related but can even be constitutive of these states. Ignorance co-constitutes trust, hope, aspiration, curiosity, suspense, thrill. For these states and attitudes to pertain the subject who is in these states must be ignorant of some fact or subject matter. It is not just that being ignorant causes these states, ignorance is one component of being in these states, albeit possibly just a small one.

And, thus, we can identify trust, hope, aspiration, curiosity, surprise, suspense and thrill as symptoms of ignorance. Ignorance is co-constitutive of these states and so it must be present for these states to obtain. But note that although these psychological states indicate ignorance, the indicated ignorance is not necessarily interesting or crucial. Trust indicates ignorance, but, by itself, this ignorance is not an interesting case of ignorance, because trust is the more significant phenomenon in this context. A parent who trusts their child saying that they went to school today and does not call the teacher to check up is ignorant about some matters regarding the child's claim, but that is not what is interesting when we look at such a case; it is the trusting attitude that is in the focus of attention. This may be because ignorance is constitutive of trust, but trust is not necessary for ignorance.

Things are different in the case of curiosity: ignorance constitutes curiosity, and curiosity is a symptom of ignorance, but an individual state of ignorance can also be constituted by curiosity. In addition, curiosity comes with an awareness of one's ignorance. Curiosity is only possible if one really does not know some *p*, if one has a question (Whitcomb 2010) and the subject wants to change this situation. In the case of curiosity, ignorance is *known* ignorance, or *reflective* ignorance. Thus, the subject is interested in overcoming her ignorance. Suspense and thrill also manifest this pull toward wanting to know – it is what makes readers of thrillers read very fast, and what produces excitement – and, therefore, in a similar way they also presuppose *known* ignorance.[42]

Curiosity comes with the drive of wanting to know, but is often also accompanied by the lingering feeling that you should not want to know, for example, because by knowing one would intrude into someone else's privacy, or one would unveil a surprise, or one could learn something about oneself that one would (should) rather not know.[43] This two-edged composition is often even stronger in suspense and thrill – knowing the end of a thriller early on destroys the pleasant suspense, but at the same time one wants to know how things go on – that is part and parcel of suspense.

4.8 The Affective Sides of Ignorance

The distinction between unknown ignorance and known (reflective) ignorance is also central for analyzing *affects* and *emotions* that *accompany ignorance*, that is, emotions that can occur together with ignorance. Here, I focus on the perspective of the ignorant subject. Emotions as symptoms of ignorance can play different roles in determining ignorance, they can be strongly indicative of ignorance, or they can be weakly indicative of ignorance, unassuming companions of ignorance, as we might say. But let me emphasize that affects and emotions are not constitutive of ignorance. They are symptoms of ignorance, but they are very weak symptoms that appear further down on the list of symptoms in identifying ignorance.

You might ask yourself why such very weak symptoms that might be unassuming companions of ignorance still appear on the list of symptoms of ignorance. They need to be included because they may be important for distinguishing and identifying manifestations of ignorance. For example, someone who is open-mindedly ignorant may experience happiness or anxiety. Both combinations are possible, and each would lead to different instances of ignorance. Moreover, emotions and affects in ignorance may be crucial for the lived experience of ignorance, and it is important to insist that there can be – and oftentimes is – a lived experience of ignorance. The lived experience of ignorance also importantly influences, and even explains, why ignorance matters to us and how ignorance matters to us. Of course, ignorance may be without an affective component but not all cases of ignorance are without affective component and, as I have said, the affective, experienced side of ignorance matters to us. Which emotion is present in a particular case of ignorance is also relevant for the reaction to that case of ignorance. Thus, we need to take that affective component seriously.

One such weakly indicative emotion is the emotion that most people will intuitively associate with ignorance: bliss or happiness. This intuitive link can be traced back to the pervasiveness of the saying "Ignorance is bliss." In the primary cases to which the saying refers, the ignorance is most probably unknown ignorance because the idea is that people are happy (in bliss) if they do not know something that might worry (etc.) them. This is most probably also the sense in which one sometimes says that children are happily ignorant, they do not know troubling and worrying facts. Another way of expressing their "happy ignorance" is to call them naïve and innocent. There are many examples of this combination of happiness and unknown ignorance in the Arts, think, for example, of Parsifal the ignorant, innocent and happy main character of the Parzival narrative of Wolfram von Eschenbach and Richard Wagner's opera. Parsifal does not know his name, he does not know who his father is, and he grows up in isolation, he is ignorant, but he is said to be innocent and happy.[44]

But reflective ignorance can also be accompanied by happiness. A researcher who has found a new question on which she wants to work knows that she is ignorant but may be happy about this ignorance. Or think of the anger of readers in the case of a journalist who unveiled the real name behind the pseudonym *Elena Ferrante*. The readers knew that they did not know who Elena Ferrante really is, and they liked this ignorance, and were angry when the journalist alleviated them of their ignorance.[45] If not knowing something is related to the subject's well-being, then this ignorance can also come with happiness. Such happy ignorance can be contentious if it takes the form of self-deception, but the contentiousness is not relevant in this section because I am not interested in assessing any states of ignorance, and rather want to look at emotions as symptoms of ignorance.[46]

Another large field of emotions related to ignorance are *shame, embarrassment and fear*. When one is told that one holds a false belief, that one does not know something or when one realizes that one holds a false belief, one often experiences shame and embarrassment.[47] And because shame and embarrassment are unpleasant emotions, subjects can also be afraid of being embarrassed about being ignorant, afraid of something finding out that they don't know some fact.

This fear of embarrassment may also lead subjects to *pretend* to know when they do not know. For example, in Jimmy Kimmel's "Lie Witness News" at the festival South by Southwest in which people were asked to say what they thought of the music some new band and people related their impressions and experiences of concerts etc., even though the band was made up by the interviewer and did not really exist (Jimmy Kimmel Live 2014). Leah Hager Cohen (2013) relates her husband's experience as a kindergarten teacher for similar evidence: when he asks 3–4-year-old children whether they can see and read the letter on the board, the children who cannot read the letter will often affirm that they can read it, but if he asks for details they cannot specify what letter it is. As Cohen notes, there is shame involved in admitting ignorance, both in the sense of lacking knowledge and in the sense of having held a false belief to be true (Cohen 2013, 15ff.).

Of course, shame is not the only way for reacting to experiencing ignorance: the ignorant interviewees and the children could have admitted their ignorance and asked for clarification, they could respond to the revelation of their ignorance by taking up an inquiring attitude, wanting to know more, being curios. But as Cohen emphasizes, such a reaction requires a special background, in particular, *self-confidence* and *privilege* (Cohen 2013, 50–52). One needs a respectful context in which one's ignorance is not treated as negative, in which one does not have to be afraid of being judged or regarded as stupid, uninformed, incompetent, etc.[48]

Ignorance can also be connected to existential fear. Patients waiting for important test results can be in such a state; they know that they do not know what the test results are going to say, and until they receive the results there is no information to alleviate their ignorance. As Kerwin (1993) and reports of patients' experiences show, in the case of particularly crucial tests, for example, cancer, such ignorance is often accompanied by fear and anxiety. This emotional reaction is an instance of *fearful ignorance*: the unknown causes fear in the subject. This may be because the unknown itself qua unknown is intimidating, or because the unknown may turn out to be disagreeable or harmful, for example, a medical diagnosis of a severe disease, or also just the first day in school, at a new job, in a new town. In less life-threatening or less unsettling instances, conscious ignorance – uncertainty – that does not come with a solution can be

100 What Is Ignorance?

accompanied by curiosity (again) and by excitement and aspiration – think again of scientists' excitement about a new field that they are starting to study. – I return to ignorance in medical contexts in Chapter 12.

Let me briefly point to another emotion that can be linked to ignorance. Another alternative to shame may be *anger* – the experience of ignorance may lead the subject to be angry with themself, or with others who have pointed out their ignorance or who sustain a particular state of ignorance. But again, as in the case of happiness – possibly an opposite of anger –, anger is not constitutive of ignorance, or necessary or sufficient for ignorance to obtain. It is just an emotion that may (and does) accompany reflective ignorance.

Clearly, ignorance can be accompanied by several and very diverse emotions. But this long and diverse list does not mean that emotions are irrelevant to ignorance, it shows, yet again, that ignorance is a complex state and that the conception of ignorance and our conceptual tools must be able to capture this complexity.

4.9 Overview of Symptoms of Ignorance

The examination of the different symptoms of ignorance has revealed a wide range of different belief states, dispositions and attitudes that occur in instances of ignorance and can be counted as symptoms of ignorance. In the case of epistemic attitudes and virtues we even saw that opposites could be symptoms of ignorance, for example, open-mindedness and close-mindedness. This does not mean that the idea of putting together a list of symptoms of ignorance is useless. It does deliver central insights about ignorance. First, a manifestation of ignorance cannot be fully captured by one single component; it also requires looking at the beliefs of the subject, the epistemic attitudes of the subject, and the affects of the subject. Second, ignorance can be epistemically valuable and epistemically bad, and it can be related to responsible epistemic behavior and irresponsible epistemic behavior.

But the list of symptoms does not deliver a collection of cardinal signs of ignorance that one might have wanted to gain and compile. The main obstacle is that ignorance is too complex and too multifaceted to be reducible to anything general and at the same time specific other than the constituents of ignorance: doxastic, attitudinal, affective and structural components. Neither of the more detailed specifications are necessary or sufficient for ignorance per se.

This result should not be surprising given the broad scope of my conception of ignorance and given the nature of ignorance itself. We can, however, collect cardinal signs of particular kinds of ignorance, for example, reflective ignorance, preferred ignorance, close-minded ignorance, and in doing so we can collect standard paradigms which we need to consider in the attempt at dealing with ignorance in Part 2 and 3. In compiling these paradigms, I will also conclude my attempts at improving the taxonomy of ignorance that I have started with at the beginning of this chapter. The different paradigms will be specified by doxastic attitudes, epistemic attitudes, epistemic virtues and vices, and affective components.

I have neglected the structural component of ignorance and only mentioned them in few cases of ignorance. This does not mean that this component is superfluous or not part of the nature of ignorance. But always including structural constituents would make this overview even more complicated and confusing. And sometimes the structural constituents are not as central as the other constituents. They will come up in the next chapter on causes of ignorance – and remember, they can be causal and constitutive of ignorance. Spelling out the structural constituents as symptoms of ignorance will then be for another occasion.

The non-exhaustive list of paradigms of ignorance that matter for how one should deal with ignorance is now complete:

A. OPEN-MINDED IGNORANCE

Open-minded ignorance simpliciter – The epistemic agent does not know something (e.g., some proposition *p*, or the details of some topic T), she is *not aware* of her particular ignorance but she is aware of her own fallibility, and therefore would be open to learning the proposition *p* and finding out about the topic T once she becomes aware of the particular instance of ignorance.

Investigative ignorance – The epistemic agent does not know something (e.g., some proposition *p*, or the details of some topic T), she is aware of her ignorance, and wants to learn and find out about it. The agent may also hold false beliefs to be true that are pertinent to her investigation and she may or may not be aware of those false beliefs.[49]

B. CLOSED-MINDED IGNORANCE

Preferred ignorance (reflective) – The epistemic agent does not know something (e.g., some proposition *p*, or the details of some topic T) and she does not want to know about the proposition *p* or the topic T. The agent is aware of her ignorance and of her not wanting to know and pursues these aims in her epistemic conduct.

Preferred ignorance (non-reflective) – The epistemic agent does not know something (e.g., some proposition *p*, or the details of some topic T) and she does not want to know about the proposition *p* or the topic T. The agent is not aware of her ignorance nor of her not wanting to know and she (implicitly) pursues these aims in her epistemic conduct.

Presumed knowledge – The epistemic agent holds a false belief to be true, and she does not know that she is wrong, she believes that her belief that *p* is true. She behaves like a knower, and does not pursue inquiry nor regards her respective beliefs as fallible.

C. COMPLETE IGNORANCE (DEEP IGNORANCE)

Cluelessness – The epistemic agent does not know some proposition *p* or the details of some topic T either because she lacks the conceptual repertoire required for holding the relevant beliefs or because she does not know that the requisite objects exist. The agent is not aware of her ignorance.

D. ALMOST COMPLETE IGNORANCE

Halbwissen – The epistemic agent has some beliefs about some state of nature/fact but her beliefs are hazy, not complete, e.g., inchoate beliefs about evolutionary biology, and she is aware of the gaps in her beliefs.

Presumed knowledge with some knowledge – The epistemic agent has some beliefs about some state of nature/fact but her beliefs are hazy, not complete, e.g., inchoate beliefs about evolutionary biology, in addition she also holds some false beliefs to be true. She is *not* aware of the gaps in her beliefs and believes that she possesses knowledge.

E. INDIFFERENT IGNORANCE

Indifferent ignorance simpliciter – The epistemic agent does not know some proposition *p* or the details of some topic T, she is aware of her own ignorance but she has determined that this ignorance and the related knowledge is irrelevant to her and, therefore, is indifferent to her ignorance and the related knowledge.

Passive ignorance – The epistemic agent does not know some proposition *p* or the details of some topic T, she is unaware of her own ignorance, but this ignorance and the related knowledge is irrelevant to her and she would not actively pursue inquiry in the relevant field if she became aware of her ignorance.

Before I end this chapter on the symptoms of ignorance let me discuss an important objection that will be looming after this host of distinctions of and variations into ignorance. A critic might reject my analysis as useless because it leads to a confusing particularist picture of ignorance. We cannot say anything principled about ignorance and symptoms of ignorance. I have collected all these different parameters and symptoms of ignorance, but they only lead us into a particularist mess.

The critic is right in noting the highly complex nature of the symptoms, and of ignorance itself, but that is just what ignorance is like. Ignorance is complex and nuanced, and that is also why the conception is complex and why *dealing* with ignorance is a demanding task. In addition, studying the symptoms of ignorance and compiling an improved taxonomy does equip us with more relevant types of ignorance that we can employ in understanding ignorance and in discussing how one should deal with ignorance.

Notes

1 Nancy Tuana's taxonomy of ignorance is even more empirical because she acknowledges that ignorance "intersect[s] with power." On that basis she develops the following distinctions:

"Knowing that we do not know, but not caring to know – [because it is] not linked to present interests" (Tuana 2006, 4).
"We do not even know that we do not know – [because] current interests/knowledge block such knowledge" (Tuana 2006, 6).
"They do not want us to know – the ignorance of certain groups is systematically cultivated" (Tuana 2006, 9).
"Willful ignorance – they do not know and they do not want to know" (Tuana 2006, 10).
"Ignorance produced by the construction of epistemically disadvantaged identities" (Tuana 2006, 13).
"Loving Ignorance – accepting what we cannot know" (Tuana 2006, 15).

I stick with Haas and Vogt's taxonomy because it is broader and less focused on motivational influences, but I will refer to Tuana's distinctions when discussing preferred ignorance.

2 Cf. St Augustine 1976, I.9, section 6. On St Augustine's conception, only God can save human beings from their ignorance (e.g., St Augustine 1941, §§52–57, 34).

3 I bracket any issues relating to whether omniscience also includes knowledge of all false propositions that they are false propositions, etc., because I do not think they are relevant to the current point of how widespread ignorance is (cf. Wierenga 2018).

4 This observation is parallel to Aristotle's observation that we do not call inanimate objects and children ignorant: they do not have the corresponding positive capacities, so it is inadequate to call them ignorant (Topics VI.9, 148a 2–8).

5 Since it is controversial how much of the claims are by Jäsche rather than Kant (cf., e.g., Conrad 1994, 62–65, Prien 2006), I was first inclined to talk of "Kant/Jäsche" as making these claims. But the *Jäsche Logic* passages on ignorance and error that are most central for my argumentation also appear in Kant's handwritten notes (Kant, HN, AA XVI), sometimes even verbatim (e.g., Kant, HN, AA XVI, 170–218, 282–294). Therefore, I talk of *Kant* making these claims.

6 Apparently, Kant brought his own copy of Meier's *Excerpt of the Doctrine of Reason* to his Logic Lectures and so it is no surprise that Kant's Logic Lectures address a number of issues from Meier's *Vernunftlehre*, including the horizon (Pozzo 2015, 17*f., Conrad 1994).
7 It is striking that Kant combines determination and judgment of the horizon, but I cannot follow up on this connection.
8 But logically perfect cognition can always turn out to be useful "for no cognition is, absolutely and for every purpose, useless and unusable, although we may not always be able to have insight into its use" (Kant, JL, AA IX, 42).
9 The studies on which the Dunning–Kruger effect is based and the effect itself have been met with ever-growing criticism but continue to have a wide popular appeal (cf. e.g., Ackerman et al. 2002, Gignac and Zajenkowski 2020, Gelman 2021, Hofer et al. 2022, but see also Anson 2018). I won't be able to enter into these discussions in this context but do want to point to these recent developments for further critical discussion of the effect in philosophical discourses.
10 For a general overview of *self-enhancement bias*, see, e.g., Krueger (1998), Weiner and Günther (2018).
11 See Hertwig and Engel (2021, 6f.) for further rationales.
12 Marshall (2015) even argues that our brains are wired to ignore and misconstrue the evidence on climate change.
13 Cf. Kruglanski and Boyatzi (2012, 218).
14 See, e.g., Kruglanski, Webster and Klem (1993).
15 The discussion could also be led using the term *lack*, instead of *absence*, without any major effects.
16 One might suggest that suspending judgment also belongs with no belief-ignorance, because in suspending, the epistemic subject neither believes that p nor does not believe that p, so there is no belief. But I think that (a) there is a difference between no belief and a suspension of belief, because no belief is nothing (a blank), whereas suspension of belief is something, namely suspension; (b) suspension is a doxastic attitude, and so I want to discuss it in the section on issues in the doxastic and epistemic attitudes.
17 Distinguishing pre-conceptual ignorance – the subject does not have command over the requisite conceptual repertoire (Le Morvan and Peels 2016, 23) – and post-conceptual ignorance – the subject possesses the relevant concepts but has not formed an attitude toward the proposition (Le Morvan and Peels 2016, 23) – may further reduce the strangeness.
18 Wilholt argues that in scientific cases deep ignorance is mostly conscious ignorance "where we do not even know any candidate answers yet (or none to which there do not seem to be immediate and decisive objections)" (Wilholt 2019, 214). The equivalent term to van Woudenberg et al.'s deep ignorance would probably be "opaque ignorance," "what we don't know we don't know" (Wilholt 2019, 197).
19 Let me emphasize that suspending as a symptom of ignorance only refers to ignorance as absence of true belief, and not to ignorance as false belief. The

Facets of Ignorance 105

subject may have false beliefs, but she does not have a false belief about Q; she doesn't know Q.

20 Ignorance with these symptoms would also tie in with Gross' conception of ignorance as knowledge of the limits of knowledge (Gross 2010).
21 The white woman may actually know and at the same time not *really* want to know that raising Black sons in the USA is different from raising white sons. This would make hers a complicated – but realistic – case of *preferred ignorance* in which her preferring to be ignorant involves denying any knowledge and true beliefs that she actually possesses. This is related to the difficult issue of ignorance ascriptions from the third-person perspective.
22 This question goes back to something along the lines of Davidson's Principle of Charity or, as he calls it, the principle of 'rational accommodation' (e.g., Davidson 2001a, 197, and 2001b).
23 For the sake of simplicity, I have identified open-minded ignorance and virtuous, good ignorance, versus close-minded ignorance and vicious, bad ignorance. My discussion of the attitudes *open-mindedness* and *close-mindedness* in Section 4.6 reveals more nuances.
24 For more on the philosophy of questions, see Cross and Roelofsen (2018).
25 One might want to object that the last claim is unjustified because the accidentally true belief that is based on a faulty deduction is still true and so it should not count as a case of ignorance. But this objection is based on a misunderstanding of what my aim is in this chapter: I do not simply want to describe instances of ignorance, but rather, I examine ignorance on the model of a syndrome. And syndromes are special in that not all of the symptoms have to be manifested for the syndrome to obtain, and it is not the case that every single symptom, independently of other symptoms, is enough to vindicate the diagnosis of the syndrome. A symptom indicates the syndrome, but the syndrome can only be identified by a conjunction of symptoms. Thus, I am not claiming that an error in a reasoning process always is an instance of ignorance; it is just a one possible indication of a manifestation of ignorance, a symptom of ignorance.
26 Le Morvan and Peels in introducing this example do not recognize that Alfred can be faulted for acquiring a false belief and for reasoning from a false belief.
27 In the history of philosophy, Hon mentions Descartes, Spinoza and St Augustine (Hon 1995, 5–6).
28 Locke in his chapter "On Wrong Assent, or Errour" defines error as "a Mistake of our Judgment giving Assent to that, which is not true" (Locke 1979, IV.xx §1). I do not employ this conception because it does not highlight the helpful objective-subjective structure. Locke also discusses error in his *Of the Conduct of the Understanding* (1996).
29 The term "error" is also prevalent in philosophy of perception, for example, the Argument from Error, and other discussions of misperception. I will not discuss this notion of error because it would lead us into different discussions. Perceptual error can be the reason for a false belief, but I won't say anything about the details of perceptual error.

106 What Is Ignorance?

30 And the German idiom "gefährliches Halbwissen" also highlights the threats that are perceived to come from Halbwissen.
31 But asking questions itself is not enough for determining whether the subject is open-mindedly ignorant or not. Remember Harvin's case of a white woman asking her how raising Black sons in the USA is any different from raising white sons. The woman asks a question but, as I have suggested in Section 4.4 on questions, her ignorance is not obviously open-minded.
32 Whitcomb, similarly, points out that curiosity can refer to "some character-constitutive way disposed to be curious" (Whitcomb 2010, 672) but also to an actual instance of ignorance where "to be curious is to have a certain sort of desire the contents of which are questions" (Whitcomb 2010, 672–673).
33 Kahan et al. have approached science curiosity by studying participants' reactions to high-quality science documentaries (Kahan et al. 2017).
34 Cf. also Pohlhaus' study of *willful hermeneutical ignorance* (Pohlhaus 2012).
35 Thanks to Jérôme Léchot and Lutz Wingert for providing this example.
36 But see also Friedman (2018) for a critical discussion of the principle and its connection to interests.
37 For example, see Cassam (2019).
38 Empirical evidence in political studies shows that knowledge and dogmatism are closely connected. As noted before, Taber and Lodge find that "people are often unable to escape the pull of their prior attitudes and beliefs, which guide the processing of new information in predictable and sometimes insidious ways" (2006, 767). They had participants who had strong views on gun control and affirmative action, read pro-and-con texts on these topics and found the prior-attitude effect, disconfirmation bias, confirmation bias, as well as a polarization effect in the participants' reactions to texts that did or did not fit their own views (Taber and Lodge 2006, see also Kruglanski and Boyatzi 2012). These biases and effects combine to being in a state of close-minded knowledge, but note that "knowledge" in these contexts probably refers to prior beliefs, independent of whether they are true or not. My examples for well-informed preferred ignorance that is based on one being true to one's principles (*being principled*) are better examples for the relation between knowledge and some form of dogmatism. One is dogmatic because one rejects the premises and/or the consequences of the topic or claim that one is ignorant about.
39 *Non-reflective indifferent ignorance* does not include explicitly taking up an indifferent position since the epistemic agent is not aware of her own ignorance. *Passive* ignorance best captures this implicit attitude; the agent is not aware of her ignorance, and she is also, we might say, in no relation to that ignorance. If she was to become aware of her own ignorance, she would not reject the evidence or try to avoid it; she would listen to it, shrug her shoulders and perhaps forget about the fact or the topic quickly.
40 Hans Blumenberg's overview of the history of curiosity from antiquity through the Middle Ages and Enlightenment until the early 20th century is an inspiring and rewarding read (Blumenberg 1985, part 3). Unfortunately, for reasons of space, I can only briefly refer to his work in this footnote. One of Blumenberg's many fascinating observations concerns curiosity's ambiguous

status in medieval philosophy. On the one hand, curiosity as wanting to know was a virtue on the Aristotelian framework. On the other hand, St Augustine grouped curiosity with vices. This dilemma has shaped much of medieval discourse on knowledge and epistemology (Blumenberg 1985, 336ff.). Nicholas of Cusa's *De docta ignorantia* (1440/1994) can also be read as an attempt to grapple with the two forces by combining the human natural desire to know and the humility of human finiteness (Blumenberg 1985, 355ff). More on curiosity in Inan (2012).

41 This list might strike some as too long and too extensive; why would a subject's behavior in discourse be relevant for ignorance? Is it even a symptom of ignorance? But in capturing ignorance as a state of a subject that is manifested in reality (as a real-world manifestation), I do not think we can restrict ourselves to only looking at a subject's belief set and her epistemic attitudes. An epistemic subject is also an epistemic agent, and epistemic agency is also found in discourse, in exchanges, in communication. And the symptoms that I list can be found in communication between epistemic subjects, and they ground or justify ascriptions of ignorance to subjects. Rejecting new evidence is a symptom of ignorance. Rejecting new evidence is not enough to ascribe ignorance or to identify ignorance, but it is one symptom of ignorance. Rejecting new evidence without good reason may be an even stronger symptom of ignorance.

42 I discuss curiosity again because juxtaposing it with other affective components leads to new facets that the virtue-perspective does not provide as easily.

43 Blumenberg's (1985, part 3) history of curiosity as vice might also explain the lingering feeling of doing something bad that may accompany curiosity. You want to know, but you know, you should not want to know.

44 See Wekker (2016) on the pernicious side of allegedly innocent ignorance.

45 Cf., e.g., Schwartz (2016).

46 According to Ravetz (1993), *pride* is another attitude or affective state that may accompany unknown ignorance. At first glance this seems like a plausible claim; someone who manifests *presumed knowledge*, that is, someone who believes she knows and is unaware of her lack of knowledge, will take herself to be a knower and assume the status and privileges that come with being a knower. But presumed knowledge itself is not enough to lead to pride; it is also compatible with happiness; one thinks one knows and therefore is happy even though one really does not know. Pride requires additional epistemic attitudes of the subject that cause her to manifest pride and ignorance. Pride, thus, just often occurs together with ignorance, but I do not think we can argue for a more systematic connection and should not include pride in the list of even weakly helpful indicators of ignorance.

47 See Graham (2015) on the function of such social emotions.

48 See Habgood-Coote, Ashton and El Kassar (2024) for receptive publics as spaces in which individuals can learn new concepts, ask questions without having to be afraid of being told off.

49 This addition is crucial so I can cover scientific error and ignorance (cf. Schickore 2005).

5 Causes of Ignorance

5.1 Getting a Clear(er) Picture of Causes of Ignorance

Getting a clear picture of the *causes* of ignorance is difficult because they are so diverse, as diverse as the manifestations of ignorance themselves, and they can be sorted in different ways. There are individual causes and structural causes: causes that can be traced back to issues in the subject and causes that can be traced back to social structures. In addition, the causes can contribute to the evaluation of an instance of ignorance – is it innocuous ignorance, is it pernicious ignorance, etc.? But as we will see, one cannot produce a clear and encompassing conception of the relation between causes of ignorance and the evaluation of ignorance. This task is just too complex since the evaluation of ignorance and the causes of ignorance are just too complex for a generalizable account. One can just talk about certain causes and potential instances of ignorance.

The different components of ignorance add further layers and complications to the initial picture. For example, for the belief component, the causes can be found in the process of belief acquisition, in the grounding of the belief. For example, the cause may be faulty evidence or faulty inferences. And the epistemic attitude of a subject may also be a cause of ignorance. In addition, the subject's motivation, interests, desires and emotions may also be causes of ignorance; for example, in instances of motivated ignorance the subject's conscious or unconscious desires and interests are causes of her ignorance.

As one might expect with these different possible causes of ignorance, ignorance is rarely, if ever, mono-causal. There is also no perfectly determined fact of the matter as to the complete picture of the causes of this-or-that particular instance of ignorance. We can just suggest an interpretation that may be more or less likely but the causes of real-world instances of ignorance will hardly ever be exhaustively covered. My overview over causes of ignorance is also not exhaustive, I only aim to present

DOI: 10.4324/9781003375500-6

a list of the most relevant causes of ignorance because they are crucial for understanding ignorance and dealing with ignorance.[1]

Let's look at an earlier example to find causes of ignorance. Rachel does not know that Japan has sand beaches. To be precise, she does not have any belief about Japan having sand beaches, and she is open-minded and curious. What is the cause of her ignorance? Why doesn't she know? What explains her ignorance? The most obvious cause are the natural limitations of human cognitive capacities: Rachel's cognitive capacities are limited for practical and performative reasons and for reasons of time – there is too much to know and too little time: the geography of Japan has not been in Rachel's focus of attention, and she does not have time to acquire knowledge about places of the world that are not immediately relevant to her life.

In the case of such ignorance of a simple factual matter, we can also cite lack of contact or interaction as a cause of her ignorance. Rachel does not have the requisite evidence. Let's assume that Rachel lives in a remote village and she has not met a Japanese citizen in her life, and she is also not interested in watching documentaries about other countries, nor in Japanese literature. The geography of Japan has also not been taught in school, or maybe she has forgotten about these lessons. This leads us to two further causes of ignorance: education and forgetting or limited memory. Limited memory, clearly, is an instance of limited cognitive capacities: there is only so much that the average human being can store and remember. Possible lapses in Rachel's education may lead us to structural causes of ignorance: Rachel's school may have been in a city that does not have enough teachers to cover all classes. Or for other cases of ignorance, there may be a deliberate decision not to teach particular topics in school or to propagate alternative narratives instead. Studies in how the Armenian genocide is denied and retold in Turkish history books are but one well-known example of such structural influences on ignorance and knowledge (cf., e.g., Çayir 2014, Altanian 2021).

Contrast these examples with Rachel having a false belief about Japan's sand beaches, she believes that Japan does not have sand beaches. This instance of ignorance has another set of causes than the first instance, because the causes for a lack of knowledge differ from the causes for holding a false belief to be true. But, of course, there is some overlap in causes: no contact with entities relevant to the subject matter, lapses in education and memory, as well as, natural cognitive limitations can also be causes of Rachel's false beliefs. Unlike in the "no belief at all" condition, however, the "false belief" condition requires that something has gone wrong with the subject's belief. The cause for the false belief may be some issue in the belief acquisition, or in the grounding of the false belief, or it may be partly caused by issues in the subject's epistemic attitudes, or in her motivation. As I said, this list is by no means exhaustive nor definitive. I just want to develop the relevant areas in which we may find causes of ignorance. Rachel's false belief that Japan does not have sand beaches can be caused by faulty evidence; for example, Rachel might have read a website with wrong information about Japan, or she might have been given wrong testimony. Or maybe she has misheard someone as saying that Japan does not have sand beaches, when the person said that Japan does have sand beaches. In these instances, the cause of ignorance is an issue in belief acquisition: faulty evidence.

Another central issue in belief acquisition that may be a cause for false belief-ignorance are faulty inferences, or more broadly faulty reasoning, for example, wrong conclusions, unwarranted generalizations. Rachel might hold the belief that European tourists generally do not go to Japan for beach vacations, and from this observation she deduces that Japan does not have sand beaches. This conclusion is neither well grounded nor justified, and so Rachel's inference is faulty.

Faulty inferences and mistakes in the exercise of one's faculties are crucial for John Locke's conception of error, for what he calls "wrong assent." Locke holds that Reason cannot make mistakes, it is the faculties that condition the mistakes. Among all errors, Locke distinguishes four causes of error:

1. Want of Proofs.
2. Want of Ability to use them [i.e., proofs, N.E.].
3. Want of Will to use them [i.e., proofs, N.E.].
4. Wrong Measures of Probability.

(Locke 1979, IV, xx, 2)

Locke observes that people have different levels of understanding and therefore may have false beliefs (Locke 1979, IV, xx, 5), and some may lack "abilities to use proofs" (Locke 1979, IV, xx, 1). These limitations may also be due to individuals not having time to think because they need to attend to urgent matters and ensure the standard of living for themselves and their family (Locke 1979, IV, xx, 2). Others may face these limitations because they live in oppressive systems that do not allow them to develop and use their faculties adequately (Locke 1979, IV, xx, 4). They do not have the relevant "proofs" or, we might say, evidence. This is another cause of error: "want of proofs" (Locke 1979, IV, xx, 2–4), the subjects lack the evidence (material) not the skills, we might say. Locke also acknowledges that people may be too lazy, may lack interest in books and study, and therefore are unable to "use proofs" (Locke 1979, IV, xx, 6).

In his *Of the Conduct of the Understanding* (1996) Locke presents a related list of three errors which I include at this point because I will return to the list in Part 2 when discussing suggestions for dealing with ignorance, in particular Locke's and Kant's suggestions.[2] But first, this is Locke's list:

> Besides the want of determined ideas and of sagacity and exercise in finding out and laying in order intermediate ideas, there are three miscarriages that men are guilty of in reference to their reason, whereby this faculty is hindered in them from that service it might do and was designed for. And he that reflects upon the actions and discourses of mankind will find their defects in this kind very frequent and very observable.
> 1. The first is of *those who seldom reason at all*, but do and think according to the example of others, whether parents, neighbors, ministers or who else they are pleased to make choice of to have an implicit faith in for the saving of themselves the pains and trouble of thinking and examining for themselves.
> 2. The second is of *those who put passion in the place of reason* and, being resolved that shall govern their actions and arguments, neither use their own nor hearken to other people's reason any further than it suits their humour, interest or party ; and these, one may observe, commonly content themselves with words which have no distinct ideas to them, though in other matters that they come with an unbiased indifference to they want not abilities to talk and hear reason, where they have no secret inclination that hinders them from being tractable to it.
> 3. The third sort is of those who readily and sincerely follow reason but, for want of having that which one may call large, sound, roundabout sense, have not a full view of all that relates to the question and may be of moment to decide it. We are all shortsighted and very often see but one side of a matter; our views are not extended to all that has a connection with it. From this defect I think no man is free. We see but in part and we know but in part, and therefore it is no wonder we conclude not right from our partial views. This might instruct the proudest esteemer of his own parts how useful it is to talk and consult with others, even such as came short of him in capacity, quickness and penetration; for since no one sees all and we generally have different prospects of the same thing according to our different, as I may say, positions to it, it is not incongruous to think nor beneath any man to try whether another may not have notions

of things which have escaped him and which his reason would make use of if they came into his mind.

(Locke 1996, §3, my emphases)

So people commit errors because they do not think for themselves and just follow the opinions of others (Cause 1), or because they let their reasoning be influenced by emotions (Cause 2), or because they draw conclusions on an incomplete basis of evidence (Cause 3). Locke's fourth cause neatly connects with heuristics and biases as we discuss them today: people use "wrong measures," such as inadequate heuristics and biases, in determining which proposition they should assent to and, thereby, acquire false beliefs. They accept doubtful propositions as principles, they assent to merely received hypotheses, they are led by their inclinations and passions and succumb to authority (Locke 1979, IV, xx, 7–17).

The literature on heuristics provides further details to issues of faulty reasoning. I have mentioned Tversky and Kahneman's research on the availability heuristic, representativeness heuristic, and anchoring and adjustment heuristic above (1974). Human beings resort to beliefs that are easily available, they use the features that they take to be representative of categories, and they use arbitrary numbers that they have just encountered as anchors when making estimates (cf. Tversky and Kahneman 1974). Such heuristics may feature as causes of Rachel's false belief.

Note that such faulty reasoning can lead to what one may call "benign ignorance," as in Rachel's cases, but, of course, it can also lead to ignorance with much more severe effects. (And remember that benign ignorance may only seem to be benign, Section 3.6.) Especially, if the beliefs are beliefs about other people and uttered in interaction. Cognitive biases can also be causes of ignorance. Elizabeth Anderson's list of biases that explain discrimination and stigmatization of Blacks in the USA provides an overview of causes for faulty inferences in practical real-world situations (2010, 46):

(1) Ingroup favoritism (ethnocentrism) – favouring the members of one's group, (2) shared reality bias – aligning one's perception and beliefs with those of other in-group members, (3) illusory correlation bias – the disposition to develop stereotypes about other groups on the basis of singular events, (4) stereotype incumbency bias – developing a bias about a person based on the job she holds, (5) power bias – the inclination of people in power to stereotype their subordinates, (6) system justification bias – the inclination to regard one's society as just.

These biases partly constitute and cause instances of preferred ignorance and presumed knowledge.[3]

Additionally, a subject's interests, desires and emotions may be causes of their ignorance. These causes may be closely connected to cognitive biases and heuristics of subjects. One's ignorance may be motivated by wanting to protect oneself from unwanted knowledge/information. As I mentioned before, many readers of Elena Ferrante's novels did not want to know the real name of Elena Ferrante, they were angry at an Italian journalist who set out to find out who Ferrante really is and came up with the name of the author. They did not want to know because they wanted to keep the mystery alive, or because they did not care about this piece of information – they were deliberately ignorant as Hertwig and Engel would say (Hertwig and Engel 2021). As Locke notes for the causes of (erroneous) beliefs: "What suits our wishes, is forwardly believed" (Locke 1979, IV, xx, 12). We influence our knowledge and assent by pausing our inquiry and not conducting it adequately. Once we have knowledge we cannot "hinder" it (Locke 1979, IV, xx, 16).

Or think of a subject who wants to protect themselves from harrowing war pictures and, therefore, say, do not attend the screening of a film on the Genocide in Ruanda. Similarly, many contemporary art museums inform guardians if the gallery room contains imagery that may be shocking to young children. Protecting someone else may also be a cause for keeping them ignorant and, thus, a cause for their ignorance.

Such protection of someone else or of oneself from unwanted knowledge can be well intended but also paternalistic or malicious and egoistic. If I think that I need to protect someone else from unwanted knowledge, I may be guilty of paternalistically interfering in another person's epistemic life. And by excessively protecting oneself from unwanted knowledge, one may be acting maliciously. For example, in an unjust society, members of the privileged group protect themselves from information that would disturb their view of their society, and that would require them to review and change the workings in their society – cf. the system justification bias. This ignorance has practical and structural consequences because the members of the privileged group are partaking in keeping alive an unjust society. This is where benign ignorance and harmful ignorance are very close. And this is why we cannot come up with a simple, generalizable conception of the evaluation of ignorance and the causes of ignorance, as I have noted at the beginning of this section.

What we should do instead, is try to understand particular forms of ignorance in which causes and evaluations overlap and to some extent even fold into one. This is what happens in deliberate ignorance and, in particular, for *motivated ignorance*. The term "deliberate ignorance" is more neutral than the term "motivated ignorance" and not all deliberate ignorance is motivated ignorance. So, what is motivated ignorance? And what does it reveal about causes of ignorance?

5.2 Motivated Ignorance

Motivated ignorance is a particularly complex phenomenon that brings together a number of causes of ignorance; individual interests and desires, as well as heuristics and cognitive biases also cause motivated ignorance. I further illuminate the nature and causes of motivated ignorance by analyzing an interaction that Cassandra Byer Harvin (1996) relates that I have introduced before and by citing current psychological research on motivated ignorance.

Let's go back to the encounter that Byer Harvis relates:

> In front of a computer in the public library, I try mightily to meet a writing deadline. But being incurably gregarious, I stop to listen to a white woman, early-50s-looking, introduce herself as a writer and ask what I am working on. Putting it simply, I say, "Raising black sons in this society." "How is that any different from raising white sons?" she replies without taking time to blink, her tone making clear that she just knows I am making something out of nothing. I politely make clear that we are not going to have that conversation. I can say it is because I am running out of time. The truth is that I am out of patience.
>
> (Harvin 1996)

In addition to the obvious insult that the woman delivers by asking this question, the question is also a clear manifestation of the white woman's ignorance: she does not know how raising Black sons in the US American society is any different from raising white sons, and she does not know that raising Black sons in the US American society is any different from raising white sons. We may say: she does not know whether p and she does not know that p, where p is "raising Black sons in the US American society is different from raising white sons."

But in analyzing this instance of ignorance it is not enough to look at the propositional level and at single propositions because it is not enough to capture the nature of that woman's ignorance. Instead, we need to see that her ignorance goes beyond not knowing that single proposition p, and we need to see that there are social and individual arrangements that foster her ignorance.

First, the woman's ignorance also extends to the everyday reality of Black lives in the USA, she does not know about the reality of *raising* Black sons, and she does not know about the reality of lives of Black sons in the USA. Second, in not knowing that raising Black sons is different from raising white sons the woman shows herself to be color-blind, since she does not see that race does make for a difference in real-world experiences. Her color-blindness may to some seem laudable because one might think that the woman is not racist, but treats everyone justly, yet her question and Harvin's reaction is a vivid argument for the observation that colorblindness is not laudable, it does not lead to less stigmatization, less discrimination, less segregation (cf. Williams 1998, Anderson 2010, 155, Medina 2013, 209–224).

What is the *basis* for this woman's ignorance? Of course, one cannot know for sure, since I am working only from the short question, but we can still uncover likely candidates. Anderson's analysis of segregation delivers plausible substantive suggestions for causes of the woman's ignorance. The bridging assumption is that the woman's ignorance is caused by effects of segregation, stigmatization and discrimination against Black people. The epistemic effects of segregation do not just concern the disadvantaged group but also the dominant group; the members of the dominant group become insular, complacent and ignorant because "they lose personal contact with the problems of the disadvantaged" (Anderson 2010, 98). Medina (2013) and Pohlhaus (2012) also point to the specific ignorance, including self-ignorance (Medina 2013, 161–185), of members of dominant groups. They do not know what the world really is like, what their role in that world is, how other individuals experience that world. For example, there is no contact between Black and White people that is not infused with stereotypes – either because the stereotypes are "practically engaged" (Anderson 2010, 62) or because the agents are inhibited by fear of the efficacy of the stereotypes. Harvin's interlocutor may not know what the lives of young Black men look like because she does not know young Black men growing up in the USA. There is a *gap* and Anderson is right to emphasize that this gap does not remain open but is filled. It is filled by stereotypes which again are shaped by segregation, stigmatization and discrimination, and by the media, social media, online discourses, films, etc. that again are shaped by segregation, stigmatization and discrimination. – Filling the gaps in this way is a very real way of human beings dealing with ignorance. – The woman's question thus is explained both by individual and structural causes, including biases in individuals' minds and public discourse (Anderson 2010, 64). And her ignorance is not just explained by these causes, it is also fostered by them.

Stereotypes and stigmatization can also work together in building up to ignorance, as this example from a school in Germany shows. A biology teacher asks a student whose parents were born in Turkey about transportation between cells, the topic of the previous lesson. The teacher asks what the name of transportation between cells is and the answer that the student is supposed to give is *osmosis*. The student has no idea what the right answer is, and the teacher wants to give him a hint by saying "Sieve. Sieve" ("*Sieb. Sieb.*" in German). The student does not understand the hint and when he still cannot answer the question, the teacher says in fake broken German something along the lines "You should learn German first." Mind you, this is a German advanced high school, a *Gymnasium*, the student, thus, must have had fairly good grades to be attending this school, and he did not just join the school but had been attending it for some years. The teacher's reaction is obviously inappropriate. It is highly unlikely that the student does not speak enough German to answer the question and infinitely more likely that the student, like other students, was simply not paying attention during the previous lesson and that is why he did not know the answer. Moreover, the teacher's supposedly helpful hint was not particularly good.

What is particularly crucial for the claim that ignorance is fostered by individual and social arrangements is that the teacher is ignorant about the reality of his students' lives; he is misinformed about what is the reason for the student being unable to answer the question (the student's ignorance), and he fills the gap by means of "stereotypic cognitive processing." To the teacher's mind the student fulfills the teacher's stereotype of a migrant student from Turkey who does not speak proper German: he "exaggerate[s] the conformity of [the student to the] group stereotype" (Anderson 2010, 45). And it is clear that the teacher is "more receptive to and better able to recall stereotype-confirming than disconfirming evidence [and] overlook[s] stereotype-independent individuating information about group members" (Anderson 2010, 45). Pragmatics might pose a problem for the example, since the teacher was speaking sarcastically, but the fact that he even suggests that the student's issue could have been not speaking proper German clearly betrays his stereotypes and biases toward this student.

Anderson suggests integration as a means to reducing segregation and its correlate effects. I submit that her suggestion can also be applied to the case of ignorance in general. If the lives of people from different communities were more integrated, they would not lack contact with another and could have normal interactions, not just out-of-the-ordinary interactions. These are steps toward dealing with ignorance and I will turn the question of how one should rationally deal with ignorance in the next chapter. But before I close this chapter and Part 1 of this study I want to mention an obvious branch of motivated reasoning that I have not discussed so far: *politically motivated reasoning*.

There are myriads of studies on politically motivated reasoning and I return to some insights when discussing the relevance of ignorance in democracy (Chapter 11). That is why, in this section, I only highlight one important finding: Beliefs that are constitutive of the subject's identity are particularly resistant to countervailing evidence. So much so that research shows that high levels in what is called *Actively Open-Minded Thinking* (Baron 2008, Stanovich and West 1997) do not lead participants to be open-minded to counter-evidence, but instead lead them to further endorse the view that comes with their political identity, for example, deny climate change when one is Republican and accept it when one is liberal or Democrat. Dan Kahan in his work with Jonathan Corbin and other authors conjectures that actively open-minded thinking enables one to recognize those beliefs that are constitutive of one's identity and where changing the beliefs would come with high "reputational cost" (Kahan et al. 2017, 181), and that this is why people who score highly in actively open-minded thinking do not change their views on identity-related beliefs.

Motivated political reasoning, thus, evinces cases in which one's political convictions influence one's reasoning process. And Kahan and Corbin suggest that

> 'beliefs' about human-caused climate change and a few select other highly divisive empirical issues are ones that people use to express who they are, an end that has little to do with the truth of what people, 'liberal' or 'conservative,' know.
>
> (2016, 4)

Other such contested issues are gun control, abortion, immigration, nuclear energy.

This concludes the first part, the study of ignorance. We have gained an overview of different constituents of ignorance and recognized the complexity and intricacies of ignorance. I have argued for the Integrated Conception of Ignorance, according to which ignorance is a disposition that is constituted by doxastic, agential and structural components. Various doxastic states, epistemic attitudes, emotions, environmental conditions, structures can take the place of these components. That means that the suggestion for rationally dealing with ignorance must be able to include these details and complexities. For example, dealing with ignorance cannot be limited to dealing with an information deficit. There must be tools for dealing with the attitudes accompanying instances of ignorance. So let's turn to look for the most promising way for rationally dealing with ignorance.

Notes

1 Epistemologist theories bring another cause of ignorance on the field: doubt and contradictory evidence. I may be ignorant because I cannot decide, because I do not know whether p or not p. Or I may be ignorant because I cannot rule out that defeaters apply to my case. Let me briefly note two such causes of ignorance: epistemic closure and defeaters.

Regarding *epistemic closure* I can be ignorant because I cannot know all that is entailed by my knowing. This point is brought up by the Harman–Vogel paradox. Imagine Tom who has parked his car on Broadway at the corner of

118 *What Is Ignorance?*

96th Street at 9 a.m. He knows that his car is on Broadway at the corner of 96th Street. But just one question may rob him of this knowledge. Does Tom know whether his car has been stolen in the meantime? He does not know whether his car has been stolen in the meantime, and *ergo* he does not know that his car is parked on Broadway at the corner of 96th Street. He has lost his knowledge by the addition of alternative possibilities and he is to some extent ignorant of whether his car is parked on Broadway at the corner of 96th Street. Strictly speaking this is not a *cause* of ignorance, but I still wanted to introduce these considerations here because the issue does look like a case of ignorance and I think we may learn from looking at the problems next to each other, see their similarities and their differences.

Epistemic defeaters can also be causes of ignorance. Say, you believe that the dress you see in a shop window is blue, but then you are told that the dress really is black; it is just the lighting conditions that make it look blue. Then your belief has been defeated by an epistemic defeater. There are also misleading defeaters, and for those defeaters it is epistemically better to be ignorant of those misleading defeaters, as Pritchard (2016) has argued. Defeaters are a popular topic in contemporary epistemology (Moretti and Piazza 2018) and it might be interesting to examine their role in epistemology of ignorance. In this study I have to postpone any such discussion for another occasion.

2 Brandt (1981) points to an interesting connection between Locke's list of errors and Kant's maxims of the *sensus communis* as presented in Kant's *Anthropology* (Kant, Anth, AA XV, 200). Brandt suggests that Locke's mistakes are "similarly structured as the Kantian maxims" (Brandt 1981, 39, my translation). I return to this connection later because Kant's maxims will figure prominently in Part 2 (Section 9.5 and Chapter 10).

3 There is a lively debate about whether there is something like implicit bias or not and how to conceptualize it, etc., but these details are irrelevant for the current issue and so I will not include the debate and its details.

Part 2
Rationally Dealing with Ignorance

6 The Framework II

What are the next steps in this project? I will now focus on the question of how one should rationally deal with ignorance. I turn to the history of philosophy for directions in how one should rationally deal with ignorance, carving out answers and testing them for their suitability. In asking how one should rationally deal with ignorance we can distinguish a first-person and a third-person perspective on the issue: How should I rationally deal with (my own) ignorance? How should we rationally deal with (our own) ignorance? And, how should other people rationally deal with (their) ignorance? I will mostly take up an involved first-person perspective on the issue: How should we rationally deal with our own ignorance? I have two reasons for that. First, the project of dealing with ignorance is not an individualistic project. And, second, a third-person perspective may become too detached from the issues at hand and it is always in danger of becoming a paternalistic project.

I work with suggestions and ideas from the history of philosophy because there are interesting suggestions around and – more importantly – because these suggestions contain many assumptions and beliefs about ignorance that shape our perception of ignorance. The prime example is Socrates' attitude toward ignorance, so-called Socratic ignorance. My aim does not lie in developing faithful interpretations of the accounts of these philosophers, rather I employ and develop the notions so that I can develop interesting and fitting suggestions for rationally dealing with ignorance.

I develop different suggestions from remarks that involve ignorance and error. Most of the texts do not aim to provide suggestions for rationally dealing with ignorance, but, as the following chapters demonstrate, they can be taken to provide directions and suggestions. The first set of suggestions are broadly virtue-theoretical: Suggestions developed from Aristotle's remarks on the nature of human beings (*Metaphysics*) and Socrates' remarks on ignorance (*Apology*). The second set of suggestions

DOI: 10.4324/9781003375500-8

are consequentialist: Suggestions from William James' Twin Goals. The third set are deontological suggestions developed from William Clifford, John Locke, Sanford Goldberg and Immanuel Kant. The order is not strictly historical but rather thematic.

What are *rational* ways for dealing with ignorance? I suggest that we should not separate epistemic and practical rationality and we should not attempt to keep epistemic and moral considerations separate. For human beings *qua* epistemic and moral agents these considerations will necessarily overlap.[1] And so what does rational mean? In the first instance I take rational to mean that something is well justified, that it comes with good reasons (cf., e.g., Gosepath 2002). But there are further facets of rationality that need to be included, too.[2] Something can be instrumentally rational, rational from a social perspective and intrinsically rational (cf. Gosepath 2002, Tugendhat 2010). Something that is instrumentally rational is rational because it contributes to achieving one's ends. Something that is rational from a social perspective is rational for specifically social reasons, for example, specific social values, but also social emotions. It might be rational in order to further social values such as honesty, or it might be rational in order to avoid such emotions such as shame. Something that is intrinsically rational is rational for its own sake, in other words: its rationality cannot be explained in terms of instrumental or social value, and it cannot be communicated to someone who does not see its rationality. I return to these distinctions later.

Since I have taken up an involved first-person perspective on dealing with ignorance, the answer that I am looking for faces a number of challenges (or must meet some adequacy conditions). First, it must be implementable from the first-person perspective. It must be formulated so that the subject can employ it for their own ignorance. That means that the answer must provide the subject with all the tools they need for addressing ignorance. This includes diagnosing ignorance and, perhaps also, equipping the subject with reactions to their ignorance. – These standards may sound abstract, but in my discussion of the different proposals, these demands will be illustrated. Second, the answer must be for human beings as they are, non-ideal, real beings who are located in the world, not idealized creatures.

And third, the answer must work for reflective and non-reflective ignorance. Here's why. Remember the obstacles that human beings face in dealing with self-evaluation bias and related types of ignorance and error in judging oneself. Adam Elga (2005) provides a vivid insight into the difficulties of reacting to the evidence on self-evaluation bias:

> I was convinced that most people overrate themselves, and had no reason to think I was an exception. I mouthed the words "I'm not as good as I thought I was." But they didn't sink in. As soon as it was time

to make dinner, write a paper, or see a friend – indeed, as soon as it was time to do anything but sit in my office brooding about the positive illusion literature – the impact of that literature on my self-evaluations completely evaporated.

Try it yourself. If you were at all convinced by the above summary of the positive illusion literature, see if it lowered your estimate of how good a writer you are. ... It is tough to make a sustained change in one's self-evaluations. Just learning that people overrate themselves does not automatically effect such a change.

(Elga 2005, 118)

Elga is bothered by the fact that in not changing one's beliefs about oneself, one goes against the following rationality norm: "One ought not have beliefs that go against what one reasonably thinks one's evidence supports" (Elga 2005, 116). But the problem is even more basic than that: One does not even know when one has "beliefs that go against what one reasonably thinks one's evidence supports" (Elga 2005, 116). The proposal for rationally dealing with ignorance should provide a solution for such issues. It should not require the subject to be mindful and reflective 24/7 since that would be highly unrealistic for human beings. But it should still consider cases of non-reflective ignorance and try to account for them. And, this is a fourth challenge, the proposal must not work with an unrealistic notion of ignorance that does not fit with ignorance in the real world. There will be idealizations, there is no avoiding them in developing general accounts, but these idealizations should be kept at a minimum and should only be justified idealizations.

Notes

1 I share Fricker's intuitions regarding the connections between ethical and epistemic considerations (Fricker 2007).
2 I employ Tugendhat's distinction of different motivations for being moral to develop these facets of rationality (Tugendhat 2010).

7 Virtue-Theoretical Answers

7.1 The Aristotelian Answer: "All Men by Nature Desire to Know" (Suggestions 1 and 2)

Even though it does not mention ignorance, the first paragraph of Aristotle's *Metaphysics* entails a straightforward suggestion for the lead question of Part 2 – how should we rationally deal with ignorance – both our own ignorance and other people's ignorance.

> All men by nature desire to know. An indication of this is the delight we take in our senses; for even apart from their usefulness they are loved for themselves; and above all others the sense of sight. For not only with a view to action, but even when we are not going to do anything, we prefer sight to almost everything else. The reason is that this, most of all the senses, makes us know and brings to light many differences between things.
>
> (Aristotle, 980a22–a27)

If, as Aristotle claims, all men by nature desire to know, then once one realizes that one does not know, that is, that one is ignorant, one's desire to know will kick in. On a more radical interpretation, one's desire to know may be said to kick in even before one realizes that one is ignorant, that one does not know some proposition p or facts in some field, but I do not think we have to ascribe this radical interpretation to Aristotle. And my critical questions for the answer developed from Aristotle's conception appear for both interpretations.

The striking implication of Aristotle's claims is that there is not much to do – epistemically or agentially – in dealing with ignorance for a subject that is ignorant because her natural desire to know will kick in whenever it is appropriate. There is, we might say, an in-built natural mechanism for rationally dealing with ignorance since human beings desire to know. The underlying assumption is that this natural desire is rational.

DOI: 10.4324/9781003375500-9

And being in a state of ignorance triggers this desire to know. Because this mechanism is natural to all human beings – and here and in what follows I read Aristotle's claim about *all men* as referring to *all human beings* – all human beings will rationally deal with ignorance, since they all desire to know. The claim applies to human nature in general and therefore also to each human being individually (cf. Cambiano 2012, 2).

Consequently, Aristotle's claim also provides material for an answer to how one should rationally deal with other people's ignorance – for them the same "natural tendency" (Cambiano 2012, 2) holds and, thus, they also have the in-built mechanism for rationally dealing with ignorance. As I have noted earlier, it is an open question, that is, how one should proceed from having observed another's ignorance, what one should *do* about the other's ignorance. Aristotle's conception can be read as entailing that one should not and does not have to interfere with other people's ignorance because one may trust their natural desire to know. On the other hand, Aristotle's pragmatic remarks in the *Nicomachean Ethics* about how education and personal experiences may impede one's development may entail that Aristotle acknowledges that not all human beings do in fact develop this in-built mechanism nor the desire to know. Thus, how one should deal with other people's ignorance in these circumstances remains an open question.

To develop the Aristotelian suggestion for one's own ignorance, we must look at the passage starting the *Metaphysics* in more detail. How does Aristotle explain the fundamental claim that "all men desire to know?" Why does the claim hold? – We desire to know why "all men desire to know."

As Hermann Bonitz notes, the knowledge that Aristotle introduces in this quotation is knowledge in a loose sense, not some specific scientific knowledge or the like (Bonitz 1849, Cambiano 2012, 3). Moreover, this knowledge is an end in itself, not just an instrumental end. As such, it is "not an object of choice and deliberation" (Cambiano 2012, 5). *Pace* Eudoxus, you do not choose to know (*Nicomachean Ethics* X 2, 1172b9–15; cf. Cambiano 2012, 5). Our desire to know is a natural tendency, and, therefore, it is objectively good and does not just appear to be good.

But what is the basis for Aristotle's claim that all men desire to know? As Cambiano points out, Aristotle does not present the claim as *endoxon*, that is, as reputable opinion, nor as *phainomenon*, that is, as an observed fact. He also does not apply the method of the *Nicomachean Ethics* that suggests that one should first discuss the difficulties of the phenomena and then try to prove the truth of as many reputable opinions about the phenomenon as possible (*Nicomachean Ethics* VII 1, 1145b2–7). Instead, Aristotle offers a justification for the claim by pointing to an "indication," what Cambiano calls a "sign," for the truth of the claim. The delight that we take in our senses, as well as the fact that we value them independently of any instrumental value is an indication for the truth of the claim. We particularly cherish sense perception by sight.[1] For the argument to work, we need to regard perception as a form of knowledge (*eidenai*).

Cambiano puts forward the following reconstruction of the argument:

> 1) sight brings to light many differences; 2) sight, bringing to light many differences, makes us know more than the other senses; 3) sight, even when pursued for its own sake, as it makes us know more than the other senses, is accompanied by delight and is preferred by us to the other senses; 4) the fact that all men take delight in perceptions and, above all, in sight is a sign that all men desire to know.
>
> (Cambiano 2012, 8)

The first sentence does not present a definition of a human being in terms of *genus* and *differentiae* (cf. *Posterior Analytics* 97a23–28, II.13). Rather, it concerns what Cambiano calls "propert[ies] pertaining only to man" (*idion*) (Cambiano 2012, 11). In the *Topics*, Aristotle explains that a property is "something which does not indicate the essence of a thing, but yet belongs to that thing alone, and is predicated convertibly to it" (*Topics* 102a18–19). On Aristotle's conception other such properties include "laughing, language, erect posture, happiness, praxis, deliberation" (Cambiano 2012, 11).[2]

Let us try to understand Aristotle's claim better and develop suggestions for dealing with ignorance from it. Aristotle's claim can be read as saying that the relation between human beings and knowledge is like the relation between amoebae and light. Amoebae naturally turn into the direction of light and in the same way human beings naturally turn from ignorance to knowledge. There is nothing that anyone has to *do* about or *undertake* in that process, that is, in rationally dealing with ignorance. The first suggestion for rationally dealing with ignorance thus can be formulated as follows:

> **Suggestion 1:** Rationally dealing with ignorance comes natural for human beings since they naturally desire to know.

But this cannot be right. The claim is easily called into question by our everyday experience, by historical events, by empirical observations. There are a sufficient number of instances in which human beings do not desire to know even though they could desire to know because there is something they do not know. This holds irrespective of whether it is in one way or another important that the subjects know or not.

One might also raise doubts about the suggestion by arguing that human beings have limited cognitive capacities and, therefore, there are natural limits to their desire to know. But this observation does not affect Aristotle's claim because he only comments on human beings' desire to know, not on their wanting to know *everything*. They take *delight* in their sense perceptions, despite their limitations, and, thus, in knowledge.

But the claim and the suggestion are unspecific and, thus, criticizable in another respect. Aristotle does not specify what kind of knowledge he talks about. As I said earlier, Bonitz suggests that *eidenai* should be read as referring to a loose understanding of knowledge, but this addition does not make the claim more specific. In fact, it becomes even more unspecific because we are led to count the input of our sense perceptions as knowledge, too. And then there are even more counterexamples available. Just think of the last time you saw something that you did not want to see because what you saw spoilt a pleasant surprise or, more harrowingly, because it was disturbing, for example, the picture of a child killed in a war torn country, or the images of people jumping from the windows of the burning World Trade Center on 9/11. You did not desire to have this perceptual input, this knowledge.

We could make the claim more specific and less prone to counterexamples by specifying *what* it is that human beings desire to know. The claim is intuitively true for all cases in which the subject is interested in knowledge, that is, in the particular piece of knowledge. In fact, this formulation comes close to a tautology because it is that obvious: All human beings desire to know what they are interested in. The claim is almost tautological because one's desires are intimately connected to one's interests. But we can ignore the tautology worry because the new formulation is more fruitful for our lead question than Aristotle's original claim and it gets us to another suggestion for how one should rationally deal with ignorance:

Suggestion 2: Desire to know all that is interesting to you.

But merely *desiring to know* may be too weak as a suggestion for rationally dealing with ignorance since there may be a disconnect between one's desire and one's (epistemic) actions.[3] One may, therefore, be inclined to modify the second suggestion:

Suggestion 2*: Try to know all that is interesting to you.

But this adaption loses the attractions of the original Aristotle-inspired suggestion and it does not overcome its problems. *Trying to know* is just as open to not succeeding and has a similar disconnect. And it loses the human *desire* to know, a significant feature of Aristotle's first sentence. There is a desire to know things. And this property of human beings is indisputable. It is just the scope that is in question and whether it is helpful for finding a way for rationally dealing with ignorance.

So let us return to Suggestion 2. How does it fare as a suggestion for how one should deal with one's ignorance? There is the worry of the disconnect between desire and action, but we can turn this worry into an advantage of the suggestion. We desire to know what is interesting to us, but we can always double check whether to pursue that desire in particular instances. In fact, it is part and parcel of the natural human desire to know to be able to step back and reflect on the desire and whether to pursue it. It comes with the human buildup as a rational being. Because human beings have rational capacities they can desire to know *and* they can step back and reflect their desire to know and whether to pursue it.

But this is also why Aristotle's original claim in its unrestricted form is easily spoilt by our everyday experience and other empirical experiences with human beings and their relation to knowledge. And it is why the relation between human beings and knowledge is not like the relation between amoeba and light. Hans-Georg Gadamer's distinction between *Welt* and *Umwelt* and John McDowell's interpretation of the distinction between first and second nature can help us understand this fundamental difference. Amoebae live in their *Umwelt* and they cannot ever leave it, they are inextricably bound to it. They cannot transcend the biological given, the biological imperatives, they cannot *not* turn to light. In contrast, human beings live in a *Welt*, more precisely they *have a world*, as Gadamer puts it (1975/2013, 460), and having a world means that one is able to distance oneself from that world. Gadamer writes:

> To have a world means to have an orientation (Verhalten) toward it. To have an orientation toward the world, however, means to keep oneself so free from what one encounters of the world that one can present it to oneself as it is. This capacity is at once to have a world and to have language. The concept of *world* is thus opposed to the concept of *environment*, which all living beings in the world possess.
>
> (Gadamer 1975/2013, 460)

Our relation to knowledge is not like the relation of amoebae to light because we are able to reflect upon us, our thoughts, our desires, our world. This status and the accompanying capacities are also natural to human beings. They are, in McDowell's terms, second nature, and second nature is also nature (McDowell 1996, xx). Second nature refers to those capacities that a being acquires in the course of a process of *Bildung* or training (McDowell 1996, 84). And for human beings, part of their second nature is to reflect in such ways. Possessing rationality is second nature to us (McDowell 1996, xx, 84–86, 91, 115–119).

Adding the concept of *second nature* to the picture opens the path for another look at Aristotle's original claim. McDowell regards Aristotle's notion of *phronesis* as a prime example of second nature, and so one might be inclined to argue that the desire of all human beings to know is also second nature and from this develop an explanation for why not all human beings manifest this desire at all times. It is only if one has gone through the process of *Bildung* that one possesses this desire to know. – Since Aristotle does emphasize the significance of education in various shapes and forms, the addition fits well with his other philosophical claims (e.g., Aristotle 1995b, book 2 *Nicomachean Ethics*). – Of course, this would entail that the original statement does not really apply to *all* human beings but only to those who have gone through the process of *Bildung*. For them it holds that they all desire to know. The *phronimos* and the *phronime* have undergone *Bildung* and so they have the desire to know.

If this conjecture is correct, we can find more material for developing the original claim and dealing with the empirical worries and objections. Someone who has the desire to know will also be a *phronimos/phronime* and, we may add, will have the capacities required for desiring to know in the right way. We, thus, would not need to add the qualification that human beings desire to know all that is interesting to them because the ability to determine what is relevant to be known would be covered by the other abilities acquired in the process of *Bildung*, that is, in becoming a *phronimos/phronime*. Rationally dealing with ignorance would amount to a human being who has gone through the process of *Bildung* desiring to know. She would simply desire to know in the right circumstances only.

This interpretation looks interesting, but I do not think that Aristotle had such restrictions and connections in mind when making the claim in the first sentence of the *Metaphysics*. This definitely speaks against the proposed interpretation as an interpretation of Aristotle's first sentence of the *Metaphysics*. Human beings can – and maybe: should, to the degree that is possible to them – improve their natural desire to know, a human being can become a *phronimos phronime* or *sophos/sophe*, but that does not mean that the natural desire only exists in human beings who have developed their natural tendency.

Robert Roberts and W. Jay Wood present another attempt at developing Aristotle's original statement into an epistemic theory. They helpfully differentiate simple "natural appetite for knowledge" (Roberts and Wood 2007, 154) and the mature form in the shape of "love of knowledge." In its simple, rudimentary form, love of knowledge is "love of cognitive stimulation," a "natural faculty-like disposition of the human will" (Roberts and Wood 2007, 169) which we already see in infants. And Roberts and Wood remark that "we are not likely to find many members of the human race who lack interest in all kinds whatsoever of cognitive stimulation or activity" (Roberts and Wood 2007, 169).

This natural faculty needs to be "matured, formed, realized, completed" (Roberts and Wood 2007, 154) so that subjects may develop the rare virtue of "love of knowledge." Just as we have seen with Aristotle's claim, their argumentative basis is mainly empirical. Children growing up in a society just naturally develop to mature their "natural appetite for knowledge." But note how Roberts and Wood assume that this development naturally leads to an aversion of false beliefs and a desire for true beliefs:

> And with further maturity, crucial distinctions come to guide the child's epistemic activities. She wants true perception and beliefs, not false ones; she wants well-grounded beliefs, not vagrant, floating ones; she wants significant rather than trivial, relevant rather than irrelevant, knowledge; she wants deep rather than shallow understanding; and she wants knowledge that ennobles human life and promotes human well-being rather than knowledge that degrades and destroys; she wants to know important truths.
> (Roberts and Wood 2007, 154–155)

Of course, their conjecture as to how the abilities of children develop is very interesting for our lead question as to how one should rationally deal with ignorance; they seem to suggest that there is an in-built mechanism for wanting knowledge, for wanting true belief and avoiding false belief. But this answer has the same downsides as the Aristotelian answer. How does this mechanism work, and how does it deal with instances in which people do not want to know, and, in particular, instances in which it is indeed better, more rational, not to know – cases that are not unlike some that we have seen in Part 1?[4]

Roberts and Wood would probably suggest that the mature lover of knowledge inadvertently develops "practical wisdom of truthfulness" (Roberts and Wood 2007, 166). And this practical wisdom consists in "a sense of which falsehoods are important to avoid, or especially important to avoid, and why, and which truths urgently need to be told" (Roberts and Wood 2007, 166). Practical wisdom comes with the ability to distinguish which truths are to be told and which not. Maybe we need to add wisdom to Aristotle's approach in order to get to an answer to how one should rationally deal with ignorance. This suggestion gets us directly to a popular approach to answering the question of how one should rationally deal with ignorance: Socratic wisdom.

Before I conclude this section on the Aristotelian Suggestion and turn to the second approach in the next section, I want to explain why I started the historical overview of answers with Aristotle's text, and I want to highlight what we have learned in examining Aristotle's approach to rationally dealing with ignorance.

I have started with Aristotle's first sentence of *Metaphysics* because his claim that all men desire to know fits very well with the widespread belief that knowledge is valuable, and, in particular, more valuable than ignorance. And it also fits with the first of the Jamesian twin goals "We must know the truth; and we must avoid error" (James 2014, 24). As we will see in the section on the Jamesian twin goals (Section 8.1), James himself describes "our belief in truth itself" as "a passionate affirmation of desire, in which our social system backs us up. We want to have a truth" (James 2014, 19). I wanted to start with Aristotle's reply – or rather a reply inspired by Aristotle; after all, Aristotle himself does not explicitly address our lead question – since it captures and undergirds the standard reaction to the lead question: ignorance should be turned into knowledge because knowledge is more valuable than ignorance, because all human beings naturally want to know.

If one reads Kant's "An Answer to the Question: What is Enlightenment?" (Kant, WIE), one understands why Aristotle's first sentence is still popular, and why it fits with widely received epistemic norms, for example, the Jamesian twin goals. Over the time Aristotle's teleological conception of human beings has fed into the notion of *human progress*. Kant writes:

> One age cannot bind itself and conspire to put the following one into such a condition that it would be impossible for it to enlarge its cognitions (especially in such urgent matters) and to purify them of errors, and generally to make further progress in enlightenment. This would be a crime against human nature, whose original vocation lies precisely in such progress.
>
> (Kant, WIE, AAVIII, 39)

Kant's claim is that making progress – participating in the enlightenment – is built into human nature. This claim is a relative of, a version of Aristotle's first sentence. I have decided to start with Aristotle's claim because it expresses a fundamental assumption that can be found throughout philosophical theories.

So, do Suggestions 1 and 2 provide a useful answer for how we should rationally deal with ignorance? I do not think so. Suggestion 1 – "Rationally dealing with ignorance comes natural for human beings since they naturally desire to know" – is too broad and merely descriptive when we are looking for normative guidance. And it is not clear that the claim is correct. Desiring to know, Suggestion 2, is not enough for determining how one should react to ignorance. We see this if we try to apply it to the paradigms of ignorance that I have carved out in Part 1. How does desiring to know help with dealing with presumed knowledge or with close-minded ignorance and open-minded ignorance? One might say that Suggestion 2 implies that one should be open-mindedly ignorant about those things that may be interesting to one, and close-mindedly ignorant about those things that are not interesting to one. But I doubt that this presents a rational and satisfactory way for dealing with this ignorance. There is also an intrinsic limitation to Suggestion 2 because desire is an attitude that is directed toward something that the subject regards as good, but it does not entail any action. And relatedly, desiring to know on its own looks too weak as a meaningful suggestion because we do not just want people to *desire* to know more. Epistemically, we want them to do more than that.

The version "desire to know all that is interesting to you" requires the epistemic subject to play a central role in determining how one should rationally deal with ignorance. And then the subject fills the details of rationally dealing with ignorance. That is also why desiring to know what is interesting to one can only work as guide for reflective ignorance, not so much for non-reflective ignorance.

But Suggestion 2 is still useful for our project because we are starting to see what we want from our answer, what it will have to include and where we might find alternative answers. For example, we want an answer that is determinate enough, both regarding the content and regarding the expectations from the subjects. "Desiring to know all that is interesting to you" is not enough for guiding our dealings with ignorance. In addition, we may also want to be able to say that someone must know something, someone should know something. We cannot make such claims about duties and obligations when the suggestion for dealing with ignorance is "Desire to know all that is interesting to you" (Suggestion 2). Duties and obligations involve much more than simply expecting people to desire to know. And, in particular, they involve more than simply expecting them to desire to know all that is interesting to them.

In further determining the desire to know, the *phronimos* and the *phronime* have played a crucial role because they have the ability to specify the content of the desire to know, so there is reason to suppose that the subject, the individual, will be central in our answer to the question of how one should rationally deal with ignorance. And, the suggestion that the subject itself is central in how one should rationally deal with ignorance may not be surprising at all: after all, Socrates' "I know that I don't know" is based on carefully examining his own epistemic status and the epistemic status of other epistemic subjects and it is frequently cited as the number one philosophical reaction to ignorance.

So the next candidate suggestion for a rational way of dealing with ignorance is Socratic wisdom. As we have just seen, the wise person is said to know how to rationally deal with ignorance. Wise Socrates knew how to deal with ignorance. Therefore, I turn to discussing wisdom as a reply to the question of how one should rationally deal with ignorance in the next section. Let us see where the second virtue-theoretic approach leads us in our quest for an answer to how one should rationally deal with ignorance.

7.2 Socratic Ignorance and Wisdom (Suggestions 3, 4, and 5)

The connection between wisdom and ignorance, and, in particular, the idea that wisdom is the best method for rationally dealing with ignorance – or having rationally dealt with ignorance – are commonplaces in philosophy. This is due to Plato's *Apology*, or rather due to Socrates being said to be the wisest of all human beings by Pythia, the Oracle of Delphi. And Socrates believes that he is the wisest of all because he is aware of his own ignorance (*Apology* 23b 2–4). Socrates knows that he is ignorant and he does not claim to know what he does not know. This has led to the term of Socratic ignorance, higher-order ignorance that consists in knowing that one is ignorant. Socratic ignorance is "ignorance as the sum of knowledge" (Ritter 1927, 1, my translation). And as Nikolai Nottelmann puts it, Socratic ignorance is "first-order ignorance without accompanying second-order ignorance" (Nottelmann 2016, 54).

Socratic ignorance is inextricably connected to wisdom. When talking to one of the statesmen, Socrates realizes that he is wiser than the statesman:

> So I withdrew and thought to myself: "I am wiser than this man; it is likely that neither of us knows anything worthwhile, but he thinks he knows something when he does not, whereas when I do not know, neither do I think I know; *so I am likely to be wiser than he to this small extent, that I do not think I know what I do not know.*"
> (Plato 1997, 21d3–7, my emphasis)

Socrates is wise because he knows that he is ignorant. In the terms of this study, he seems to be able to rationally deal with his ignorance.

What does that mean for our lead question? Can we get another Suggestion from Socratic ignorance and wisdom? The most obvious suggestion is, that, trivially, wise people know how to rationally deal with ignorance. That just comes with being wise.

Suggestion 3: Be wise (or: Become wise) because wise people know how to rationally deal with ignorance.

But, of course, this suggestion is not particularly helpful for the non-wise. We have to unpack wisdom and being wise to get closer to the answers and suggestions that we could gain from Socratic wisdom.

Socrates knows that he is ignorant, so another suggestion for rationally dealing with one's ignorance may be

Suggestion 4: Know that you are ignorant.

But this suggestion is hardly helpful because it presupposes that one is knowledgeable and ignorant at the same time. And it does not specify the object or topic of ignorance. Most importantly, it does not specify what one should do based on that knowledge. Is it enough to be content with that recognition? How should or would the recognition translate into dealing with reflective and non-reflective paradigms of ignorance? For reflective preferred ignorance it seems to allow one to stay ignorant, similarly for presumed knowledge. In other words: knowing that one is ignorant is enough, according to that suggestion. But this is neither rational nor satisfactory. The suggestion is too static and passive to be a helpful suggestion.

Another crucial feature of Socratic ignorance is that Socrates is humble. He admits to his ignorance and he does not claim to be wise. Thus, the rational way for dealing with ignorance may be to be humble.

Suggestion 5: Be humble.

But we may well want more than this because merely being humble is not enough for the rational reaction to ignorance. Just like merely knowing that one is ignorant is not enough. One will also have to know what one is knowledgeable about, what one is not knowledgeable about, when to be humble and when to acknowledge that one is indeed knowledgeable etc. Again, this would be a demanding task for the epistemic agent, requiring capacities similar to those of Aristotle's *phronimos* and *phronime*. Simply being humble, thus, is not enough for rationally dealing with ignorance, it is a promising candidate, but it is not enough all by itself.

This is also why an adapted suggestion based on Duncan Pritchard's notion of intellectual humility is also not enough.

Suggestion 5*: Be intellectually humble.

Pritchard explains that intellectual humility "requires … that, in being aware of one's epistemic limitations – in being aware of the general level of one's ignorance – one is appropriately sensitive to the possibility of error, and so revises one' s beliefs accordingly" (Pritchard 2016, 141). But even though Pritchard is more specific as to how intellectual humility is crucial for ignorance and error – namely, one should be aware of one's ignorance and "sensitive to the possibility of error" and one should "revise one's beliefs accordingly" (Pritchard 2016, 141), we are none the wiser because mere sensitivity to the possibility of error does not mean that one finds one's errors, nor does awareness of one's ignorance mean that one knows what to do about it. "Revis[ing] one's beliefs accordingly" presupposes that one knows when and how to revise one's beliefs. Pritchard's suggestion is that one should be what I have called reflectively open-mindedly ignorant, or that one should be in a state of investigative ignorance. The agent knows that she is ignorant and attempts to address this ignorance. But Pritchard himself also notes that sometimes reflective close-minded ignorance is epistemically more valuable than unrestricted open-minded ignorance: it may be better to not (want to) know many trivial truths and to know only one important truth about a subject (Pritchard 2016, 141). Generally, the suggested attitude is rather defensive – the agent is open for her own fallibility, for her having done something wrong epistemically, for her believing wrongly. I do not think that this is a valuable, forward-looking suggestion for addressing ignorance. It may be a building block of a suggestion, but, again, by itself it is not enough.

The problems of the suggestions from Socratic ignorance show that the idea that Socratic wisdom and Socratic ignorance are good entry points for how one should rationally deal with ignorance relies heavily on Socrates and his wisdom. His humility is not as essential as it seems. Socrates' particular epistemic and practical capacities and his wisdom do most of the work in intuitively explaining why *wisdom* is the key to rationally dealing with ignorance. So for the proposal to work we need to explicate these capacities.

Ryan (2018) proposes two interpretations of the humility theory of wisdom that say more about why Socrates is humble and wise, but as she herself notes, they ultimately fail as explications of wisdom and as interpretations of Socrates' wisdom. Neither "S is wise iff S believes s/he is not wise" nor "S is wise iff S believes S does not know anything" (Ryan 2018) work as a theory of wisdom. We should not yet give up on the Suggestions developed from Socratic ignorance but try to develop them. Let us also check other explications of wisdom and whether they offer any lead on why the wise person (or: the sage) is supposed to be excellently equipped for dealing with ignorance, and what capacities are required for this excellent position.

How do other authors explicate wisdom? Let me note at the outset that it is surprising that few explications of wisdom (*sophia*) mention the issue of ignorance, or suggest that wisdom involves knowing that one is ignorant or humble about one's cognitive capacities. The *locus classicus* for wisdom is Aristotle's *Nicomachean Ethics*, in which he distinguishes practical wisdom, consisting in *techne* and *phronesis*, and theoretical wisdom, consisting in *epistēmē* and *nous*. Many authors focus on either form of wisdom. It is not particularly clear whether Socrates' wisdom is theoretical wisdom or practical wisdom. Since it is concerned with epistemic matters, one may suppose that it belongs with theoretical wisdom, but Aristotle's conceptions of *epistēmē* – scientific knowledge or understanding – and *nous* – grasp of first principles – do not fit Socrates' wisdom. This also becomes clear in *Metaphysics A* (at the end of the section discussed in the previous section on Aristotle's suggestions) when Aristotle notes about wisdom that "all men assume what is called wisdom to deal with the first causes and the principles" (*Metaphysics A* 981b25). This is not what Socrates' wisdom consists in, at least not primarily.

But wisdom is not unique to Aristotle's theory. Recently, the notion has become more prevalent in contemporary epistemology, especially in virtue epistemology. Jason Baehr helpfully distinguishes three interpretations of wisdom (*sophia*):

a   the explanatory understanding account of *sophia*
b   the cognitive faculty conception of *sophia*
c   the intellectual trait conception of *sophia*.

The *explanatory understanding account* regards wisdom as a cognitive state that amounts to "deep explanatory understanding" (Baehr 2014, 312). To be wise is

> to grasp, relative to a given "epistemically significant" domain D, (1) that which is fundamental to D, (2) how the fundamental elements of D stand in relation to each other, and (3) how they stand in relation to the non-fundamental elements of D.
>
> (Baehr 2014, 312)

Wisdom here clearly is limited to theoretical wisdom and similar to Aristotle's conception.

On the *cognitive faculty conception*, *sophia* refers to the particular cognitive capacities that make the particular knowledge available to the wise subject (Baehr 2014, 313). Baehr does not go into much detail about this conception, because he thinks that these capacities would still need to be adapted to explain how they are a form of wisdom. They must be well-developed, educated capacities.

But Ryan's conception of wisdom as deep rationality may be read as a cognitive faculty conception that counters Baehr's criticism of cognitive faculty conceptions. Ryan suggests the following conception:

> S is wise iff
>
> 1. S has a wide variety of epistemically justified beliefs on a wide variety of valuable academic subjects.

2. S has a wide variety of justified beliefs on how to live rationally (epistemically, morally, and practically).
3. S is committed to living rationally.
4. S has very few unjustified beliefs and is sensitive to her limitations.

(Ryan 2018)

Note that Ryan is one of the few authors who explicitly includes awareness of one's cognitive limitations, that is, Socratic wisdom, in her conception of wisdom. Her conception also unites theoretical and practical wisdom.

On the third conception, the *intellectual trait conception*, wisdom

is a disposition to act or inquire in *sophia*-relevant ways out of a desire for "deep explanatory understanding of epistemically significant subject matters" and a belief that acting or inquiring in these ways is likely to promote the goal in question.

(Baehr 2014, 315)

Wisdom is a meta-intellectual virtue that involves a desire to know for its own sake and "an understanding of how best to *pursue* deep explanatory understanding or how best to negotiate the terrain and demands of *inquiry* aimed at such understanding" (Baehr 2014, 315, emphasis in original) as well as a disposition to act on this understanding.

This notion of *wisdom* may connect up nicely with Aristotle's notion of the human desire to know as discussed in Section 7.1. Zagzebski, for example, explains *sophia* as a "firm and abiding desire for deep and significant theoretical knowledge" that is accompanied by the "corresponding disposition to pursue such knowledge in active and intelligent ways" (Baehr 2011, 308; cf. Zagzebski 1996). But, again, no mention of ignorance.

In contrast, the psychological approach to wisdom by Paul Baltes and Ursula Staudinger and the Berlin Wisdom Paradigm do mention "the limits of knowledge and the uncertainties of the world" (2000, 123) as a topic of wisdom. This is not exactly *ignorance* but "limits of knowledge" is close enough to ignorance. Baltes and Staudinger develop an implicit psychological theory of wisdom that is based on "cultural-historical and philosophical analyses of the wisdom concept" (2000, 123). Their list of seven properties of wisdom mentions "knowledge about the limits of knowledge and the uncertainties of the world" (Baltes and Staudinger 2000, 123) as one of the properties of wisdom. Of course, this description is reminiscent of Socratic knowledge of one's own ignorance.

More particularly, Baltes and Staudinger suggest wisdom is expertise in, what they call, the "fundamental pragmatics of life": knowledge and judgment about the essence of the human condition and the ways and means of planning, managing and understanding a good life (Baltes and Staudinger 2000, 124). Like some of the philosophical conceptions, their psychological conception also locates wisdom on a meta-level. Wisdom is a meta-heuristic, that is,

> a heuristic that organizes, at a high level of aggregation, the pool (ensemble) of bodies of knowledge and commensurate, more specific heuristics that are available to individuals in planning, managing, and evaluating issues surrounding the fundamental pragmatics of life.
> (Baltes and Staudinger 2000, 132)

Wisdom, on this approach, has seven properties:

> (a) Wisdom represents a truly superior level of knowledge, judgment, and advice; (b) wisdom addresses important and difficult questions and strategies about the conduct and meaning of life; (c) wisdom includes knowledge about the limits of knowledge and the uncertainties of the world; (d) wisdom constitutes knowledge with extraordinary scope, depth, measure and balance; (e) wisdom involves a perfect synergy of mind and character; that is, an orchestration of knowledge and virtues; (f) wisdom represents knowledge used for the good or well-being of oneself and that of others; and (g) wisdom, although difficult to achieve and to specify, is easily recognized when manifested, although difficult to achieve and to specify.
> (Baltes and Staudinger 2000, 123)

We have now seen different philosophical conceptions and one psychological conception of wisdom. Only one of the philosophical conceptions (indirectly) mentions Socratic ignorance, and the psychological conception of wisdom mentions limits of knowledge. Can we gage any further suggestions for how one should rationally deal with ignorance from these conceptions, in addition to Suggestion 3 – be wise (or: become wise) because wise people know how to rationally deal with ignorance?

One option is to simply apply the different conceptions to the case of ignorance. For example, the meta-intellectual virtue *wisdom* that involves an understanding of how to pursue inquiry aimed at deep explanatory understanding may be read as also including the ability to address one's ignorance. But this proposal is not satisfying because it does not say in more detail *what is involved in addressing one's ignorance*. It is no better than Suggestion 3. In addition, it is too restricted because it focuses on "deep explanatory understanding" when we have seen in Part 1 that ignorance is not just ignorance about first principles etc. We face the same problems with the other conceptions. We need more details as to how the wise person addresses her own ignorance.

A major issue for the question of what current conceptions of wisdom have to say about rationally dealing with ignorance lies in whether these conceptions separate moral and intellectual wisdom and moral and intellectual virtues or not. Roberts and Wood (2007) suggest that there is no strict separation between moral and intellectual virtue (Roberts and Wood 2007, 180) and, as we have seen earlier, they argue that "the practical wisdom of truthfulness" (Roberts and Wood 2007, 166) is intimately linked to dealing with falsehood and truth: "the practical wisdom of truthfulness is a sense of which falsehoods are important to avoid, or especially important to avoid, and why, and which truths urgently need to be told" (Roberts and Wood 2007, 166).

Nozick's explication of practical wisdom as "what you need to understand in order to live well and cope with the central problems and avoid the dangers in the predicaments human beings find themselves in" (Nozick 1990, 267) provides much more details. Unfortunately, these details are geared to practical wisdom only, but they could be translated into an amended list of "what a wise person needs to know and understand" (Nozick 1990, 269) that includes wisdom as truthfulness along the lines of Roberts' and Wood's proposal. Nozick explains:

> Wisdom is not just one type of knowledge, but diverse. What a wise person needs to know and understand constitutes a varied list: the most important goals and values of life – the ultimate goal, if there is one; what means will reach these goals without too great a cost; what kinds of dangers threaten the achieving of these goals; how to recognize and avoid or minimize these dangers; what different types of human beings are like in their actions and motives (as this presents dangers or opportunities); what is not possible or feasible to achieve (or avoid); how to tell what is appropriate when; knowing when certain goals are sufficiently achieved; what limitations are unavoidable and how to accept them; how to improve oneself and one's relationships with others or society; knowing what the true and unapparent value of various things is; when to take a long-term view; knowing the variety and obduracy of facts, institutions, and human nature; understanding what one's real motives are; how to cope and deal with the major tragedies and dilemmas of life, and with the major good things too.
>
> (Nozick 1990, 269)

We would need some description like this one for getting helpful suggestions for rationally dealing with ignorance like a wise person. But the philosophical conceptions that we have encountered, including Roberts and Wood's conception, do not provide any material for such suggestions.

The psychological conception by Baltes and Staudinger has more details about the acquisition of wisdom based on their empirical work on what are conditions of wisdom. Since wisdom is a multifaceted concept, it is based on "microfactors" and "macrofactors" (Baltes and Staudinger 2000, 127) and Baltes and Staudinger surmise that wisdom is not really a trait of an individual but rather "collectively anchored" (Baltes and Staudinger 2000, 130). For an individual to acquire wisdom they require "guidance by mentors or other wisdom-enhancing 'voices' of society [and] the experience and mastery of critical life experiences" (Baltes and Staudinger 2000, 127) as well as "the orchestration of several characteristics: cognitive, motivational, social, interpersonal and spiritual" (Baltes and Staudinger 2000, 127).

This list seems helpful, but I surmise that these details are not too helpful for a person who wants to become wise: First, she is dependent on an intricate interplay between internal and external forces, second, she must meet those "critical life experiences," and whether she faces such experiences is probably contingent. Third, it is not clear how wisdom as "expertise in the fundamental pragmatics of life" (Baltes and Staudinger 2000, 124) translates into rationally dealing with ignorance. This ability just seems to be a byproduct of becoming wise.

To some extent these issues seem to be inherent to wisdom and so we will most probably not find a convincing detailed conception of wisdom as a means for dealing rationally with ignorance and its acquisition because wisdom is an abstract notion in which the development of the wise agent and the actions of the wise agent do most of the work. Similarly to Aristotle's *phronimos* and *phronime* who just know what to do in the respective situations. And Aristotle's *phronimos* and *phronime* are also somewhat dependent on happy conditions – in addition to their own involvement – for becoming a *phronimos* or *phronime*. So we will always be back to Suggestion 3: "Be wise (or: Become wise) because wise people know how to rationally deal with ignorance." We might rephrase the suggestion as:

Suggestion 3*: Emulate the sage.

But this version, too, remains unhelpful as a suggestion for dealing with ignorance. Like the other versions, it lacks the details that explain for the non-wise how to proceed. First, again, it is unclear what *being wise* entails for dealing with preferred ignorance and presumed knowledge, open-minded and close-minded ignorance. Should one act like a wise person, or as one thinks a wise person would act? There is no obvious clue involved in being wise. The guidance is now implicit in being wise.

Second, the unavoidable, unsurmountable issue for the non-wise is, as Julia Annas puts it, "How do we get from here to there?" (Annas 2008,

12) For practical wisdom, once we recognize our defectiveness we can develop "ethical aspirations which propel [us]" (Annas 2008, 27) and choose the sage as our ideal.

> The best life is one in which we are virtuously active, aspiring towards an ideal as best as we can, not seeking to get there and then stop, but finding the reward of virtue to be in the virtuous activity itself.
>
> (Annas 2008, 27)

For theoretical wisdom this also means that *we*, the individual, the epistemic agent have to have the impulse in ourselves. The epistemic agent needs to do the work in getting closer to wisdom. She needs to initiate the process. We do not know what this process would involve and we do not know where it leads us. We are back to a process like *Bildung* that is required for becoming wise. Kant's suggestion for dealing with ignorance will pick up on the problems that human beings have with acquiring wisdom – it is very difficult for them to become wise – but he also has a solution for the problem – go for an alternative, the second best option, the maxims of the *sensus communis* (cf. Kant, Anth, AA VII, 200). These maxims are "1. To think for oneself. 2. To think oneself (in communication with human beings) into the place of every other person. 3. Always to think consistently with oneself" (Kant, JL, AA IX 57). I return to this suggestion in Section 9.5 and Chapter 10.

There are limitations to the Aristotelian approach and the Socratic Wisdom approach, two central virtue-theoretic approaches to the question of how we should rationally deal with ignorance, so let's look at a consequentialist approach to rationally dealing with ignorance.

Notes

1 I will not enter into the discussion as to why we particularly value sight according to Aristotle since this issue is not relevant for the leading question of how one should deal with ignorance.
2 One might have expected that the *Ergon* argument plays a bigger role in explaining Aristotle's fundamental claim: The *ergon* of human beings is rational activity and so the best human life is life lived according to reason (*Nicomachean Ethics* I 1097b22–1098a19). And the desire to know is one way of living life according to reason, so it is part of fulfilling the human *ergon*. But Aristotle does not make this connection. Zagzebski considers whether true belief could be good for us and thus figure as a constituent of *eudaimonia* (Zagzebski 2003, 140–141), but she notes that such claims would need to be adapted to inquiry instead of Aristotle's notion of contemplation, and so she concludes that "this route has promise, but it is complicated" (Zagzebski 2003, 141). For a convincing account that explains how *theoria* is the best mode of human life, see Braun (2014).

3 One may want to suggest that desire and action are intrinsically linked – similarly to one's aims and ones' means on a Kantian instrumental conception (cf. Kant, G, AA IV, 417; Korsgaard 1997; Kolodny and Brunero 2018) – but I do not think that this connection is plausible.
4 I will examine aversion to false belief and desire for true beliefs as suggestions for rationally dealing with ignorance in the section dedicated to the Jamesian twin goals (Section 8.1).

8 Consequentialist Answers

8.1 James' Twin Goals: "Believe Truth! Shun Error!" (Suggestions 6 and 7)

Another (very) obvious candidate for providing us with a good suggestion for rationally dealing with ignorance are James' goals "We must know the truth, and we must avoid error" (James 2014, 24), or more briefly "Believe truth! Shun error!" (James 2014, 24).[1] As Feldman notes, these suggestions belong to the group of epistemic duties (Feldman 2002), but they also determine the goals of epistemic activities and thus may lead to a consequentialist answer for how we should rationally deal with ignorance. That's why they appear in this section on consequentialist approaches rather than in the deontology section. Locke might be also studied in this section, because, as we will see, he focuses on truth as the goal of epistemic conduct. But since he formulates his conception in terms of obligations and duties and has God and the natural endowed capacities as the background to these duties, he fits better in the section on deontological answers.

These goals are often called "twin goals" suggesting that they belong together, that they are separate but intimately connected. Some authors even go so far as saying that believing truths or striving for truth is the same as avoiding error. Clifford's suggestion about carefully examining evidence can be read as making such claims. This position is certainly a minority view, and in introducing the two goals, James himself already notes that the goals are "separable laws" and lead to differences in people's "intellectual li[ves]":

> There are two ways of looking at our duty in the matter of opinion – ways entirely different, and yet ways about whose difference the theory of knowledge seems hitherto to have shown very little concern. *We must know the truth; and we must avoid error* – these are our first and great commandments as would-be knowers; but they are not two ways of stating an identical commandment, they are two separable laws. Although

DOI: 10.4324/9781003375500-10

it may indeed happen that when we believe the truth A, we escape as an incidental consequence from believing the falsehood B, it hardly ever happens that by merely disbelieving B we necessarily believe A. We may in escaping B fall into believing other falsehoods, C or D, just as bad as B; or we may escape B by not believing anything at all, not even A.

Believe truth! Shun error! – these, we see, are *two materially different laws*; and by choosing between them we may end by colouring differently our whole intellectual life.

(James 2014, 24, my emphases)

But nevertheless a majority of authors mentions the two goals in unison and in conjunction, see these examples:

There is one and only one epistemic goal, and that is the dual goal of attaining true belief and avoiding false beliefs.[2]

(Ahlstrom-Vij 2013b, 277)

In short, our distinctively epistemic goal is to get at the truth, and so, in the broadest terms, what promotes this goal has epistemic value. The acquisition of true belief, and the avoidance of false belief, are thus two core epistemic goods which determine epistemic value, in that whatever promotes truth in one's beliefs, and the avoidance of error, will have epistemic value.

(Pritchard 2016, 135)

The book's overarching ambition is to articulate and defend a picture according to which the normativity in question reflects the sorts of social expectations epistemic subjects are entitled to have of one another as epistemic subjects – as subjects who mentally represent the world as being a certain way, and who aim in these representations at truth and the avoidance of error.

(Goldberg 2018, 13)

These are just the standard goals that people (epistemic subjects) are said to pursue naturally. Apparently, the descriptive variant of these views is also standardly held in sociology. Linsey McGoey explicitly sets out to argue against the widely held claim that social actors "have an obvious interest in expanding knowledge and eradicating ignorance" (McGoey 2012, 571). And, remember also Hertwig and Engel who argue against the focus on low-cost knowledge in the "economics of information" (Hertwig and Engel 2021). The next suggestion for our lead question thus is:

Suggestion 6: Strive for truth and avoid error.

So, how does this popular suggestion fare as an answer to how one should rationally deal with ignorance?

The twin goals appear to provide adequate detail for dealing with ignorance, but, at second glance, one really does not know *what* one should do.[3] A particular problem germane to the twin goals is that, as James notes, the two goals are "materially different" (James 2014, 24) and, therefore, they lead to two sets of epistemic behavior: On the one hand one may favor truths, on the other hand one may find it more important to avoid error. The person who favors truths, is "ready to be duped" (James 1979, 24) in exchange for more truths. The person who fears error is willing to miss out on some truths because she is afraid of getting falsehoods on her pursuit of truths. Ultimately, she is afraid of "being duped" (James 1979, 24). In a very fitting image James compares this paradoxical attitude to that of a general who warns his soldiers of fights: "It is like a general informing his soldiers that it is better to keep out of battle forever than to risk a single wound. Not so are victories either over enemies or over nature gained" (James 2014, 25).

In effect, these issues show that the twin goals and, thus, Suggestion 6 – "We must know the truth, and we must avoid error" – are not helpful as a suggestion for how one should rationally deal with ignorance. Its two components are in tension and, therefore, cannot commend a certain course of action.

But I do not want to give up on a twin goal-related suggestion quite so easily. I will discuss three suggestions for how we should weigh the two goals, including James' suggestion. Ultimately, the proposals do not get us to one satisfying answer, but we do learn more about what constituents the answer must have, and we find further inspiration for where we might look for the best suggestion for how one should rationally deal with ignorance.

James notes that one's position toward risk is central in determining how one reconciles the two goals. A skeptic wants to keep the risk down and, therefore, does not want to make a decision. For science, James suggests, the best approach is to have both an "eager interest" and a "nervousness lest [one] become deceived" (James 2014, 26) which amounts to the position of "dispassionately judicial intellect" (James 2014, 27). In moral and personal relations James leaves room for passions, the heart and the will to also decide what to believe. In these instances "faith in a fact can help create the fact" (James 2014, 29, emphasis deleted) – and we can translate faith into the involvement of passions, heart, desire and will. In religion, too, one should not have to keep the will out of thinking and deciding. So, in effect, James weighs the two goals by determining the topic of the belief and the decision. The *topic* determines which considerations should be primary.

Pritchard (2016) also points out that the relation between the two goals is somewhat complicated. An equal weight view on which one should simply maximize true beliefs and minimize false beliefs fails because not all true beliefs improve one's belief set. We cannot just say that between two belief sets the belief set with more true beliefs is better than the belief set with fewer true beliefs. Only particular true beliefs are relevant for the quality of one's epistemic status. There are beliefs that have "more content" (Pritchard 2016, 139) than others. In addition, as I have noted before, ignorance and false beliefs may have non-epistemic value – for example, some may want to remain ignorant about the personality of this partner's ex. Pritchard argues that ignorance – though not error in particular – may also have epistemic value: not knowing about misleading defeaters is epistemically valuable (Pritchard 2016, 136). And being ignorant of small and trivial truths and knowledgeable about one important truth is epistemically more valuable than knowing all the small and trivial truths – knowing a higher quantity of truths – and not knowing the important truth (Pritchard 2016, 139–141).[4]

But Pritchard's observations do not help improve Suggestion 6, they just evince that it is not enough to just go for true belief *simpliciter*, and that the epistemic agent must add details, she must decide whether to go for truth or not and whether to go for false belief and/or ignorance or not. Pritchard provides examples for reflective close-minded ignorance, the scientist who does not want to know trivial truths prefers not to know. And, as I have noted earlier, his notion of intellectual humility amounts to *reflective open-minded ignorance*, that is, reflective ignorance. But how one should get into these stances, how one decides to be investigatively ignorant or prefers to be ignorant when it is appropriate remains unanswered.

Moreover, by focusing merely on maximizing true belief and avoiding false belief the approach is too simplistic. Epistemology is not just about truth-conduciveness, and as the different cases of ignorance have shown, ignorance can be valuable and true belief can be pernicious. The consequentialist answer that focuses on truth and falsehood cannot capture these facets and nuances.[5]

Wayne Riggs' discussion of epistemic goals is more helpful in that respect, he even has an explanation for why theories like Pritchard's cannot say more about how we should get into the attitude of investigative ignorance. Overall, Riggs' observations concerning the twin goals are similar to James' remarks about the role of wanting to take risks. Riggs compares the epistemic situation concerning true and false belief to the production of a widget in a company in which Mr. Nervous produces hardly any output but high-quality output, and Ms. Careless produces much output and has a higher number of deficiencies in her output. His article, at the same time, goes significantly beyond James' observations because he also discusses how current epistemology, especially theories of justification and theories of knowledge handle the twin goals – of course, this is not a disadvantage of James' original text because he could not have known about these positions, he was "pre-conceptually ignorant" (Le Morvan and Peels 2016, 23). These theories mainly focus on the aim of believing truth, or striving for knowledge, but their epistemic norms actually tacitly prioritize avoiding falsehood. If you favor avoiding false beliefs, you set high epistemic standards so that false beliefs can be avoided (cf. Clifford's suggestion in Section 9.1). If you favor more truths, you endorse lower standards so that you can find more truths and are not busy trying to avoid the false beliefs. Of course, hardly any theories of justification and knowledge – if any at all – endorse lower standards, and so their views would have to focus on avoiding falsehoods, but in their statements and norms they focus on the pursuit of true belief and knowledge instead.

Riggs suggests that we should not be surprised that these epistemological theories do not say anything about avoiding falsehoods or avoiding ignorance since they are only concerned with evaluating actual belief and, therefore, are unable to deal with "hypothetical belief" and "sins of omission" (Riggs 2003, 348). This explanation also applies to Pritchard's conception discussed earlier. Feldman also presupposes this particular emphasis when he distinguishes duties to believe particular propositions and duties to have the attitude (belief, disbelief, suspension) that is supported by the evidence (Feldman 2002, 368).

But let us return to the search for an answer to the question of how one should rationally deal with ignorance. Riggs' contribution helps explain why I have not found much supporting material in traditional 20th- and 21st-century epistemology: the authors are concerned with evaluating belief and *ignorance* does not fit their object of study. At the same time, it is curious that the twin goals that do address concerns of ignorance and error are still mostly cited conjointly.

8.2 Understanding as a Goal for Dealing with Ignorance

Riggs proposes that the two goals need to be balanced by a third goal, either an epistemic goal or a non-epistemic goal. He introduces understanding as an epistemic goal that can balance the twin goals, that is, balance *caution* and *acceptance*. From this modification we can develop another consequentialist answer for rationally dealing with ignorance.

> **Suggestion 7:** Believe truth and shun error relative to their significance for you developing understanding.

On Riggs' conception *understanding* is "understanding of the world and one's place in it," (2003, 350) it comes with an "appreciation for order, fit, and pattern. It requires that one 'see' how thing[s] fit together and why they are the way they are" (2003, 350). The value of true belief and the disvalue of false belief could then be explained in terms of their role for the subject's understanding.

The avid reader will of course have recognized the parallels to Aristotle's *phronimos* and *phronime* and to the content of *theoretical wisdom*. In effect, Riggs suggests that the subject must have something like a meta-intellectual virtue along the lines of wisdom to be able to adjudicate and weigh the twin goals. So we are back to the Aristotelian approach and Socratic Wisdom. Riggs has wed the consequentialist approach and the virtue-theoretic approach. But we have seen that these approaches, individually, do not get us what we want for our answer to the lead question. We do not want to hear that the *sage* knows how to deal with ignorance. The consequentialist additions "believe truths" and "shun error" are also not helpful – they do not adequately guide one's epistemic action and ignorance may be epistemically and non-epistemically valuable.[6] And even in conjunction, the virtue-theoretic and the consequentialist approach cannot overcome these issues.

Another prominent alternative rival conception is a deontic approach to how we should rationally deal with ignorance. Epistemic duties determine how we should rationally deal with ignorance. These duties may guide the epistemic agent in rationally dealing with ignorance. In the next chapter I discuss how epistemic duties may provide an answer to how one should rationally deal with ignorance. There are different accounts of epistemic duties; they differ in particular in which deontic authority of the duties they presuppose, for example, humanity in the case of William Clifford, God in the case of John Locke, Reason in the case of Kant. Note that in the section on epistemic duties I will mainly develop an account of why epistemic duties hold. Which epistemic duties are germane to the question of how one should rationally deal with ignorance will take a backseat since it is to an important part dependent on who or what the deontic authority is and why epistemic duties concerning knowledge even hold. I cannot adequately address these issues in this book.

Notes

1 Feldman notes the parallel and the differences to Locke's duty to "seek the truth" (2002, 363).
2 I will not discuss whether truth is the only epistemic goal and determines epistemic value or not (see, e.g., Ahlstrom-Vij 2013c).

3 Lutz Wingert similarly notes that a signed commitment to searching for the truth – at the University of Frankfurt one used to sign such a statement when one received the PhD from the university – is empty. He notes that after those recommendations one does not know how to go on (Wingert 2019, 3).
4 Daniel Whiting argues for the stronger claim that false belief is bad independent of its content, "believing the false has content-independent disvalue" (Whiting 2013, 222).
5 One can also apply Berker's objections against epistemic consequentialism (Berker 2013), even though Berker finds deontic claims in epistemic consequentialism and focuses on reliabilism as the primary variety of epistemic consequentialism.
6 For more suggestions on the epistemic value of ignorance and error, see, e.g., Klein (2008), Bortolotti (2015), Bortolotti and Sullivan (2017).

9 Deontological Answers

The discussions so far have shown that the "just so" answers from virtue-epistemology and consequentialism are not enough: the rational way for dealing with ignorance does not just come naturally as the Aristotelian answer has suggested, nor does "Be wise, be like Socrates" spell out into an option that is attainable for all human beings. And the consequentialist is also too vague because they do not specify how one should go about striving for truth and avoiding falsehood, nor is the consequentialist focus well justified. From William Clifford, John Locke, Immanuel Kant and Sanford Goldberg we can develop the third strand of answers to how one should rationally deal with ignorance: deontic accounts. Such accounts argue that there are duties or obligations that human beings have to obey to (or to follow) in rationally dealing with ignorance. These duties or obligations are not necessarily epistemic duties, in fact, they are often claimed to be moral duties. Note that these accounts rarely discuss ignorance specifically. Most of the time they talk about duties concerning evidence. But as we will see, Clifford and Locke, in particular, formulate duties and obligations regarding true and false beliefs. And we can develop further deontic suggestions from Goldberg on what one "should have known" (Goldberg 2017b) and from Kant's maxims of the *sensus communis*.

We find indications for and traces of such epistemic duties in our reactions to someone not knowing what they should know. The most well-known case is that of a doctor who should know the standard protocol for treating a disease that is common within her field of expertise. Another case is that of a meteorologist having an obligation to know the fundamental weather phenomena required for her to prepare correct calculations of the weather forecast. But such expectations are not restricted to professional contexts. In non-professional contexts, too, there are things that people, arguably, should know. If Peter does not know his partner's birthday, his

DOI: 10.4324/9781003375500-11

interlocutors are likely to say, "You should know Kim's birthday." Or imagine Sarah who is going to the rainforest on a three-week vacation, but she has no idea about the rainforest, its nature, animals, plants etc. She does not even know that the air in rainforests is humid. Upon finding out about her ignorance her interlocutors are likely to say: "When you're travelling into the rainforest, you should know fundamental details about rainforests."

These examples evince that there are epistemic duties and these epistemic duties may provide a further set of answers to the question of how one should rationally deal with ignorance, namely by fulfilling these epistemic duties. The crucial question is why these epistemic duties hold. In other words: what is the deontic authority behind these epistemic duties? This question is important because it will help adjudicate the different proposals for duties regarding ignorance.

Roberta Cutler Klein, in a very interesting, largely forgotten article, observes that a number of epistemologists "[take] for granted the notion that people are subject to some sort of intellectual requirement vis-à-vis truth" (Klein 1987, 79). Roderick Chisholm is one such epistemologist since he states that an epistemic agent is subject to a "purely intellectual requirement, that of trying his best to bring it about that, for every proposition p he considers, he believes that p if and only if p is true" (Chisholm 1977, 14).[1] Such requirements hold because epistemic agents are intellectual beings:

> One might say that this is the person's responsibility or duty *qua* intellectual being. (But as a requirement it is only a *prima facie* duty; it may be, and usually is, overridden by other, nonintellectual requirements, and it may be fulfilled more or less adequately.) One way, then, of re-expressing the locution "p is more reasonable than q for S at t" is to say this: "S is so situated at t that his intellectual requirement, his responsibility as an intellectual being, is better fulfilled by p than by q."
>
> (Chisholm 1977, 14, I have deleted a footnote)

Chisholm (1977, 14–15) and Klein also mention William James' twin goals "we must know the truth; and we must avoid error – these are our first and great commandments as would-be knowers" (James 2014). But we have seen why the twin goals don't make for adequate suggestions for dealing with ignorance. Klein also quotes Descartes, whom she also takes to imply that human beings must aim for truth. In this chapter, I will present deontic approaches to ignorance, philosophers postulating intellectual requirements regarding ignorance and how they justify this requirement.

152 Rationally Dealing with Ignorance

In principle, we find four major candidates for deontic authorities:

1 Humanity or mankind, as proposed by Clifford.
2 God, as proposed by Locke.
3 Epistemic community, as proposed, for example, by Bernard Williams (2004), Peter Graham (2015) and Sanford Goldberg (2017b).
4 Reason and the subject herself, as proposed by Kant.

I will discuss these options in turn, starting with Clifford's proposal.

9.1 Clifford's Duties to Mankind (Suggestion 8)

William Clifford summarizes his own suggestion regarding epistemic duties as follows: "It is wrong always, everywhere, and for anyone, to believe anything upon insufficient evidence" (1999, 77). His answer to our lead question of how one should rationally deal with ignorance is just this general piece of advice:

> **Suggestion 8:** "It is wrong always, everywhere, and for anyone, to believe anything upon insufficient evidence."

Clifford develops this duty from the example of a ship-owner who gives a ship to refugees for a sea crossing, even though he does not know whether the ship is in good shape for this journey. According to Clifford, the ship-owner is guilty, irrespective of whether the refugees safely reach the harbor with that ship or not, because the ship-owner has acted upon insufficient evidence and has silenced his doubts about the condition of the ship. The ship-owner has failed to fulfill the above duty. This duty holds for everyone, "not only the leader of men, statesman, philosopher, or poet" (Clifford 1999, 74). And the duty is not simply a duty to the refugees or to oneself but it is *a duty to mankind* (Clifford 1999, 74).

The obvious question is why this duty to mankind – a fairly demanding duty and a large deontic authority – holds. Clifford explains that just one false belief, one badly founded belief, has negative effects on the individual's belief set and on her faculties (Clifford 1999, 73). And since, as he claims, one's words and phrases are "common property" (Clifford 1999, 73–74), false beliefs will also have negative effects on society and mankind. In particular, for the individual and society a false belief may turn into a bad habit (Clifford 1999, 76), and "we weaken our powers of self-control, of doubting, of judicially and fairly weighing evidence" (Clifford 1999, 76).

> No real belief, however trifling and fragmentary it may seem, is ever truly insignificant; it prepares us to receive more of its like, confirms

those which resembled it before, and weakens others; and so gradually it lays a stealthy train in our inmost thoughts, which may someday explode into overt action, and leave its stamp upon our character for ever.

And no one man's belief is in any case a private matter which concerns himself alone. Our lives are guided by that general conception of the course of things which has been created by society for social purposes. Our words, our phrases, our forms and processes and modes of thought, are common property, fashioned and perfected from age to age; an heirloom which every succeeding generation inherits as a precious deposit and a sacred trust to be handled on to the next one, not unchanged but enlarged and purified, with some clear marks of its proper handiwork. Into this, for good or ill, is woven every belief of every man who has speech of his fellows. An awful privilege, and an awful responsibility, that we should help to create the world in which posterity will live.

(Clifford 1999, 73–74)

Assuming that there are such enormous repercussions from one individual false belief, someone who does not avoid acquiring and maintaining faulty beliefs, who instead avoids getting information, avoids testing her beliefs, commits a "sin against mankind" (Clifford 1999, 77).

What does that mean for our question of how one should rationally deal with ignorance? According to Clifford, one *must* – "should" would clearly be too weak for Clifford's conception – try to believe on sufficient evidence, one must strive for good, reliable evidence, one must examine and weigh one's evidence carefully. In addition, one has to put one's beliefs to test so as to avoid damaging one's belief set and one's faculties.

These suggestions are not all off track and, unlike the Aristotelian answer and the wisdom answer, they do contain clear epistemic instructions. In fact, you will see that the instructions regarding evidence return in subsequent proposals; but, clearly, Clifford's particular brand of suggestion is far too strict. He does not introduce any prima facie caveats. Nor does he not at all acknowledge the non-culpable limitations of human beings that may keep them from "always, everywhere" avoiding "to believe anything on insufficient evidence." There are a large number of beliefs that I hold without sufficient evidence and where it is not detrimental to my belief set, nor to my faculties that I do not possess sufficient evidence. Quite to the contrary, it is conducive to the quality of my faculties, their activities and their products that I do not have all the available sufficient evidence (cf. Harman 1986, 15 on clutter-avoidance). And James has famously argued – against Clifford – that one may be justified in believing certain beliefs without adequate evidence (James 2014). I have discussed such cases of positive illusions and the beneficial role of ignorance for trust in Sections 4.1 and 4.7. Clifford's claims about the duty as a duty against mankind can also be rebutted. As we have seen in the paradigms of ignorance, there may be well-justified cases of preferred ignorance that are justified with a view to the good of mankind – for example, research that leads to improved biological weapons. In addition, and quite significantly, Clifford does not explain adequately, why this duty should be a duty to mankind. It is a gross exaggeration – and self-aggrandizing – to claim that my one false belief will have detrimental effects for mankind.

But note that the particular suggestion that how one deals with *one's evidence* matters for rationally dealing with ignorance, itself, is not at all that bad. It is just Clifford's story of why the duties hold and his story of the deontic authority, which is not convincing. Locke's discussion of error and epistemic duties avoids the issue of scope because, for him, epistemic duties only hold for things of "maximal 'concernment'" (Locke 1979, IV, xx, 3; Wolterstorff 1996, 63). And with Goldberg we can develop an account of why and how communities can expect an individual of that community to know. I will discuss these two deontological approaches next.

9.2 Locke's Alethic Obligation to God (Suggestion 9)

John Locke is very much concerned with two issues "(1) what is the scope of human knowledge? and (2) how ought we to govern our assent when we lack knowledge?" (Wolterstorff 1994, 172) Thus, it is not surprising that he is one of the few philosophers to engage directly with the issues of error and ignorance.[2] In his *An Essay Concerning Human Understanding* (1979) and in *Of the Conduct of the Understanding* (1996) he discusses the causes of "wrong assent" and "errour" [sic] (Locke 1979, IV, xx). And he notes that human beings are subject to, what Wolterstorff in his interpretation of Locke's epistemology calls, an "alethic obligation" (Wolterstorff 1996, 63).[3] This obligation is the primary obligation that human beings have to meet regarding beliefs: they should "aim at getting things right, at getting in touch with reality" (Wolterstorff 1996, 65). Locke restricts the obligation to fundamental moral and religious matters (Wolterstorff 1996, 70), but I think that, ultimately, we can extend it to epistemic matters, too. On the one hand, Locke states that the obligation holds for everyone because everybody has *some* time to consider fundamental religious matters, at least on Sundays (Locke 1979, IV, xx, 3, Wolterstorff 1994, 186):

> No Man is so wholly taken up with the Attendance on the Means of the Living, as to have no spare Time at all to think of his Soul, and inform himself in Matters of Religion.
>
> (Locke 1979 IV, xx, 3)

But on the other hand, Locke also admits that the alethic obligation may be trumped by other more urgent matters, especially for people who do not have much time at their leisure.[4]

You will have (at least) two follow-up questions concerning the alethic obligation: First, why and on what basis does the alethic obligation hold? What is the deontic authority for the obligation? Second, what does the alethic obligation consist in? We find most of the material for the answers in this long quotation from Locke's chapter xvii "Of Reason" in *An Essay Concerning Human Understanding*:

> Faith is nothing but a firm Assent of the Mind: which if it be regulated, as is our Duty, cannot be afforded to anything, but upon good Reason; and so cannot be opposite to it. He that believes, without having any Reason for believing, may be in love with his own Fancies; *but neither seeks Truth as he ought, nor pays the Obedience due his Maker, who would have him use those discerning Faculties he has given him, to keep him out of Mistake and Errour*. He that does not this to the best of his Power, however he sometimes lights on Truth, is in the right but by chance; and I know not whether the luckiness of the Accident will excuse the irregularity of his proceeding. This at least is certain, that he must be accountable for whatever Mistakes he runs into: *whereas he that makes use of the Light and Faculties God has given him, and seeks sincerely to discover Truth, by those Helps and Abilities he has, may have this satisfaction in doing his Duty as a rational Creature, that though he should miss Truth, he will not miss the Reward of it*. For he governs his Assent right, and places it as he should, who in any Case or Matter whatsoever, *believes or disbelieves, according as reason directs him*. He that does otherwise, *transgresses against his own Light, and misuses those Faculties, which were given him to no other end, but to search and follow the clearer Evidence, and greater Probability*.
>
> (Locke 1979, IV, xvii, 24, my emphases)

The alethic obligation is an obligation toward God since God has equipped human beings with the capacities required for avoiding errors and ignorance.[5] As Wolterstorff emphasizes, this is a moral duty, not an epistemic duty (Wolterstorff 1996, 64). At the end of the above passage Locke also hints at what the alethic obligation consists in: it is about "follow[ing] the clearer Evidence, and greater Probability." Locke's talk of evidence is obviously reminiscent of Clifford's emphasis on evidence.

Wolterstorff suggests that the demands of the alethic obligation can be translated into three principles:

Principle of evidence: Acquire evidence for and against the proposition such that each item of evidence is something that one knows and such that the totality of one's evidence is satisfactory.

(Wolterstorff 1996, 67, Locke 1996, §7)

Principle of appraisal: Examine the (satisfactory) evidence one has collected so as to determine its evidential force, until one has "perceived" what is the probability of the proposition on that evidence.

(Wolterstorff 1996, 73)[6]

Principle of proportionality: Adopt a level of confidence in the proposition which is proportioned to its probability on one's satisfactory evidence.

(Wolterstorff 1996, 79)[7]

In addition, one should be indifferent so as to avoid the errors mentioned in Section 5 (cf. also Wolterstorff 1996, 104): lack of evidence, inappropriate usage of evidence, being unwilling to use evidence, and employing "wrong measures of proportionality" (Locke 1979, IV, xx, 1). I suggest adding the *principle of indifference* as another principle to Wolterstorff's list of principles. In his *Of the Conduct of the Understanding* Locke specifies this indifference:

> I have said above that we should keep a perfect indifference for all opinions, not wish any of them true, or try to make them appear so; but being indifferent, receive and embrace them according as evidence, and that alone, gives the attestation of truth.
>
> (Locke 1996, §34)

The principles, in addition to being part of meeting the moral duty toward God, appear to be self-evident to Locke (Wolterstorff 1996, 80). They are self-evident to "lovers of truth for truth's sake" (Locke 1979, IV, xix, 1).

But Wolterstorff points out that Locke's argument that the principles are self-evident is not convincing (Wolterstorff 1996, 80ff.). In addition, the three principles cannot be explained coherently, especially the Principle of proportionality is problematic (Wolterstorff 1996, 80f.). I will not enter into a detailed exegesis of the principles and just take them as they are without discussing these problems in detail. And it seems that there is something about having *satisfactory evidence* that is crucial for dealing rationally with ignorance. Clifford mentions this component, and now Locke refers to it, too. In the field of *belief acquisition* and *belief maintenance* rationally dealing with ignorance is closely tied to one's dealings with evidence. Let us keep the principle of evidence, the principle of appraisal and the principle of proportionality in the group of candidates for an answer to how one should rationally deal with ignorance.

Locke also proposes a cure for what Wolterstorff calls "wounds of the mind" (Wolterstorff 1996, 94).[8] Note that to Locke these are not "wounds" of Reason because Reason itself is infallible, it is in employing our faculties that mistakes occur, for example, by deciding not to look at some object, or by not looking and listening carefully.[9] In turn, this means that by looking and listening carefully one can be cured from related errors. In addition, one should check carefully what one accepts as a principle because principles are particularly strong and persistent (Locke 1979, IV, xx, 8–11). Indifference, finally, helps us rule out the effects of passion and interests.

Locke's suggestion can be framed thus:

Suggestion 9: Follow these principles to rationally deal with ignorance and error: (L1) Indifference (belief acquisition and maintenance), (L2) Principle of evidence, (L3) Principle of appraisal, (L4) Principle of proportionality. In other words: Look and listen carefully, check your principles, and be indifferent to rule out the effects of passion.

These principles look particularly useful for dealing with motivated reasoning, preferred ignorance and presumed knowledge because they give more detailed advice and leads for addressing error and ignorance. And they appear to work for reflective and non-reflective ignorance since they also include what one may call *precautionary measures*.

So Locke's principles are promising candidates for the answer to our lead question but there is a fundamental problem with the conception that leads me to reject Suggestion 9 as proposed by Locke. Locke has God as the deontic authority for the alethic obligation and the related principles and it is not clear whether the principles hold without this assumption. And then why should one follow the principles if one does not think they are part of an obligation that we have toward God? We can keep Locke's principles on the list for answers as to how one should rationally deal with ignorance, but we will have to continue looking for another relevant deontic authority. I do not think we can put forward a conception based on the alethic obligation to God; it will not generally be accepted as binding, nor is it clear whether it even is binding.[10]

One option might be to put evolution in the place of God: Human capacities have developed throughout evolution and so one should actualize those capacities according to nature. This proposal would amount to a deontological version of the Aristotelian teleological suggestion (Section

7.1), but, as in the case of Aristotle, it is not clear whether an evolutionary story can provide the normative or deontic material for such a proposal.

Another issue with the Lockean suggestion is its addressee: The epistemic agent has a central role in determining how one should rationally deal with ignorance, just as it was in the Aristotelian Answer and the Socratic Answer from Wisdom. The agent must remain indifferent, the agent has to examine the evidence, etc. Locke locates the standards for the principles in the agent herself since she is a "lover of truth for truth's sake" (Locke 1979, IV, xix, 1). But this agent is very idealized – human beings do not just value truth for truth's sake. And in addition, the proposal is individualistic in a problematic sense: the agent does everything related to the principles by herself. These are two further problematic assumptions that one should avoid. Next, I turn to a more community-based deontological answer.

9.3 Epistemic Duties as Other-Regarding Duties (Suggestion 10)

In his article on "epistemological duties" Richard Feldman observes that most duties, in general, have an institutional source or a contractual source, yet, there are no such sources for epistemic obligations (2002, 366f.). There is no contract that anyone has signed concerning epistemic obligations or duties. It may, thus, seem that there are no epistemological duties. But, as I have suggested at the beginning of this chapter on epistemic duties, we can see a *social* basis for epistemic obligations in people's reactions to problematic instances of ignorance. Remember again, the doctor who should know the standard treatment for her patient, or Peter who should know his partner's birthday.

Feldman suggests that "things of certain kinds, simply in virtue of being of that kind, have certain duties" (Feldman 2002, 367), for example, parents in virtue of being parents have parental duties. The problem with this solution for how there can be epistemic duties is that Feldman's proposal cannot adequately distinguish desirable actions and required actions. This is most probably because Feldman does not think there is anything like a deontic authority for epistemic duties. In order to be able to say which epistemic obligations are desired and which are required, we, thus, still need a deontic authority – *pace* Feldman. In what follows, I discuss another possible epistemic authority: epistemic communities. In order to carve out these explications of epistemic duties I work with four examples that I have introduced at the beginning of these sections on epistemic duties: *Doctor's case*, *Meteorologist's case*, *Partner's birthday*, *Travelling the rainforest*.

The argumentative basis for explaining that one's epistemic community is the deontic authority in our epistemic obligations is the claim that if the epistemic community is justified in saying "You should have known" or "You should know," then there is a corresponding duty for the subject that faces the "You should have known" or "You should know" reaction, namely a duty to know. Sanford Goldberg has developed a convincing account of the base of "Should have known" replies (2017b, 2018, ch. 6), and his observations provide a fruitful starting point for spelling out duties to know as *other-regarding duties to know*.

Goldberg focuses on "You should have known" cases in which the subject did not have the evidence to know that p but still *should have known that p*. The doctor's case is one of those cases (Goldberg 2017b, 2865). There are two justifications for saying that the doctor should have known the treatment protocol. She should have known because of her professional, institutional role of being a doctor. And we, for example, as her patients, are entitled to say "You should have known" because the doctor and we are participants in a shared practice, the practice of relying on experts such as the doctor. Our entitlement is both moral and epistemic (Goldberg 2017b, 2891–2892) and, correspondingly, the "should" is also both moral and epistemic. Participating in a shared practice generates our entitlement to say "You should have known"; this is a *practice-generated entitlement* (Goldberg 2017b, 2868).

Such a practice may also be instituted by two people who are in an interpersonal relationship. The relevant "practices … emerge in … interpersonal relationships: our friends, partners, business relations, and so forth" (Goldberg 2017b, 2868) and such interpersonal practices can also justify the entitlement to say "You should have known." This reasoning is not limited to particular practices but also extends to epistemic and moral standards in general. The members of a community are entitled to particular expectations because there are certain general epistemic and moral standards (Goldberg 2017b, 2868). For example, we have minimal epistemic expectations such as

> expect[ing] that people know all sorts of things about the state of their immediate environment through the use of their sensory modalities; we expect them to make simple categorical identifications on this basis, and in this way come to know of at least some of the objects they are 'observing' or expect[ing] competent reading by those whose reading competence is mutually recognized.
>
> (Goldberg 2017b, 2880)

The entitlements hold because of their particular significance for the respective practice: if one were to question the entitlement, one would question the practice at large (Goldberg 2017b, 2869). The entitlement to expect the other agent to satisfy a certain epistemic condition is constitutive of the very practice that the subjects engage in. For example, if we were to question whether we may say "You should have known" to our family doctor, we would question the medical practice at large, including the practice of relying on experts. Thus, the expectations are not epistemically grounded but grounded on the existing normative practices.

Goldberg's conception is capable of explaining the reaction in the first three cases – *Doctor's case, Meteorologist's case, Partner's birthday*. Our practice-generated entitlements and shared moral and epistemic standards entitle us to expect the doctor to know the standard treatment protocol and to expect the meteorologist to know fundamental weather phenomena relevant for producing the weather forecast.[11] And they entitle Peter's partner (and maybe us) to expect him to know her birthday. Being in a loving intimate relationship usually also includes knowing when the other person's birthday is. More generally, we can say that being in a close relationship comes with a number of shared practices, like knowing the birthdate of one's partner.[12] That's why Peter's partner may expect him to know their birthday.

Goldberg does not talk of duties to know nor of obligations to know, but I suggest that his remarks about the entitlement to expect someone to know and to say "You should have known" can be employed to explain how and why there are duties to know. The doctor has a duty to know the standard protocol because she participates in a shared practice in which she is the expert on medical treatment and her patients and her colleagues expect her to know the standard protocol and are entitled to expect her to know the standard protocol. I submit that this is no major change to Goldberg's "Should have known" conception, I just refer to the flipside of the medal. If I am legitimately expected to know, then I should know. And if I should know, then I have a duty to know.

We can thus develop the following suggestion for rationally dealing with ignorance:

Suggestion 10: You have a duty to know what you are expected to know.

Two worries will immediately arise. What does *knowing* in a duty to know amount to? Is it a duty to be informed? Is it a duty to heed one's evidence? Is it a duty to seek evidence? Is it a duty to strive for truth and avoid falsehood? Such epistemic duties would certainly be interconnected since they all address elements in the epistemic life of an agent. But they are not reducible to just one of them. So the duty to know does not reduce to being informed. It is more advisable to understand *knowing* broadly as an epistemic state of a subject that includes epistemic processes, for example, acquiring concepts, and understanding of, say, phenomena – as do Haas and Vogt (2015). I propose to treat *know* as an umbrella term for the epistemic actions like, being informed, acquiring and heeding evidence. A duty to know, thus, consists inter alia in acquiring and possessing concepts, developing understanding, awareness of truths.

Second, one might object that not every "should" gives rise to a duty. If I want chocolate cake, I should buy chocolate cake, but I do not have a duty to buy chocolate cake. But this objection does not take seriously the interpersonal expectations that infuse the "should" in the "should have known" cases. The "should" is not merely instrumental but instead based on and infused by the expectations of the other participants of the practice which generates the entitlement to expectations of one another. Therefore, the "should" in "should have known" cases or in related "should know" cases *does* generate a duty to know.

These particular duties are *other-regarding duties to know* because they have their basis in the context of shared practices. The meteorologist has the duty to know fundamental weather phenomena relevant for producing the weather forecast because she has the role of an expert in the practice of weather forecasting. Peter has the duty to know his partner's birthday because they are in a close relationship, they have established shared practices, including that of knowing the other's person birthdate.

Let me emphasize that duties to know as other-regarding duties are not exclusively moral duties; their "should" is not just a moral "should." Rather, duties to know are both moral and epistemic: the "should" in "you should have known" is both a moral and an epistemic "should" because it holds on the basis of moral and epistemic standards.[13] The epistemic and the moral components are also seen distinctly in particular instances of duties to know in which the moral component is less pertinent and we would still say that the subject has a duty to know. In particular, this concerns cases in which the "You should have known" reaction is not obviously other-regarding, but still warranted, like the *Traveling the rainforest* case – Sarah travels the rainforest and she does not know that the rainforest is humid. This and related cases do not fit the model of other-regarding duties. Sarah does not fail to meet an other-regarding duty nor is it obvious that she fails to meet a moral duty, but our reaction may still be warranted.

So our reactions to someone not knowing are not enough for developing an account of how one should rationally deal with ignorance. It is *too* community-oriented one might say. We need an account that is not merely individualistic and not too community-oriented. There are two directions for looking outside the individual (and avoiding individualism) and anchoring the approach in the individual (and avoiding collectivism): including the world outside the individual and including an intersubjective perspective. We find these two approaches in the work of Kant – by focusing on the horizon one includes the world and by following the maxims of the *sensus communis* one becomes intersubjectively connected. Let's look at the approaches in turn.

9.4 Determining, Demarcating, and Extending One's Horizon (Suggestion 11)

Let's go back to Kant's remarks about ignorance from Section 4.1. The notion of a horizon plays a key role, and the horizon also is crucial for a Kantian suggestion for dealing with one's ignorance. – Let me note at the start that this is not the Kantian suggestion that I will endorse, but it is interesting and worth spelling out. – Ignorance is determined in relation to the horizon. And there are three ways of determining the horizon. The horizon is logically determined if it is related to the "interest of the understanding" ("das Interesse des Verstandes," Kant, JL, AA IX, 41). The horizon is aesthetically determined if the cognition is related to taste, and if one looks at the interests of feeling (Kant, JL, AA IX, 41). On this approach, science is put in relation to the taste of the public and to the unlearned. This approach determines what human beings ("man") are permitted to know. The horizon is practically determined if it is related to the interest of the will (Kant, JL, AA IX, 41). In the practical determination, cognition captures what effect "a cognition has on our morality" (Kant, JL, AA IX, 41). The approach determines what human beings ("man") ought to know.

In sum, the horizon determines and judges – evaluates, we may say – *what a human being can know, what a human being is permitted to know* and *what a human being ought to know*. But Kant does not say how the aesthetical approach determines what man is permitted to know, so I will bracket these claims. As I have noted before, there are two ways for logically determining a horizon: determination from the object's perspective, determination from the subject's perspective. If the horizon is determined from the object – the objective horizon – there is a historical horizon and a rational horizon. Kant notes that the historical horizon is infinite because our historical cognition is unlimited. The rational limit is determined by the limits of the objects of cognition of reason, or mathematical cognition (cf. Kant, CPR, AA III).

If the horizon is determined from the subject's perspective – the subjective horizon –, there is the absolute/universal horizon and the particular/conditioned horizon. The absolute/universal horizon is determined by the limits of human cognition in general. The particular/conditioned horizon is what Kant calls the private horizon, and this horizon is determined by an individual's gender, class, standing, etc. The private horizon can also be generalized to a horizon of science and a horizon of "healthy reason" (JL, AA IX, 41).

Kant uses the horizon to determine the character of our ignorance: Something can be beyond, outside or beneath one's horizon: "What we cannot know is beyond our horizon, what we do not need to know is outside our horizon" (JL, AA IX, 42). And what we ought not know because it would be harmful is *beneath our horizon*. The two latter differentiations are always relative to the individual. Kant then employs the relation between *Erkenntnis* and horizon to specify which attitude we should take toward our ignorance: Ignorance that is based on some *Erkenntnis* being *beyond* our horizon is never culpable, ignorance that is based on *Erkenntnis* being *outside* our horizon is even permitted. Finally, logically perfect cognition can always turn out to be useful, "for no cognition is, absolutely and for every purpose, useless and unusable, although we may not always be able to have insight into its use" (Kant, JL, AA IX, 42).

As in the case of the horizon, ignorance is further determined by the object or by the subject. If one determines ignorance starting from the object, there can be *material ignorance* – lack of historical cognitions – and *formal ignorance* – lack of rational cognitions. If one determines ignorance starting from the subject, ignorance is scientific or common. *Scientific ignorance* includes insights into one's ignorance, *common ignorance* doesn't come with insights into one's ignorance, the subject doesn't even know that she is ignorant. Awareness of one's own ignorance requires a scientific stance because it is only via the mediation of the sciences that one can be aware of one's ignorance. "For one can never represent his ignorance except through science, as a blind man cannot represent darkness until he has become sighted" (Kant, JL, AA IX, 44). But it is doubtful that this analogy is right. First, Kant clearly misconstrues blindness and underestimates a blind person's perception – they do not need to be "sighted" in order to represent darkness. Second, it is not clear that one needs science to represent one's ignorance, especially if one thinks of ignorance relative to the private horizon. It is not clear that one needs the sciences for that. What one certainly would need is conceptual capacities or Reason, and one may deduce such requirements from Kant's theory of perception and related conceptual theories of perception (cf. e.g., McDowell 1996). But one does not need science.

There is a suggestion for dealing with ignorance in these remarks about ignorance and horizons. According to Kant, the rational way for dealing with one's ignorance as determined by one's horizon is to know the scope of one's horizon and to extend it (JL, AA IX, 42). Kant presents eight recommendations for demarcating and extending one's horizon:

1 One should determine the horizon when one is able to do so on one's own.
2 One should not change the horizon too easily.
3 One should not compare one's own horizon with other people's horizons, and one should not judge other people's horizons.

4 One should not want to know too much or too little. "For he who wants to know too much ends by knowing nothing, and conversely, he who believes of some things that they do not concern him, often deceives himself" (JL, AA IX, 43).
5 One should "determine in advance the absolute horizon of the whole human race" (JL, AA IX, 43).
6 One should determine the position of science in *Erkenntnis* in general.
7 One should examine what one's best and most pleasurable capacities are, which capacities one needs or does not need in regard to certain duties.
8 "One should of course always seek to expand his horizon rather than narrow it" (JL, AA IX, 43).

These recommendations can be taken up as suggestions for dealing with one's ignorance, via demarcating and extending one's horizon. In this list we, thus, find suggestions for dealing with what Riggs has called "hypothetical beliefs" rather than only evaluating beliefs as current epistemological theories mainly do (Riggs 2003, 348).

Suggestion 11: Demarcate and extend your horizon in order to rationally deal with your ignorance.

Kant has further suggestions: quite generally, one should aim to know the limits of human cognition and, thus, our ignorance as "proved from principles" and not as particular – the task of the *Critique of Pure Reason* (Kant, CPR, AA III, A 761/B789). The philosopher has recognized the limitations of human cognition and, thus, is ignorant in a scholarly or "artful" way (Kant, JL, AA IX, 44). In fact, scholars who are aware of their ignorance are not guilty of being ignorant as Kant argues, with reference to Socrates' ignorance.

And Kant emphasizes that ignoring things may be good: "There is a distinction between not knowing something and ignoring something, i.e., taking no notice of it. It is good to ignore much that it is not good for us to know" (Kant, JL, AA IX, 45). This obviously ties in with preferred close-minded ignorance, one of the paradigms of ignorance. And it parallels Pritchard's explanation that ignorance may contribute to epistemic value and epistemic goods.

We can, thus, adapt the above suggestion:

Suggestion 11*: Know the limits of human cognition in a principled way and demarcate and extend your horizon in order to rationally deal with your ignorance.

This suggestion avoids some of the issues raised in other suggestions because it says what one should do – demarcate and extend one's horizon. But, at the same time, the suggestion is too vague because it does not say what demarcating and extending one's horizon consists in. In addition, the suggestion is still too individualistic and does not harness the intellectual powers of other individuals or intersubjective insights. Fortunately, Kant has another candidate suggestion that is more intersubjective. We get to it by looking at Kant's observations about error.

9.5 Dealing with Error and the *Sensus Communis* (Suggestion 12)

Kant does not just address ignorance (*Unwissenheit*), he also distinguishes *ignorance* and *error* and specifically addresses how we can avoid errors and deal with errors. As we have seen before, to Kant, error ultimately consists in a confusion between truth and merely apparent truth, more particularly "the merely subjective is confused in judgment with the objective" (Kant, JL, AA IX, 54). According to Kant, the cause of error lies in sensibility unduly influencing judgment and us judging, even though we are not able to judge (Kant, JL, AA IX, 53–54). And these characteristics of error also determine how we should deal with it – both after an error has occurred and in order to avoid error.

First, it is central to discover and explain the source of the illusion.

> To avoid errors – and no error is unavoidable, at least not absolutely or without qualification, although it can be unavoidable relatively, for the cases where it is unavoidable for us to judge, even with the danger of error – to avoid errors, then, one must seek to disclose and to explain their source, illusion.
>
> (Kant, JL, AA IX, 56)

It is crucial to do more than just disproving the errors because the same illusion may lead to different errors. Only if the illusion is uncovered and explained, can we ensure that it does not lead to other errors. Kant surmises that one might feel better if one learns that the illusion has been leading others into errors, too (Kant, JL, AA IX, 56).

By comparing our judgments with other people's judgment, we can find indications for error: if we disagree with other people's judgments, that is a reason for us to examine our own judgments and methods. Yet, Kant emphasizes that mere disagreement is not a sufficient reason for *dismissing* one's judgments, "for one can perhaps be right about the thing but not right in manner, i.e., in the exposition" (Kant, JL, AA IX, 57). In addition to other individuals as "external touchstone" (Kant, JL, AA IX, 57), one can turn to the *sensus communis* to discover errors of

166 *Rationally Dealing with Ignorance*

the understanding. The *sensus communis* can provide one orientation in thinking. Both *orientation* and *sensus communis* are crucial notions in this study and for finding a way for rationally dealing with ignorance. *Orientation in thinking* is a very apt formulation for what one wants in rationally dealing with ignorance. And the *sensus communis* gets us to a suggestion for rationally dealing with ignorance that is adequately broad and specific and that I take to be, ultimately, the right suggestion. Kant's remarks on "orientation in thinking" (OOT, AA VIII) will return later in explicating the final proposal.

In the *Jäsche Logic* Kant presents three general rules for avoiding errors that are candidates for another answer to our question of how one should rationally deal with ignorance.[14]

> Universal rules and conditions for avoiding error in general are: i) to think for oneself, 2) to think oneself in the position of someone else, and 3) always to think in agreement with oneself. The maxim of thinking for oneself can be called the enlightened mode of thought; the maxim of putting oneself in the viewpoint of others in thought, the extended mode of thought; and the maxim of always thinking in agreement with one self, the consequent or coherent mode of thought.
>
> (Kant, JL, AA IX, 57)

It is striking that these three rules also appear in *The Critique of the Power of Judgment* (CPJ) and *Anthropology from a Pragmatic Point of View* (Anth). Kant presents these three rules as the maxims of the sensus communis in *The Critique of the Power of Judgment* and as the maxims that lead to wisdom in the *Anthropology*. In the *Anthropology* Kant even lists the maxims twice (Kant, Anth, AA VII, 200, 228). In *The Jäsche Logic* the *sensus communis* is mentioned as a "touchstone" in the paragraph just before the one listing the rules for avoiding error (Kant, JL, AA IX, 57). But Kant himself does not make this intertextual connection explicit[15] – neither in *The Critique of the Power of Judgment* nor in the *Jäsche Logic* nor the *Anthropology*.

The first maxim, Kant writes, "is the maxim of a reason that is never passive" (Kant, CPJ, AA V, 294); reason is not passive because it is self-legislating. Clearly, this maxim is intimately connected to the demands of the Enlightenment, for example, the epistemic subject must not be a slave to epistemic authorities (e.g., Kant, WIE, AA VIII). Kant fittingly calls it the enlightened mode of thought. Thinking for oneself requires that one be a thinking epistemic agent. The second maxim holds for a subject that goes beyond her cognitive limitations and thinks about her own judgments from a general viewpoint. She can take up this general viewpoint by taking up the perspective of other subjects (Kant, CPJ, AA V,

294). This is the extended mode of thought. And this is the crucial intersubjective, community-oriented step that other individualistic suggestions have not made.

The third maxim builds on the first two maxims and is developed by a continuous realization of the first two maxims. Kant summarizes the maxims in *The Critique of the Power of Judgment* as follows: "One can say that the first of these maxims is that maxim of the understanding, the second that of the power of judgment, the third that of reason" (Kant, CPJ, AA V, 295). Kant does not say why thinking in accord with oneself is crucial for avoiding error, nor why it is crucial for the *sensus communis*. I will offer an interpretation that goes beyond Kant's own remarks. By introducing Ernst Tugendhat's notion of *intellectual honesty* as a disposition that consists in acknowledging the possibility that one's own beliefs are false and in accepting "a dynamic of clarifying and justifying"[16] (Tugendhat 2010, 109, my translation), I am able to explain why consistency is one of the maxims of the *sensus communis* and why it is crucial for rationally dealing with ignorance (Sections 10.1 and 10.2).

Let me say more about the second maxim by way of a detour via Locke's list of errors in *Of the Conduct of the Understanding*. As Reinhard Brandt notes, there is a striking connection between Locke's list of three errors and the three maxims. Brandt even suggests that "it can hardly be doubted that Locke's text, modified by Kant, is the model for the three maxims" (Brandt 1981, 40, my translation). One indication is that Locke and Kant both use the rare biblical image "Gosen" (Brandt 1981, 40, fn. 7).[17]

I have introduced Locke's list of errors in Section 5.1 on causes of ignorance and will now return to the third error on the list because it helps illuminate the significance and impact of the second maxim. The third error in *Of the Conduct of the Understanding* (1996) consists in not realizing that one's own viewpoint is necessarily restricted and in not taking any countermeasures against this restriction. Let me give you the relevant section again, with Locke's suggestion for how one should react to these restrictions. You will see that Locke provides a fitting description for why we need to include other perspectives and how we can include other perspectives which is exactly what Kant's second maxim amounts to:

(iii) The third sort [of error, N.E.] is of those who readily and sincerely follow reason but, for want of having that which one may call large, sound, roundabout sense, have not a full view of all that relates to the question and may be of moment to decide it. *We are all shortsighted and very often see but one side of a matter; our views are not extended to all that has a connection with it. From this defect I think no man is free.* We see but in part and we know but in part, and therefore it is no wonder we conclude not right from our partial views. This might instruct the proudest esteemer of his own parts how useful it is to talk and consult with others, even such as came short of him in capacity, quickness and penetration; for since no one sees all and we generally have different prospects of the same thing according to our different, as I may say, positions to it, it is not incongruous to think nor beneath any man to try whether another may not have notions of things which have escaped him and which his reason would make use of if they came into his mind. ... In this we may see the reason why some men of study and thought that reason right and are lovers of truth do make no great advances in their discoveries of it. *Error and truth are uncertainly blended in their minds ; their decisions are lame and defective, and they are very often mistaken in their judgments ; the reason whereof is, they converse but with one sort of men, they read but one sort of books, they will not come in the hearing but of one sort of notions ; the truth is, they canton out to themselves a little Goshen in the intellectual world where light shines and, as they conclude, day blesses them ; but the rest of that vast expansion they give up to night and darkness and so avoid coming near it.* They have a pretty traffick with known correspondents in some little creek ; within that they confine themselves and are dexterous managers enough of the wares and products of that corner with which they content themselves, *but will not venture out into the great ocean of knowledge to survey the riches that nature has stored other parts with, no less genuine, no less solid, no less useful than what has fallen to their lot in the admired plenty and sufficiency of their own little spot, which to them contains whatsoever is good in the universe.*

(Locke 1996, §3, my emphases)

In *The Critique of the Power of Judgment* Kant explains that by thinking oneself in the position of everyone else one acquires a general viewpoint that allows one to reflect one's own opinions, beliefs and judgments.[18] This process of extending one's cognition is unique because it does not proceed analytically like standard metaphysics at Kant's time (Brandt 1981, 40). In a new move, both Locke and Kant suggest that one should extend one's thought (Kant, JL, AA IX, 57) by looking at the beliefs of other epistemic subjects, by confronting oneself with other judgments. Brandt emphasizes that by extending one's thought one does not just achieve control of one's own judgments through other judgments, one also gains more *Erkenntnis* (Brandt 1981, 41).

The second maxim is a tool for *diagnosing one's own ignorance and errors* despite the necessary limitations that come with the first-person perspective on one's own ignorance that we have encountered before. One may even suggest that the second maxim allows the subject to be genuinely open-minded, one *opens one's mind* by taking the perspective of other subjects, by thinking in the "extended mode of thought." The third maxim requires the thinker to combine their thinking and the thinking of other individuals, it is like the conclusion to the first two maxims.

The three maxims determine what the *sensus communis* does and what it consists in. From Kant's explanation we understand why the *sensus communis* is a good tool for addressing and avoiding errors. Kant writes:

> By "sensus communis"[19] however, must be understood the idea of a communal sense, i.e., a faculty for judging that in its reflection takes account (a priori) of everyone else's way of representing in thought, in order as it were to hold its judgment up to human reason as a whole and thereby avoid the illusion which, from subjective private conditions that could easily be held to be objective, would have a detrimental influence on the judgment.
> (Kant, CPJ, AA V, 293–294, B157)

By activating the *sensus communis* one avoids making judgments that are influenced by one's subjective conditions, and instead includes humanity as a measure and co-deciding entity in the process of judging. That is how one *finds and avoids* errors. Again we see that Kant, unlike most contemporary epistemologists, is able to deal with "hypothetical beliefs" and "merely possible judgments."

The role of the *sensus communis* and in particular the significance of humanity for judgment must be further elucidated by Kant's suggestion how one should orient oneself in thinking. But first, in the context of this study, I suggest we can gage another suggestion for rationally dealing with ignorance:

> **Suggestion 12:** Follow the maxims of the *sensus communis*: 1. Think for oneself; 2. Think in the position of everyone else; 3. Always think in accord with oneself.

I submit that, ultimately, this is the most promising suggestion for rationally dealing with ignorance and error. I call it the *Maxim-based Answer*. The suggestion is specific but not too specific and not too broad. We have three maxims that one can stick to. The maxims are particularly suitable for the present study because they allow for more complex and sophisticated stances toward ignorance and error and do not simply call for avoiding ignorance and error. Such sophisticated stances are required by the paradigms of ignorance. In addition, the maxims come with a tool for diagnosing and identifying one's own ignorance: by taking the position of everyone else (maxim 2) one is able to find when one does not know something or when one holds a false belief, etc. At the same time, the Maxim-based Answer does not just impose duties on the subject nor are they duties imposed by another authority. Instead, since the rules are maxims, they are self-legislated by the subject herself. This is another advantage of Suggestion 12.

The three maxims and the Maxim-based Answer for rationally dealing with ignorance need more unpacking. We also need to consider why Kant's suggestion for avoiding errors should work for ignorance, too. I will turn to the notion of a maxim and Ernst Tugendhat's considerations regarding intellectual honesty to elucidate the Maxim-based Answer.

Notes

1 Note that Chisholm makes these claims only in the second edition of his *Theory of Knowledge* (1977), but not in the first (1966) and the third (1989). In some parts the three editions of his *Theory of Knowledge* differ significantly (1966, 1977, 1989).

2 Wolterstorff emphasizes that Locke "perceived himself as philosophizing in a situation of cultural and social crisis, [and] he set out to address himself to that crisis" (Wolterstorff 1996, 4). The crisis was induced by Locke and his contemporaries feeling that they could not anymore turn to the writings and doctrines of religion in understanding the world (Wolterstorff 1996, 3).

3 Wolterstorff notes that Locke does not explicitly state that the alethic obligation is toward God, but suggests that the cited passage lends itself to being read that way (Wolterstorff 1996, 64).

4 Wolterstorff conceptualizes these excusing conditions as a "practical inability" (1996, 70). He notes that, according to Locke, "each of us ... for many of the propositions that come to mind, is *obligated not to* try to do his or her best. Doing his or her best would require neglecting other more weighty obligations" (Wolterstorff 1996, 70, emphasis in original). But the passages on this topic can also be interpreted more critically since Locke may be taken to suggest that they are *unable* to engage in fundamental religious matters. Locke writes: "T'is not to be expected, that a Man, who drudges on, all his Life, in a laborious Trade, should be more knowing in the variety of Things done in the World, than a Pack-horse, who is driven constantly forwards and backwards in a narrow Lane, and dirty Road, only to Market, should be skilled in the Geography of the country. Nor is it all more possible, that he who wants Leisure, Books, and Languages, and the Opportunity of Conversing with variety of Men, should be in a Condition to collect those Testimonies and Observations, which are in Being, and are necessary to make out many, nay most of the Propositions, that, in the Societies of Men, are judged of the greatest Moment; or to find out Grounds of Assurance so great, as the Belief of the points he would build on them, is thought necessary. So that a great part of Mankind are, by the natural and unalterable State of Things in this World, and the Constitution of humane Affairs unavoidably given over to invincible

Ignorance of those Proofs, on which others build, and which are necessary to establish those Opinions: *The greatest part of Men, having much to do to get the Means of Living are not in a Condition to look after those of learned and laborious Enquiries*" (Locke 1979, IV, xx, 2, my emphases).

5 St Augustine, too, argues that one is guilty of a sin if one does not use one's God-given capacities appropriately (St Augustine 1993, book 3).

6 "To conduct such appraisal, one must consider such matters as the following: 1. The number. 2. The integrity. 3. The skill of the witnesses. 4. The design of the author, where it is a testimony out of a book cited. 5. The consistency of the parts, and circumstances of the relation. 6. Contrary testimonies" (Locke 1979 IV, xv, 4, Wolterstorff 1996, 75).

7 "One might assume that, to a particular probability, a certain level of confidence has an inherent aptness (fittingness, rightness, propriety); and one might then hold that one's task is to see to it that one's level of confidence in the proposition 'fits' its probability, on one's satisfactory evidence" (Wolterstorff 1996, 80).

8 Wolterstorff justifies the "medical metaphor" by pointing out that "Locke himself regularly uses the medical metaphor of disease" (Wolterstorff 1996, 94, fn.78). He explains that Locke speaks of "the variety of distempers in men's minds" (Locke 1996, §38), and he says that there are perhaps as many "weaknesses and defects in the understanding, either from the natural temper of the mind, or ill habits taken up … as there are diseases of the body, each whereof clogs and disables the understanding to some degree, and therefore deserves to be looked after and cured" (Locke 1996 §38, Works II, 349). As one would expect, he also regularly speaks, as in that last passage, of "cures" and "remedies" (e.g., Locke 1996, §41, Works II, 388–389).

9 As I have mentioned in the Introduction, such issues also appear for Descartes and Spinoza who also hold that cognitive capacities are divine *qua* being God-given. Cf. e.g., Garrett (2013).

10 Locke's suggestion will be particularly interesting to formal epistemologists because it contains the reference to probabilities in belief and, thus, is amenable to probabilistic, say, Bayesian frameworks and talk of ignorance in terms of credence. See, e.g., Pettigrew (2016) for an attempt at formalizing the Jamesian twin goals. Note that formal epistemology also has the so-called *Lockean Thesis* that "says that one should believe a proposition A just in case one's degree of belief for A is sufficiently high" (Huber 2016).

11 Note that these expectations are relative to the state of the disciplines and the standards of expertise at the time of the cases. For example, a meteorologist in the early days of meteorology is not expected to know that she needs to include the North Atlantic Oscillation (NAO) in preparing the weather forecast.

12 For further support as to why Peter may be said to have a duty to know his partner's birthday, see Smith (2005): "We expect the participants in such relationships [viz. love and friendship, N.E.] to place a special importance on the needs and interests of their beloveds, and … failures of awareness seem to call into question the presence of that evaluative commitment" (2005, 245).

172 Rationally Dealing with Ignorance

13 As noted before, Goldberg makes a related observation about the nature of the entitlement to expect others to know being both a moral and an epistemic entitlement (Goldberg 2017b, 2891f.).
14 Readers who are worried whether the *Jäsche Logic* is really faithful to Kant's logical claims are reminded that Kant gives the same three rules in his handwritten notes (Kant, HN, AA XVI, 294). See also Chapter 4, endnote 5.
15 See Jüngel (2005, 4) on "self-citations" as signs of topics and issues that are central for Kant and other authors.
16 All translations of Tugendhat (2010) are mine.
17 And Locke also uses the term of a "touchstone" that every person has, but for him it is natural reason rather than other thinking beings (Locke 1996, §3).
18 These components are also crucial for explaining how aesthetic judgments can be subjective and objective; cf., e.g., Ginsborg (2006).
19 Note that Kant in this passage does not use the term *common sense* but only the Latin expression *sensus communis*. The *sensus communis* is not the same as simple *common sense*. Though later in *The Critique of the Power of Judgment* Kant also uses the term *common sense*.

10 The Maxim-Based Answer

10.1 Developing the Maxim-Based Answer

In this chapter I spell out my own proposal for rationally dealing with ignorance. The Maxim-based Answer holds that one should (1) think for oneself, (2) think in the position of everyone else, and (3) think in accord with oneself. Kant introduces these maxims as tools for avoiding error. My proposal extends and explicates these maxims so that they can be applied to ignorance, by elaborating "thinking in the position of everyone else" as the tool of intersubjective, social thinking.

What follows from the fact that the three sentences, the rules for the *sensus communis*, are maxims? First of all, it means that they are rules. Then, as Harald Köhl points out, maxims are "subjective cardinal propositions of the will" (Köhl 1990, 47, my translation). They are subjective in that they are commitments of a person as to what she wants to do in a particular situation. The subject commits to acting in a particular way when they get in that particular situation for which their commitment holds. Consequently, maxims cannot claim to be intersubjectively valid (Köhl 1990, 47) and they are something that one *actively* commits to. They are not rules that one just finds oneself with, they are "rules imposed upon oneself" (Kant, G, AA IV, 438). In settling on these rules from a first-person singular perspective, one attempts to define oneself and decides to settle for an intention and a decision (Köhl 1990, 49). Consequently, maxims do not have truth-values; they are not truth apt. If one does not act according to one's maxim, one did not have a false belief, but simply did not act according to one's maxim. Yet, maxims are intimately connected to normative sentences: maxims imply normative statements. If I have given myself maxim M for situation S and situation S comes, then I should act according to maxim M – if I am consistent (*konsequent*).

You might be worried that these demanding features of maxims make them *too* demanding. How can one expect that every being gives herself the maxims of the *sensus communis* in a conscious, deliberate act? Köhl's discussion of maxims in the ethical case also emphasizes this problem. As he puts it succinctly, "The assumption that we always act according to maxims that we have consciously given ourselves is empirically wrong. We do not make maxims for everything. Not everyone of us is a Kant" (Köhl 1990, 60, my translation).

But Köhl is not deterred by the problem of how we can expect every being to consciously give herself the maxims for her actions and instead points to a solution. First, we do not need to examine every maxim to morally evaluate a person, the character (which is connected to the maxims) is enough. And he suggests that maxims are conclusions based on (life-)experiences that make our lives easier. They provide shortcuts that simplify our lives. Thus, they are what he calls, following Freud, "cultural achievements through which structure can come into our life" (Köhl 1990, 61, my translation).

Köhl does not make this claim, but I think we may surmise that the active decision to commit to a maxim, to give oneself a maxim (or maxims) is not as important as it may initially seem. As constituents of culture, we may acquire them culturally, and they may be second nature to us. A version of the second nature argument that I have introduced in discussing Aristotle's answer ties in well (Section 7.1).

Let me now show that Kant's list of rules, originally designed to avoid error, can also be extended to cover error *and* ignorance. My argumentation has two strands. One strand works from within Kant's writings, the other strand works with my own considerations on error and ignorance.

We can gain indirect support from Kant via the connection between the maxims and wisdom, one of our (former) natural candidates for rationally dealing with ignorance. When Kant introduces the three maxims for thinkers in the *Anthropology*, he observes that the cognition of thinkers differ in how they answer the questions of the three cognitive faculties: "What do I want? (asks understanding) What does it matter? (asks the power of judgment) What comes of it? (asks reason)" (Kant, Anth, AA VII, 227).

So cognitions (literally, "people's heads," Anth, AA VII, 228) are different, but the three maxims can be made into "unalterable commands" (Anth, AA VII, 228) that work for everyone and they lead to wisdom. Kant admits that wisdom "as the idea of a practical use of reason that conforms perfectly with the law" (Anth, AA VII, 200) is probably too high a demand for human beings, but the three maxims are the best way for producing wisdom (Anth, AA VII, 200).[1]

Kant's article "What does it mean to orient oneself in thinking?" (OOT, AA VIII) provides further grounds for saying that these maxims and the *sensus communis* are the best approach for dealing with error *and* ignorance. In his handwritten notes on logic, Kant also connects orienting oneself and the *sensus communis* when he writes in a comment in brackets that one gets orientation by the common sense (HN, AA XVI, 293). In the article on orienting oneself in thinking, Kant enters into a debate about how one can have knowledge of God. Moses Mendelssohn had argued that one can have rational knowledge of God and Kant rejects this claim. But as Onora O'Neill (2015) points out, this is but one aspect of the article. Kant more generally explains how human beings with their limited cognitive abilities can conduct inquiry and orient themselves. This issue obviously is highly relevant to anyone who wants to know how to deal with ignorance.

In the article, Kant starts from geographical orientation and notes that one orientates oneself geographically by means of a subjective distinction, a distinction within the subject (O'Neill 2015, 158). The same holds for orientation in thinking; here, maxims take the role of subjective distinctions. And the subjective distinction is "created by agents who adopt maxims in order to make good a deficiency or need in their ordinary cognitive capacities, so that they can regulate their thought and action" (O'Neill 2015, 161). We can recognize the concerns about the possibility and reality of error and ignorance in the maxims' concern with the deficiencies of ordinary cognitive capacities.

So, it is in the maxims which enable orientation in thinking that the subject addresses ignorance and error. As we have just seen, these maxims are subjective because they are determined by the subject herself. Since these maxims must not be arbitrary, Kant must be able to explain how they can be lawlike and have universal scope. And Kant's solution is that the maxims must be "*followable* in thought or *adoptable* for action by any others who are to consider, entertain, adopt and reject them" (O'Neill 2015, 167, emphasis in original). The standard for one's maxims in orienting oneself in thinking must, thus, be "followable" or "adoptable" by all others, otherwise one cannot communicate with others about the maxims.

According to O'Neill, one can develop as a supreme principle for reason a negative strategy: "Reject principles that are unfit to serve as principle for all" (O'Neill 2015, 167). I suggest that the three maxims of the *sensus communis* are principles that fit this strategy, they "combine lawlike form with universal scope" (O'Neill 2015, 165) and they are "fit to serve as principle for all" (O'Neill 2015, 167).[2] And Kant combines individual thinking and collective thinking insofar as the "capacity to orient ourselves is a shared rather than a solitary task" (O'Neill 2015, 154).

Now we can see how in the *sensus communis* one can be said to "hold [one's] judgment up to human reason as a whole" (Kant, CPJ, AA V, 293): It is by following maxims that are followable and adoptable by others that I make my thought and judgment available to human reason as a whole. This interpretation further substantiates the Maxim-based Answer, which consists in following the maxims of the *sensus communis*.

The *sensus communis* is a necessary condition for the communicability of our cognition (cf. Kant CPJ, AA V 238–239) – but as Kant notes in the *Jäsche Logic*, the maxims of the *sensus communis* are also the best way for addressing and avoiding errors. I conjecture that the *sensus communis* is also a necessary condition for addressing and reflecting our fallibility – our errors and our ignorance. If I think for myself and think in the position of everyone else and always think in accord with myself, I am able to deal with errors and ignorance.[3]

On to the second strand of the extension to ignorance. – Note that this is not in Kant, but I think we are warranted in developing Kant's basic notions and claims further even if his texts did not license these extensions. These extensions are valuable and helpful for the present project. – I suggest that the three maxims can also be applied to dealing with ignorance and not just to error because error is an instance of ignorance. When committing an error, there is something that one does not know, and there may be structures that co-constitute the specific error, just as in ignorance in general. Moreover, there is a structural similarity between error and ignorance: Ignorance is like hypothetical beliefs because ignorance can be co-constituted by absences or gaps or by beliefs that one could have and not just actual beliefs. Error consists in beliefs that one has but also in beliefs one should have, or in attitudes one has and attitudes that one should have. It is thus similarly complex.

We can employ the maxims for dealing with instances of ignorance in which we *know* that we are ignorant – searching out other perspectives, taking up other perspectives, and combining these perspectives and thinking for oneself. And as a general stance that we should always be prepared to take up explicitly or take up dispositionally as epistemic agents, we can also employ it for instances of ignorance of which we are not aware, that is, non-reflective ignorance. This is the diagnosing power of the maxims that I have mentioned earlier. In employing the tools in that way, we take up an intersubjectively grounded position. Note that the proposal also fits with the Integrated Conception of Ignorance because it recognizes the individual as located in communities and in interaction with other individuals thus realizing the adequacy conditions for an account of ignorance (Section 3.4). I'll say more about the intersubjective component in developing intellectual honesty as a stance related to the Maxim-based Answer and in discussing objections against the proposal (Chapter 10).

10.2 How Is This a Rational Approach to Dealing with Ignorance?

Let me start this section with an important caveat that gets us to the issue of why this is a rational approach to dealing with ignorance. This is the caveat: The Maxim-based Answer is not intended to provide a fool-proof account nor does it come with a guarantee for success. Someone who manifests White Ignorance may take themselves to be thinking for themselves, thinking themselves in the position of everyone else and thinking in accord with themselves. But their selection of relevant other perspectives is distorted and biased. We can say that they did not extend their thought in the right way because they did not take the stance of *humanity* but of White people. And the Integrated Conception of Ignorance enables us to explain how structures and systems obstruct people's perspectives and how people use the structures and system to obstruct and limit their perspectives. It is a social process and not just an individual process.

But how is the Maxim-based Answer still a rational suggestion or a rational approach to dealing with ignorance? Again there are two strands: one Kantian, one non-Kantian. On the Kantian argumentative strand the suggestion is rational because maxims are rules that a rational being imposes upon themself (cf. Kant, G, AA IV, 438) and thus the three maxims are rational, too. It's the typical Kantian rationality approach. But even if one does not like the Kantian approach, there is a very convincing route to arguing for the rationality of the approach. In fact, there are even three routes: an instrumentalist-pragmatic route, a social route and a realist non-instrumentalist route. I employ Tugendhat's distinctions of motivations for being intellectually honest that in turn refer to the taxonomy developed by Gosepath (1992): one can be pragmatically motivated, or one can be socially motivated or one can be motivated by the intrinsic value of knowing the truth (as opposed to being delusional or ignorant). When I am *pragmatically motivated (instrumentally motivated)* to follow the three maxims (aka the Maxim-based Answer), I recognize that it is the best approach to reaching my aims regarding my dealings with ignorance. I'm more likely to take the right stance toward ignorance – reflective and non-reflective – when I think for myself, take other perspectives and think accordingly. And I'm more likely to avoid errors. I might also be more likely to identify my own non-reflective ignorance and know how to address my reflective ignorance.

When I am socially motivated, I am motivated by expectations from other community members and by social values such as honesty and accuracy (cf. Williams 2004). This is the familiar topos of expectations from other community members that we encountered in Goldberg's "Should have known" study. I'm expected to make correct statements about when I'll be arriving at a friend's house, I'm expected to give accurate descriptions when I tell a tourist asking me for the way that I know the way to the train station. We are also expected to have basic knowledge about the town we live in or sometimes also more demanding knowledge, say, about the effects of climate change. And we are also expected to have well-justified views about justice, political issues, etc. These views are the basis for our participation in democracies. – I return to this topic in Chapter 11. – The social motivation also works because of social reactions to our epistemic states (and our actions); one may feel shame if one does not know what one is (rightly) expected to know, or one may be held accountable if one does not know what one is rightly expected to know. On this conception one is motivated to adopt and follow the three maxims because they are the best way for implementing social values such as honesty and accuracy and for avoiding social reactive attitudes if one fails to meet social expectations. Note that the communicative, intersubjective face of the second maxim would also entail that one manifests social relations in following the maxims. The Maxim-based Answer is inherently social and thus complements the social motivation.

But Tugendhat also adds what I call a "realist non-instrumentalist motivation": One can be motivated by wanting to be connected to reality, wanting to know how things really are, not believing falsehoods or being delusional. The motive for taking up the Maxim-based Answer in this case is that it enables one to not be deluded about the world or oneself, but one is not instrumentally motivated. It is simply how one behaves or acts in avoiding delusions and being related to the world as it is. Again, there is no anti-delusion guarantee in the Maxim-based Approach, but it is the best approach one has.

These motivations are three different explanations for why taking up the Maxim-based Approach is rational. There are arguments for each explanation and the related theory. I won't discuss which explanation is best. All that matters is that there are different respects in which it is rational to pursue the Maxim-based Approach in dealing with ignorance. And which motivation an individual pursues is ultimately an empirical question. For this project we only need to see that the approach itself is rational.

In the present study of determining how one should rationally deal with ignorance *intellectual honesty* (*Intellektuelle Redlichkeit*) plays a crucial role for undergirding and substantiating my proposal that the Maxim-based Answer is the best suggestion for rationally dealing with ignorance. We learn more about the motivation of rationally dealing with ignorance from this study of intellectual honesty.

And we can also explicate the practice(s) *behind* Kant's maxims by including intellectual honesty in the conception. Tugendhat describes intellectual honesty as accounting for one's own beliefs about oneself and one's beliefs about the world. In being intellectually honest one has a disposition that consists in allowing for one's own beliefs to be false. Intellectual honesty is "the attitude of being open for reasons that speak against one's own belief" (Tugendhat 2010, 98, my translation). One is open for one's own epistemic and cognitive fallibility. This disposition can be further differentiated into *intellectual honesty in a formal sense* and *intellectual honesty in a substantial sense*. Intellectual honesty in a formal sense refers to a stance toward one's own beliefs (irrespective of their content). Intellectual honesty in a substantial sense consists in avoiding pretense.

Importantly, intellectual honesty *simpliciter* is not restricted to aiming at truth or searching for the truth, rather, it consists in examining the beliefs that one holds. One aims to avoid false beliefs in one's own belief system, both in individual and collective belief systems (Tugendhat 2010, 101). And in fact, wanting to acquire more knowledge is a secondary aim (Tugendhat 2010, 101). The background to this practice is what Tugendhat describes as giving in to a "dynamic of clarifying and justifying" (Tugendhat 2010, 109) that is informed by a dynamic of reacting to a lack of justification and accuracy in one's beliefs (Tugendhat 2010, 98).

I submit that the practice of intellectual honesty and the accompanying background "dynamic of clarifying and justifying" form the background to Kant's maxims. Thinking for yourself and taking up the perspective of other subjects only make sense against the background of the dynamic of clarifying and justifying and intellectual honesty. And now we have another explanation for why Kant says that the third maxim, being consistent with oneself, ultimately consists in following the first and the second maxim. In thinking for yourself and taking up other people's perspective you put intellectual honesty into practice; in other words, you actualize intellectual honesty.

Tugendhat observes that since intellectual honesty is so demanding and may lead to unwelcome results – for example, I may find out that I hold false beliefs about myself; say, I am overly self-confident or I am not as nice a person as I think I am – the motivation *against* being intellectually honest is stronger and more obvious than the motivation *for* being intellectual honest. And so he asks why human beings are still motivated to be intellectually honest and he discusses the three motivations that I have introduced earlier to explain why the Maxim-based Approach is rational. The most obvious motivations are pragmatic/instrumental considerations and moral or social considerations. Having right beliefs and avoiding false beliefs in my belief set is advantageous because it allows me to achieve my aims and fulfill my desires. I have to know how things really are in order to achieve my aims and not be deluded (cf. Gosepath 1992). Moral and social considerations that motivate being intellectually honest build on the social value of honesty and accuracy (cf. Williams 2004). Pragmatic and social and moral considerations overlap. The subject is motivated to be intellectually honest because she wants to avoid being called to account and, in particular, she wants to avoid the shame of being called to account (Tugendhat 2010, 107).

But there is also a non-instrumental motivation for intellectual honesty. Paradigmatically, we find this non-instrumental motivation in Socrates when he realizes that his own beliefs that are directly and indirectly related to the Good are unclear and biased and must be cleared up. In doing so he does not aim at truth but at avoiding false beliefs in his belief set. Tugendhat suggests that Socrates actualizes intellectual honesty in the substantive sense since he wants to avoid pretense and false beliefs about the good. – This form of intellectual honesty is not motivated by pragmatic or moral considerations because it sets out to question just those considerations. Tugendhat surmises that the motivation for this form of intellectual honesty lies in wanting to counter delusion and mania (2010, 109) and is grounded in the observation that a life of pretense, a life of as-ifs is less valuable than a real life, an honest life, an authentic life, as we might say even though Tugendhat does not employ this term.

This form of intellectual honesty, substantial intellectual honesty, is unavoidably circular (Tugendhat 2010, 110–111). The non-instrumental value of intellectual honesty and substantial intellectual honesty can only be recognized by those who already recognize the evidence in favor of intellectual honesty. Those who like being in the opaque, who like it when things are opaque cannot be *talked into* recognizing substantial intellectual honesty to avoid pretense. They can only value intellectual honesty because of a social reason, namely wanting to avoid shame (Tugendhat 2010, 111), but *not* for a non-instrumental reason.

Let me close this section by briefly pointing to advantages to the conception. My interpretation of the Maxim-based Answer for dealing with ignorance and error comes with a number of advantages and productive starting points. As I have said earlier, it is neither too broad nor too specific. Moreover, it is flexible because it does not advantage truth nor condemns false belief and ignorance. It allows that false belief and ignorance are acceptable, for example, because they are outside our horizon. The maxims are self-legislated and subjective and, therefore, do not depend on a foreign deontic authority.

But the maxims are also objective and, thus, the Maxim-based Answer does not regard dealing with ignorance as a solitary task but includes the epistemic community in the project. And as we have seen in the list of epistemic conduct and actions that instantiate open-minded ignorance and close-minded ignorance, the others – the community, one's interlocutors, the second person – play a crucial role in one's dealing with ignorance. One can tackle the limitations of one's first-personal perspective by following the second maxim, in particular. Of course, one cannot indefinitely overcome the limitations, but triangulation with other subjects is a sure way to avoid the limitations or work around them.

In taking the perspective of others in thinking one is also open-mindedly ignorant. This stance may also include listening to other people, not silencing them, etc. One is close-mindedly ignorant in not listening to other people's evidence. In taking the perspective of others, one is *rationally* dealing with ignorance because one follows reason (one's own rationality) and one gives and takes reasons. As we will see in the next chapter, it is constitutive of living the three maxims that one engages in the practice of giving reasons and explaining. This is as rational a practice as one can get. And this practice also allows one to justify and explain instances of close-minded ignorance that may be warranted.

In addition, the Maxim-based Answer puts the epistemic subject and epistemic agency in the center of attention. There are things that an epistemic subject can do in dealing with ignorance and error and those epistemic actions are constituted and actualized by the epistemic subject herself and other epistemic subjects. This setup leads to two problems that I will have to address: First, the setup seems to be restricted to dealing with reflective ignorance because the maxims are very conscious. By discussing how one should deal with uncertainty in medicine I will outline how the three maxims are also appropriate for dealing with non-reflective ignorance (Chapter 12). Second, such a proposal puts a lot of weight, expectations and pressure on the epistemic subject in rationally dealing with ignorance.

In order to further explicate and refine the conception of the Maxim-based Answer I discuss three sets of worries. I address these worries in turn, starting with the first worry. In replying to the worries, I will further elucidate the Maxim-based Answer.

1 The Pessimist Objection. Epistemic subjects qua human beings continuously fail to adequately deal with ignorance and error. Therefore, the proposed conception is destined to fail. There is no *rational* way of dealing with ignorance.
2 The Objection from Those Who Just Do Not Care. How do you deal with an epistemic subject who rejects the demands placed on her by your suggestions?
3 The Objection from Overdemandingness, from Arrogant Elitism and from Intellectualization. On the proposed conception dealing with ignorance requires self-mastery, self-discipline, self-denial and intellectualism. Doesn't this amount to Arrogant Elitism and isn't it too demanding for human beings?

10.3 Objections against the Maxim-Based Answer

10.3.1 The Pessimist's Objection

The first worry wants to pull the rug out from my attempts at finding a principled way of rationally dealing with ignorance. Human beings continuously fail to rationally deal with ignorance and error, therefore there is no definitive answer to my quest.[4] It is a *pessimist* who puts forward the worry.[5] The *agnostic* position is closely connected to this pessimistic stance, but it also differs significantly. The agnostic is equally impressed by the reality and possibility of failure, but, unlike the pessimist, they do not deny the possibility of determining a way for rationally dealing with ignorance and merely suspend judgment on that question. The agnostic suspends judgment on whether human beings are able to rationally deal with ignorance and whether an epistemological project trying to outline how one should rationally deal with ignorance could ever succeed. They also suspend judgment on how to rationally deal with ignorance.

But these are not the only positions that one can take toward wanting to find a way for rationally dealing with ignorance and dealing with ignorance. There is also the *naïve optimist* who holds that things will just turn out fine. One can succeed in determining a way for rationally dealing with ignorance. And there is also someone that I propose to call the *reflective optimist*. The reflective optimist holds that there is no getting around dealing with ignorance and that trying to succeed in detailing a way for *rationally dealing with ignorance* will be the best option for dealing with ignorance. This is the stance I suggest we should take up.

Note that the agnostic position is practically untenable since one cannot *not* deal with ignorance. One just cannot get around dealing with one's ignorance, because, say, if one does not try to overcome one's reflective ignorance, one decides to overlook or ignore one's ignorance and, thereby, also deals with one's ignorance. One does not necessarily explicitly endorse this strategy, but one endorses it implicitly. So there is no avoiding turning a strategy for dealing with ignorance into practice, and one cannot suspend judgment on the issues of ignorance.[6]

The pessimist position is certainly tenable, it is just destructive in spirit and I do not think that it should rationally be endorsed, because it denies the epistemic powers and the potential of human beings. Moreover, I do not think that one is warranted in taking up the pessimist position. At the beginning of this study, I have detailed how this is a non-ideal project, but at this point I want to emphasize that it is also an idealist's project because it builds on – and believes in – the epistemic potential of human beings. We should not be naïve optimists, because such a view would ignore the evidence on ignorance and the detrimental effects of ignorance. But we can be realist about human beings and their cognitive abilities, without denying the negative traits of human beings.

The pessimist is passive whereas the realist can still be an agent. We see this feature of pessimism clearly if we consider an instructive parallel. We find the dynamic, the setup and the attitudes (pessimist, agnostic, optimist) paralleled in how people deal with disappointment in personal relationships, for example, after having been betrayed once again by another person, say, a friend, a lover or another close person. The pessimist's position is the reaction of a disappointed subject who vows to never trust anyone again because all human beings are bound to disappoint her. The agnostic position is that of the disappointed subject who does not know whether she should or can ever trust anyone after the incidents. She does not condemn and reject all human relationships based on trust – that is the pessimist position – but the agnostic also does not enter into any trusting relationships because she does not know whether she will be disappointed or not. And so, in order to avoid being disappointed, which is very likely, she thinks, she does not trust others. The naïve optimist on the other hand simply ignores the disappointment and naïvely continues to be open for close relationships that build on trust.

Such naïve optimistic behavior may be gullible and foolhardy, but I do not think that an optimist per se is foolhardy and that is why I have distinguished above between the naïve optimist and the reflective optimist. The reflective optimist is not gullible, and so after having been disappointed by a close person, the reflective optimist continues to be open for close relationships, but they are careful about whom they trust. They do not trust just anyone. Like the pessimist and the agnostic, they learned from previous experiences, but they do not conclude that there is no basis for trust and personal relationships at all. And they do not abstain from entering into personal relationships or trusting someone.

One may wonder about the reflective optimist's motivation. And again, we can employ Tugendhat's picture. One strong reason would be an instrumental reason: they know that personal relationships are valuable for a good life. But they may also have a prudential reason: they know that it would be an exaggeration to avoid all close relationships because of their previous experiences. Another reason is rooted in their self-trust and autonomy: they know that they would weaken and disarm themselves if they react like the pessimist and the agnostic because they would allow those disappointing experiences to determine how they act rather than deciding themselves and determining themself how they act in personal relationships. The pessimist and the agnostic choose to be passive and inert because of their experiences. The reflective optimist wants to remain active.

You will have recognized why I take the parallel to be instructive. The structure is parallel to the situation presented by the pessimist objection. The pessimist is equally disappointed in human beings, their cognitive capacities and their epistemic conduct. One may be a pessimist about the potential for dealing with ignorance and reject (and avoid) all suggestions for action; one may be an agnostic and be paralyzed by the situation and abstain from all suggestions for action; one may be a naïve optimist who thinks that human beings just will be able to deal with ignorance; or one may be a reflective optimist who thinks that human beings can rationally deal with ignorance by following the right suggestions (say, Kant's three maxims) and accepting the cognitive limitations and fallibility of human beings. This stance manages to value and strengthen human epistemic agency because it rests on the assumption that human beings as individuals have the capacities for rationally dealing with ignorance. Those capacities constitute epistemic agency. The reflective optimist, thus, boosts their own epistemic agency and epistemic agency in general. This is the stance I suggest we should take up.

As you will have realized, my project is driven by a motivation akin to reflective optimism: all of the suggestions that I have discussed, including my favored suggestion, are based on the assumption that there is a way of rationally dealing with ignorance open to human being, and that epistemic agency is available to epistemic subjects (epistemic agents) and that such agency is key in finding the rational way for dealing with ignorance. Both accepting pessimism and accepting agnosticism amount to giving up epistemic agency and, thus, epistemic self-determination and self-control – for no good reason. One gives away or binds one's epistemic powers like Ulysses when the fear of the alleged Sirens is exaggerated. I insist that the reality of ignorance and error are no good reason for giving away our epistemic powers and epistemic agency.[7]

The pessimist reaction is, thus, circumscribed and unmasked as unattractive and unwarranted, but it will return in a different shape – the Objection from Those Who Just Do Not Care in the next section.

10.3.2 The Objection from Those Who Just Do Not Care

The Objection from Those Who Just Do Not Care notes that the Maxim-based Answer has no power to convince anyone to follow the maxims in rationally dealing with ignorance. Those who do not care about ignorance and error can and will just ignore the maxims.

Tugendhat's discussion of moral, social, pragmatic vs. non-instrumental motivations for intellectual honesty and the unavoidable circularity of substantive intellectual honesty show the way to replying to this objection. Just as in the case of intellectual honesty, we can at most convince skeptics (or even deniers) by pointing them to instrumental motivations, for example, the pragmatic consideration that it is best for realizing one's wishes and desires that one knows how things really are – in the world and within oneself – and that one thinks for oneself, thinks from the perspective of other subjects and thinks consistently with oneself. If you hold false beliefs, or if you are even deluded, it is much more difficult and perhaps even arbitrary whether you achieve your goals. A practically rational subject will want to avoid this situation (cf. again Gosepath 1992). But you cannot convince anyone of the *non-instrumental* value of the three maxims if they do not recognize the reasoning behind the non-instrumental value of the three maxims. Just as you cannot convince anyone of the value of substantive intellectual honesty who does not recognize the non-instrumental value of living a life without pretense and delusion and avoiding mania.[8]

For some my reply may seem to lead directly to another objection, the Objection from Arrogant Elitism that I discuss in the next section, because it sounds as if I hold that only those who are intelligent enough or enlightened enough can recognize the maxims and understand my proposal. I hope that this impression has not come up and, if it has, I will dissolve it in responding to the next objection.

Before that let me highlight another parallel that helps me further explicate my reply to the second objection. My reply so far has been that there is no way to convince those who do not want to acknowledge the reasoning behind the three maxims and the importance of rationally dealing with ignorance. You need to acknowledge the basic reasoning in order to accept my argumentation. I can point to instrumental considerations, but I cannot convince anyone by non-instrumental considerations. And my reasoning in favor of the Maxim-based Answer has been based on a mixture of non-instrumental considerations and instrumental considerations. The objection really involves three subjects: the fellow epistemic subject, the un-epistemic subject and the an-epistemic subject. The distinction is intended to parallel the distinction of the moral, the unmoral and the amoral subject. Those who just don't care are like unmoral and amoral subjects.

Again we can take this differentiation from a similar argument that Tugendhat gives in explaining how one can or cannot convince an amoralist of a moral theory in his *Lectures on Ethics* (1993).

> Here we find a specific togetherness of motives and reasons. That we even want to be a good member of society and, i.e. that we even want to belong to a moral community in the first place (that we even want to be able to make moral judgments) is ultimately an act of our autonomy, and *there can only be good motives for this, no reasons*. We have, as we will see, the strongest motives for the lower level of contractualist

morality – a level which is still the level of the amoralist –, and we only have good motives (but no conclusive motives) to also take up the level of actual morality. The dispute with the amoralist can thus only be led by giving motives. This is different in the dispute with other concepts of morality, there judgments stand against judgments. And only there can we speak of reasons. In this realm there can be no absolute justifications. The morality of universal and equal respect, the morality of non-instrumentality is in some sense indeed in limbo: one cannot demonstrate more than that it is the plausible (justified best) concept of the good, and that itself presupposes that one wants to be able to make moral judgments.

That means that the objectivity of the judgments that belong with this moral can only claim to be plausible. That is less than mere justification, but it is more than an intuition without justification and without considering other concepts. You might feel that this is disappointing, but as a philosopher one cannot apologize to the moral consciousness as it is for not being able to make it stronger than it is. Especially since we will see that a stronger justification is not just unavailable but nonsensical.

(Tugendhat 1993, 29–30, my translation and my emphasis)

Tugendhat distinguishes arguing with the amoralist and arguing with another moralist who defends a different moral theory. As I have noted, we should distinguish an *an-epistemic subject* who does not care about any epistemic norms, considerations, expectations nor about rationality, an *un-epistemic subject* who does not meet epistemic norms and epistemic expectations and who does not rationally deal with ignorance, and an *epistemic subject* who endorses another account of epistemic norms and dealing with ignorance. In trying to convince the epistemic subject I can offer reasons for accepting the Maxim-based Answer. But in trying to convince the un-epistemic subject I can only appeal to their motives and to instrumental considerations, and I cannot hope to convince them with any non-instrumental considerations nor any reasons.[9]

The parallel between the moral and the epistemic case is instructive, but it also has limitations, mainly, because moral community and epistemic community are not obviously identical. I cannot address the relationship between moral and epistemic communities in adequate detail because this is a topic in its own right. Let me just point out some issues. First, it is not obviously true that just by being a member of an epistemic community I am subject to the epistemic norms and demands of that community, or that I am an advocate and addressee of the epistemic norms.[10] Goldberg has argued that other members of the epistemic community have "legitimate expectations regarding [the] epistemic condition" (Goldberg

2017b, 2863) of other participants of an epistemic practice in an epistemic community, but we would need to look at the interplay between the expectations and rejecting any questions about why one has not met those expectations.

Second, there is the question of sanctions in moral and epistemic communities. Moral communities can sanction members who do not obey the norms, but it is disputed whether such sanctions are available or employed in epistemic communities. Excluding unreliable community members can be seen as a form of sanctioning. But, ultimately, most instances of sanctions in epistemic communities are based on the role obligations of the subject and, therefore, the sanctions seem to stem from the role obligations rather than from the membership in the epistemic community as is the case in moral communities.

Third, we would have to look at epistemic communities more closely. What *is* an epistemic community? How are they constituted? How do they work? Who are their constituents? What are their norms? Do they have any basic principles? How do blame and praise work in epistemic communities?[11] I cannot even begin to adequately address these issues in this context and, therefore, I will focus on how my proposals deals with people who just do not care or people who, like Bartleby, the Scrivener, would rather not rationally deal with ignorance (Melville 1985).

As I have noted earlier, I submit that I (and we) cannot convince the Bartlebys of our days from my proposal or from even rationally dealing with ignorance. We can relate the instrumental reasons and motivations to them, but it is up to them to implement these reasons and motivations into their lives. Everybody is free to be irrational, for example, by not reacting to the best reasons available, they are free to go against advice, and they are free to not take reasons seriously (cf. Wesche 2011, 195).

Wesche construes a similar problem for Tugendhat's conception of intellectual honesty. Tugendhat cannot (and does not) explain what it is that makes someone recognize intellectual honesty as an intrinsic value. Such insight and recognition may be just accidental, they may be arbitrary (Wesche 2011, 194)[12] and then intellectual honesty just becomes "a curse that cannot be influenced" (Wesche 2011, 194). This lacuna is an argumentative gap in Tugendhat's theory and he has to face up to "fatalism" and "circularity" (Wesche 2011, 195).

To some extent I face the same problem, but I can offer parts of a story here, namely the story of being initiated into epistemic practices and rationally dealing with ignorance being second nature to one (Section 7.1). In being brought up as a member of an epistemic community a subject acquires the capacities required for participating in the community, they become second nature to her. And these capacities may also include recognizing intellectual honesty as an intrinsic value. I will discuss this option in my reply to the third set of objections.

On the other hand, I think we need to accept that there is a circularity to the three maxims and to something like intellectual honesty; if anyone does not want to be impressed by the reasons for adopting the maxims (or any other set of suggestions for rationally dealing with ignorance), any influence is intrinsically limited. To some extent this is the flipside of an advantage of the Maxim-based Answer: the subject gives herself the maxims, they are self-legislated. They are subjective and not intersubjective. But I think it is worth biting this bullet.

And, let me emphasize that these limitations do not have to discourage the subject herself nor the community who is faced with a subject who is unphased by any reasoning in favor of rationally dealing with ignorance. We can talk to people about disagreements, even if things are much more difficult when someone believes wrongly on the fundamental level of epistemic conduct.

Another issue – and fact of reality – is that subjects may also cancel their membership in the community in a one-sided cancellation. In effect, this is what their rejection of the Maxim-based Answer or the rejection of any epistemic norms amounts to. They do not want to meet the expectations of the community and, ultimately, this means that they do not want to be a member of that community and cancel their membership. They do not respect shared standards and underlying norms and maxims. For example, if I decide to lie whenever I feel like it, I stop being a trustworthy member of the epistemic community, and I cancel my membership in that community. Similarly, if I knowingly form my beliefs on the basis of insufficient or inadequate evidence.

At the same time, the other members of the community can – and need to – react to my cancellation. They can ignore it, though this might make them gullible since they do not take the cancellation into account and rely on unreliable evidence and unreliable epistemic agents. This in turn would impact the quality of their own belief set. And, of course, it would also impact the collective belief set.[13] Alternatively, the other members may try to convince the former member or the non-member that they should join the community. Relatedly, they can also pursue an integrative approach on which they continue addressing the non-member as a member and try to include her in the activities of the community. But they will have to be cautious in this approach so that they are not too gullible and accidentally harm their own community or allow the non-member to harm the community.

The potential danger of the non-member for the epistemic community may be a reason for actively excluding the non-member from the community, another possible reaction to the non-member. In a way, this exclusionary move seems superfluous because the non-member has already cancelled their membership, but there may be reasons related to motivation, security and self-ascertainment of the epistemic community for cutting the connection with the non-member themselves.

Again a parallel with practical philosophy, in this case with political philosophy, is helpful. A democratic community may be justified in excluding members who pursue anti-democratic strategies and aim to destroy the democratic community because their own undemocratic behavior would save the democratic community. It may be crucial for the democratic community to expel the anti-democratic member herself and to not allow the anti-democratic member to cancel the membership in a one-sided act. In a similar way, it may be crucial for the epistemic community to expel the non-member herself to make sure that the non-member does not harm the epistemic community. But note that this situation only pertains in particular conditions, namely if the non-member is a threat to the functioning of the epistemic community.

For epistemic communities this may be someone like Fred Singer who notoriously questions scientific studies even though he lacks the relevant expertise for a justified verdict. For instance, he mimics the IPCC (Intergovernmental Panel on Climate Change) report and issues what he calls a "Non-Governmental International Panel on Climate Change" (NIPCC). "The NIPCC produces reports modeled exactly on the IPCC's reports: the same size and length, the same formatting – and, of course, reaching precisely the opposite conclusions" (O'Connor and Weatherall 2018, 134). In doing so, Singer ignites distrust by questioning reliable results with unreliable objections. As we have witnessed multiple times, such localized distrust may easily spread to other fields and it may become global. This is a version of the dynamic that influences versions of the Pessimist's Objection (Section 10.3.1). I submit that an epistemic community may be ultimately justified in excluding individuals like Fred Singer from the community. And they need to do as much as they can to guard themselves, their community and their members, against the influence of such subjects. I submit that following the Maxim-based Answer in rationally dealing with one's own ignorance and errors is a promising way for guarding oneself against such influences. And in telling others about those maxims, teaching the maxims, one may be able prepare one's community for such influences and guard them against it.

This reply leads to the third objection since in my remarks I have presupposed that everyone can learn to follow the maxims and everyone can follow the maxims. The third objection criticizes my proposal because the maxims are not for everyone and so my proposal looks elitist.

10.3.3 The Objection from Overdemandingness, from Arrogant Elitism and from Intellectualization

The third objection actually consists in three objections that are closely related and criticize the conception of human beings that the proposal and my project at large propound: the Objection from Overdemandingness, the Objection from Elitism, the Objection from Intellectualization.

The first objection, the Objection from Overdemandingness, argues that the proposal is too demanding for epistemic agents. One cannot always think for oneself, think from the perspective of another and think consistently with oneself. Human beings are not like lovers of knowledge as envisioned by Roberts and Wood. On their conception

> the lover of knowledge may have some of the impulses of the prejudiced – an anxiety about putting his pet beliefs in jeopardy, a certain aversion to long drawn-out investigations, and so forth – but he also has a counterbalancing love of the intellectual goods, discriminated according to their significance, relevance, and worthiness, and he has a toughness of self-discipline that allows him to override these less worthy motivations when they threaten his intellectual life, with more or fewer efforts of self-management.
>
> (Roberts and Wood 2007, 163)

These expectations from the lover of knowledge are clearly unrealistic and elitist. And if my proposal includes these assumptions, it should be replaced by a more relaxed approach.

But this worry can be easily calmed down. I agree that the perspective that Roberts and Wood sketch is frightening; I am sure that it also invites the Objection from Elitism and the Objection from Intellectualization, but my proposal does not lead to their outline and their demands and views. Of course, some self-discipline is involved in rationally dealing with ignorance and error, but my proposal and the activity of rationally dealing with ignorance and error does not turn one into a self-disciplined, self-denying human being who eschews trivial hobbies, trivial conversations, trivial TV shows, etc. Rather, my proposal emphasizes the influence of the epistemic agent on her (epistemic) conduct and her life.

In addition, the maxims allow for latitude since the subject may follow them more strictly in some contexts and less strictly in other contexts, for example, when her ignorance is less relevant. One may allow oneself to introduce Kant's latitude in imperfect duties[14] at this point of the discussion.[15]

The objection is worried that we all have to be super-experts in rationally dealing with ignorance and become disciplined (boring) lovers of knowledge as described by Roberts and Wood, but this would be like demanding that every human being must exercise so much and so well that she can participate in the Olympics. Or that we must all be super-brains. That is not what my proposal wants nor what it entails. The proposal is based on an insight about human beings as fallible creatures and, therefore, it would be inappropriate – even foolish – if my proposal put up demands that are impossible to meet. The proposal avoids being overdemanding because the three maxims are formal requirements and not connected to any particular knowledge content or minimal knowledge standards and because it emphasizes latitude.

A related objection, the Objection from Arrogant Elitism, criticizes the proposal because it indulges in problems and solutions that are only relevant for educated people who have undergone university education and are privileged enough to think about ignorance and to follow the three maxims. But the objection draws an overly simplistic picture of ignorance and the challenges that it raises. Ignorance concerns everyone, privileged and marginalized subjects alike. As previous discussions of willful ignorance, close-minded ignorance have shown, privilege often comes with the opportunity and the arrogance of not addressing one's own ignorance and not having to think about one's own ignorance thus perpetuating an unjust status quo (cf. Medina 2013, Harvin 1996). So thinking about rational ways of dealing with ignorance is not an indulgence but a social necessity. And more generally, ignorance is part of the human condition, of human existence and, therefore, it is a very human issue that is not elitist at all. By emphasizing the power of the epistemic agent qua rational being in rationally dealing with ignorance, the proposal also allows the epistemic agent to determine how she proceeds in rationally dealing with ignorance.

The Maxim-based Answer is also not elitist because it does not set up a canon of things that must be known, it just provides a formal suggestion for the best way of rationally dealing with ignorance, based on the most basic human cognitive capacities. The proposal also does not aim at perfectionism nor does it propound perfectionism, it just builds on the assumption that there is a way of rationally dealing with ignorance – we can be active in rationally dealing with ignorance and are not condemned to being passive. In addition, this path is open to all human beings. Everyone can follow the three maxims. In fact, as we have seen, this is one of the conditions of Kant's maxims. Moreover, I have noted that the maxims do not have to be determined and legislated explicitly (cf. Köhl 1990).

The final, related objection, the Objection from Intellectualization, challenges my previous replies and my proposal because they misconstrue human lives, they intellectualize human lives when they are much more driven by practical concerns. If one follows the three maxims, one is always busy with following the maxims, and one loses all livelihood and the irrational and rational bits that also constitute human life. But the proposal does not entail that human beings are all intellectual and not practical, quite to the contrary, it recognizes that practical considerations also infuse epistemic and cognitive concerns. In addition, the objection itself fails to adequately capture human beings. Their cognitive sides are not tangential to being human. On many conceptions of what it means to be human, *being rational* is a crucial feature of being human. And being cognitively fallible, and that includes being subject to ignorance and errors, is particularly distinctive of being human.

As we have seen earlier, human beings do not always make the best choices in rationally dealing with their ignorance, but they are able to learn how to deal with ignorance. One way of rationally dealing with ignorance is adopting Kant's three maxims. And these maxims are not something that is foreign to human beings or that is externally imposed upon them. They are maxims for human beings attuned to their fallible existence. As I have argued earlier, following these maxims can also be conceived as second nature to human beings.

Having developed and defended the Maxim-based Answer as the answer to how one should rationally deal with ignorance, I now want to apply the conception to two real-world contexts: democracy and medicine.

Notes

1 In the context of the second mention of the three maxims in the *Anthropology* section, Kant explicitly mentions the role of understanding and reason for dealing with error *and* ignorance. But he does not directly connect the three maxims with these roles of understanding and reasons. "Understanding is positive and drives out the darkness of ignorance the power of judgment is more negative, for the prevention of errors from the dim light in which objects appear. – Reason blocks the sources of errors (prejudices), and thereby safeguards understanding through the universality of principles" (Kant, Anth, AA VII, 228). Since I do not want to implement Kant's distinction between understanding and reason, I do not discuss this interesting passage in more detail. Suffice it to say that it is the task of reason and understanding to deal with – and get rid of – ignorance *and* error.
2 There may be some tension between the maxims as maxims, that is, as subjective, and the claim that the maxims are lawlike and have a universal scope. But I think we can reduce this tension if we distinguish between the maxims having universal scope, being followable and them being intersubjective. Everybody can give themselves the maxims and they are followable, but that does not mean they are intersubjective.
3 Sophia Rosenfeld (2011) in her book on common sense describes Kant's *sensus communis* as the "faculty of judgment that leads us, without reflection, to make [the] comparison [with the judgment of humanity as a whole] or to think from a universal standpoint" (Rosenfeld 2011, 223). And the *sensus communis* "is thus also the source for a social feeling, a sense of sharing something with others, that Kant describes as the 'necessary condition of the universal communicability of our knowledge' [(5: 239)]" (Rosenfeld 2011, 223).

Kant's conjecture has important implications for our main question of how one should rationally deal with ignorance because it points to a faculty that makes us think from a universal standpoint and compare our judgment with other judgments, which is part of addressing and avoiding *error* on Kant's Three Maxims Suggestion. And I submit that it is also fruitful for dealing with *ignorance* more generally.

4 A pessimist could also argue that there is no answer at all, but I find it more attractive to work with a weaker version of the claim since it is less implausible.

5 Note that this pessimism is not Kathryn Norlock's "nonideal pessimism" (2019). This pessimist is closer to what Norlock calls cynicism, the view that one cannot act in a hopeless situation. Non-ideal pessimism is pessimist because it does not think that there is any progress in humankind, but it still thinks that agency is possible and even called for. What I call *reflective optimism* is related to non-ideal pessimism because it also presupposes human beings as non-ideal, fallible agents. Norlock's non-ideal pessimism just starts from a different topic, the ineliminability of evil caused by humans, and therefore ends up with a different name and a different conception, the main direction of the argument still is similar.

6 As Descartes notes in his *Meditations*, suspending judgment or action is not really a live option in practical cases: by not deciding and not acting, one does act (Descartes 2017, 71).

7 A critic might object that this route gets us directly into an individualistic setup in which people simply decide on a case-by-case basis how they deal with ignorance. There are no standards by which we can judge what one should do about ignorance and error; deciding is up to the individual. And so it looks like I am licensing rampant arbitrariness.

But the objection and these conclusions are based on an incomplete picture that fails to take the subject and epistemic agency seriously. Epistemic agents can make justified or unjustified, good or bad decisions in dealing with ignorance and error, and those decisions can be context-dependent and case by case and individualist without also being arbitrary. In addition, epistemic agents can follow rules and principles in making such decisions. There is no arbitrariness.

The principles of my choice are, as I have explained earlier, Kant's principles of the *sensus communis*. The agent's epistemic conduct is not arbitrary because it is the conduct of a rational epistemic agent; it is justified by that agent who follows the maxims of the *sensus communis*. The particularist picture of the critic is incomplete because it does not recognize that epistemic agency comes with standards of action and epistemic norms that one is subject to and that there are maxims that can guide us.

8 Tilo Wesche helpfully notes in discussing Tugendhat's conception of intellectual honesty that "individuals are free to allow themselves to be impressed by reasons or not" and therefore "no one can be made to take reasons more seriously than they want to by reasons" (Wesche 2011, 195, my translation). Thanks to Martin Hurni for pointing me to Wesche's text.

9 Wingert (1997) criticizes Tugendhat's proposal, and from his criticism we can take further important insights for the answer to the second objection and a

difference between the epistemic and the moral realm. Wingert argues that it is no "motivational miracle" (Wingert 1997, 502, my translation) that people fulfill their (moral) obligations. Fulfilling one's obligations is simply in the interest of everyone who lives with others, and an individual cannot but recognize herself and others as "voluntative" (Wingert 1997, 527, my translation). His insights are based on a crucial observation about the difference between vertical and horizontal relationships in morality. On a vertical conception, one presupposes that morality consists in a vertical relationship between the individual who is confronted with the moral demand and some social authority that asserts the demand. A horizontal conception, in contrast, also includes the horizontal relationships between the subjects of moral demands as beings that need morality and as advocates and addresses of moral demands (Wingert 1997, 505). Wingert insists that this intersubjective conception is more appropriate and meets the challenges modern morality faces. As we have seen in my elaboration on Kant's maxims and the significance of epistemic agency and epistemic autonomy, this intersubjective component is also central in my proposal and in Kant's Three Maxims Suggestion. The principles, albeit not intersubjective, must be followable by everyone, and other subjects and their perspectives are explicitly included in the second maxim. In addition, the maxims are self-given, self-legislated. There is, thus, no vertical authority involved; there is only the horizontal relation that Wingert highlights.

10 As Wingert has argued for the moral case (1997, 505).
11 E.g., Bruner (2013).
12 My translations for quotations from Wesche (2011).
13 Here there are *really* potentially destructive effects for the collective belief set; unlike in Clifford's exaggeration that one single false belief is destructive for the collective belief set.
14 Cf. for Kant's duties (Timmermann 2018).
15 John Locke provides a valuable justification of latitude and of not being too demanding in one's expectations from others. In exercising their freedom, their epistemic agency, the subjects develop and improve their abilities:

> It will possibly be objected, Who is sufficient for all this? I answer, more than can be imagined. Everyone knows what his proper business is and what, according to the character he makes of himself, the world may justly expect of him; and to answer that, he will find he will have time and opportunity enough to furnish himself, if he will not deprive himself by a narrowness of spirit of those helps that are at hand. I do not say to be a good geographer that a man should visit every mountain, river, promontory and creek; upon the face of the earth, view the buildings and survey the land everywhere, as if he were going to make a purchase. But yet everyone must allow that he shall know a country better that makes often sallies into it and traverses it up and down than he that, like a mill-horse, goes still round in the same tract or keeps within the narrow bounds of a field or two that delight him. He that will enquire out the best books in every science and inform himself of the most material authors of the several sects of philosophy and religion, will not find it an infinite work to acquaint himself with the sentiments of mankind

concerning the most weighty and comprehensive subjects. Let him exercise the freedom of his reason and understanding in such a latitude as this, and his mind will be strengthened, his capacity enlarged, his faculties improved; and the light which the remote and scattered parts of truth will give to one another still so assist his judgment, that he will seldom be widely out or miss giving proof of a clear head and a comprehensive knowledge. At least, this is the only way I know to give the understanding its due improvement to the full extent of its capacity, and to distinguish the two most different things I know in the world, a logical chicaner from a man of reason. Only, he that would thus give the mind its flight and send abroad his enquiries into all parts after truth must be sure to settle in his head determined ideas of all that he employs his thoughts about, and never fail to judge himself and judge unbiasedly of all that he receives from others either in their writings or discourses. Reverence or prejudice must not be suffered to give beauty or deformity to any of their opinions.

(Locke 1996, §3)

Part 3
Applications

11 Ignorance in Democracies

In this chapter I discuss ignorance in the social, communal and political context. My case study explicates the fundamental claim that ignorance is pervasive in democracy. I do so by introducing the Integrated Conception of Ignorance and the Maxim-based Answer into the debate about citizen ignorance; a debate which is arguably stuck in reverse. In the current political and social landscape the claim that ignorance is pervasive in democracy will be heard as an uncontroversial, albeit lamented, empirical claim about citizen ignorance in real-world democracies, but I argue that it should also be taken seriously as a consequential theoretical claim about democracies and theories of democracy in general. Ignorance is pervasive because it is a fact about human beings that they are not omniscient. They are ignorant *qua* being limited and finite human beings. Once we recognize the nexus between ignorance and democracy, (a) we will understand *democracy* better, (b) we will understand *ignorance* better, (c) we will be able to develop a clearer understanding of what being a citizen of democratic societies amounts to, and (d) we will be better equipped to recognize what is needed to sustain democracies.

The main aim of this chapter, thus, is to explicate the pervasiveness of ignorance in democracy, and draw consequences for the right way of dealing with ignorance in democracy. Let me safeguard against two possible misunderstandings: I do not want to argue for the simple-minded claim that because ignorance is pervasive, all ignorance in democracy is acceptable. And I do not want to argue that because ignorance is pervasive, we should get rid of democracy and replace it by other forms of government such as epistocracy. In fact, in properly explicating how ignorance is pervasive in democracy, I will develop material for rejecting these latter claims that have been put forward in different forms but quite persistently for more than 2,000 years – for example, by Ilya Somin (2016) and Jason Brennan (2016), but long before that, of course, by Plato, Joseph Schumpeter and many others. For the sake of simplicity I focus on more recent forms of this criticism that I label the "Argument from Citizen Ignorance against Democracy".

I first formulate the Argument from Citizen Ignorance against Democracy, then I reject the Argument by pointing out that its conceptions of *ignorance* and of *democracy* are too restricted and by developing the observation that citizen ignorance *qua* human ignorance is part and parcel of democracy. After that, I reply to the objection that I defend epistemic laziness by pointing to the difference between descriptive and normative components of the picture of ignorance and democracy. This chapter also serves as an example for how epistemology and theory of democracy (political philosophy) can complement each other and work together.

My working definition of democracy will be Abraham Lincoln's Gettysburg formulation: democracy is "government of the people, by the people, for the people" (Lincoln 1953[1863]). This definition is sufficiently broad to cover different theories of democracy and it contains crucial elements of democracy like egalitarian values, equal vote, autonomy of people. I deliberately employ this broad definition and do not focus on particular forms of democracy since, as I claim, ignorance is a pertinent issue for *all* forms of democracy. Against the standard assumption (and *pace* Weinshall 2003), it does not just affect deliberative theories of democracy.

11.1 Reconstructing the Argument from Citizen Ignorance against Democracy

When Donald Trump won the US presidential election in 2016, the default reaction substantially consisted in explaining his success by voters' ignorance. The populist rise in Europe and on other continents is often also implicitly, if not explicitly, linked to citizen ignorance. Quite generally, unfavorable voting results or low voter turnout always invite references to voter ignorance or citizen ignorance.[1] And, of course, this argumentative strategy is not new. Walter Lippmann has discussed political ignorance in the 1920s and his criticism still rings true today: "the accepted theory of popular government ... rests upon the belief that there is a public which directs the course of events. I hold that this public is a mere phantom" (Lippmann 1922). Then, there is also Joseph Schumpeter's (1976) pessimistic picture of citizens in democratic states that may strike some as having a grain of truth:

> The typical citizen drops down to a lower level of mental performance as soon as he enters the political field. He argues and analyzes in a way which he would readily recognize as infantile within the sphere of his real interests. He becomes a primitive again. His thinking becomes associative and affective.
>
> (Schumpeter 1976, 262)

These and related claims are supported by evidence of two kinds of shortcomings of people: first, evidence of political ignorance and, second, evidence of citizen irrationality as in biases etc. Most studies on political ignorance are for the USA, for example, the items on this list from Brennan's *Against Democracy* (2016):

- During election years, most citizens cannot identify any congressional candidates in their district.
- Citizens generally don't know which party controls Congress.
- Immediately before the 2004 presidential election, almost 70 percent of US citizens were unaware that Congress had added a prescription drug benefit to Medicare, though this was a giant increase to the federal budget and the largest new entitlement program since President Lyndon Johnson began the War on Poverty.
- In the 2010 midterm presidential election, only 34 percent of voters knew that the Troubled Asset Relief Program was enacted under George W. Bush rather than Barack Obama. Only 39 percent knew that defense was the largest category of discretionary spending in the federal budget.
- Americans vastly overestimate how much money is spent on foreign aid, and so many of them mistakenly believe we can significantly reduce the budget deficit by cutting foreign aid.
- In 1964, only a minority of citizens knew that the Soviet Union was not a member of the North Atlantic Treaty Organization. (Yes, that's right: NATO, the alliance created to oppose the Soviet Union.) Keep in mind this is just a short time after the Cuban Missile Crisis, in which the United States almost went to (nuclear) war with the USSR.
- Seventy-three percent of Americans do not understand what the Cold War was about.
- Most Americans do not know even roughly how much is spent on social security or how much of the federal budget it takes up.
- Forty percent of Americans do not know whom the United States fought in World War II.

(Brennan 2016, 25f., references omitted, N.E.)[2]

Studies for other countries are less numerous, but they do exist. In 2016 Ipsos Mori studied people's false beliefs about "key issues and features of the population in their country" (Ipsos Mori 2016).[3] The German weekly newspaper *Die Zeit*, together with economists, has reviewed economic ignorance of people (Heuser and Djahangard 2018a, 2018b, Heuser 2018, Radbruch 2018). Other studies about students' knowledge or ignorance concerning the history of the GDR and the Federal Republic of Germany reveal that most students did not know who built the Wall in 1961 or the difference between dictatorship and democracy (FAZ 2008).[4]

Such evidence is taken to show that citizens lack the requisite political knowledge, that is, they do not know fundamental facts about politics in their country, their state or worldwide. They are ignorant about political issues, players, and what Delli Carpini and Kelter call "rules of the game" (Delli Carpini and Keeter 1996, 65).

The second shortcoming is traced back to people using unreliable heuristics and irrational factors in making decisions and being subject to biases. It goes under the heading "Irrationality." I have discussed such findings in Section 4.1.2. For example, Phillip Converse has identified "the nature of the times" heuristic (Converse 2006[1964], 16) and the "issue public" heuristic. In "the nature of the times" heuristic, "parties or candidates were praised or blamed primarily because of their temporal association in the past with broad societal states of war or peace, prosperity or depression" (Converse 2006[1964], 16). The "issue public" heuristic finds that people vote on the basis of just one issue of concern to them, disregarding any connections to other issues and not building up a broader picture of politics (Converse 2006[1964], 54).

Danny Oppenheimer and Mike Edwards provide an encompassing overview over people's biases in politics (Oppenheimer and Edwards 2012, 39–59). Who people vote for is influenced by appearances. For example, height matters for who people vote for. In addition, electoral decisions can be influenced by associative priming, such as music or a flag in the background; framing affects voters' decisions; form matters more than content, for example, fluency increases perceptions of truth. Brennan also cites ample evidence that confirmation bias, motivated reasoning, intergroup bias, etc. distort people's political decisions (Brennan 2016, 43ff.)

In addition, these irrational, unjustified decisions and opinions are found to be unstable over time (Converse 2006[1964], 51–52). Converse found that people changed their views without good reasons, say, an extraordinary event. This finding is telling and important for democracy because, as Converse concludes, it shows that "large portions of an electorate do not have meaningful beliefs, even on issues that have formed the basis for intense political controversies among elites for substantial periods of time" (Converse 2006[1964], 51–52).

In order to reconstruct the Argument from Citizen Ignorance against Democracy, we need to understand why ignorance is so readily accepted as a threat to democracy. Why does evidence on citizen ignorance lead authors to reject democracy or to introduce countermeasures? Knowledge and democracy are intimately connected and citizens mediate or even embody this connection. If, as the empirical evidence suggests, citizens are largely ignorant, but democracy presupposes knowledgeable citizens, then citizen ignorance is a threat to democracy. In theories of democracy, knowledge and democracy can be connected in two different ways: (a) knowledge is one of the conditions for (good) democracy, (b) knowledge is an outcome of democracy.

Knowledge figures as a condition for democracy since knowledge is required for making appropriate choices in elections, you need to know who the candidates are, what their views are, how their views relate to your views, etc. Moreover, knowledge is required for successful participation, especially in deliberative democracy, since as Talisse puts it "deliberative democracy requires that citizens' deliberations begin from true, or at least justified, premises" (Talisse 2004, 456). And, as Claus Offe notes in agreement with Cass Sunstein, knowledge is also required for "autonomous preference formation" since it "flow[s] from decisions 'reached with a full and vivid awareness of available opportunities, with reference to all relevant information, and without illegitimate or excessive constraints on the process of preference formation' (Sunstein 1991: 11)" (Offe 2003, 313). The knowledge that underlies these kinds of roles of knowledge in democracy is both knowledge about the world and knowledge about oneself (cf. Offe 2003, 298). This is what one may call the procedural role of knowledge in democracy, following Kaye's remarks about the procedural justification of democracy (cf. Kaye 2015, 317).

The second connection between knowledge and democracy takes a consequentialist approach to democracy (cf. Kaye 2015, 317) and holds that knowledge is the result of democracy. Some defenders of participatory and deliberative democracy argue that participating in democratic processes leads to the production and acquisition of knowledge in the subject and in society. Knowledge, thus, is the result of democracy in at least two ways. On the one hand, a subject that participates in democracy acquires more political knowledge (e.g., Gutmann 2007, 525). On the other hand, democratic processes are said to be the best procedure for getting good decisions and even truths.[5]

We now have got the material for the Argument from Citizen Ignorance against Democracy and can reconstruct the argument as follows:

> P1: Democracy requires citizens to be knowledgeable about politics (issues, players, rules of the game) in order to be able vote proficiently.
> P2: There is strong evidence of widespread political ignorance of citizens (lack of political knowledge, irrationality, unstable opinions).
> P3: Citizens do not have the knowledge (competences) required for voting proficiently.
> C1: Citizens cannot fulfill their democratic roles adequately. (from P1, P2, P3)
> C2: Democracy is deficient and therefore should be replaced by another form of government.

The argument deduces consequences for democracy at large from problems at the micro level, that is, the citizen level. And, intuitively, issues at the

204 Applications

micro level are bound to affect the whole structure. Offe specifies the danger: "Democracies can fail to come into being for lack of appropriate dispositions among citizens, and they can self-destruct because of a decline in civic competence or the breakdown of background conditions that are conducive to it" (Offe 2003, 297). But as Offe also evinces in his article, one may be moved by these worries without jettisoning democracy at large. And as I will go on to show, there is even no need to be moved by the Argument from Citizen Ignorance because it is invalid.[6]

11.2 Rejecting the Argument from Citizen Ignorance against Democracy

We should reject the Argument from Citizen Ignorance against Democracy because its premises are fundamentally flawed. The basic concepts *ignorance*, *citizen ignorance* and *democracy* are significantly misconstrued. Once we correct these flaws, the Citizen Ignorance Argument is defused and we are able to reconceive ignorance in democracy, and see which kinds of ignorance are a threat to democracy and which ones are not.

The most obvious way to react to the argument is by questioning the evidence, the setup of the studies, etc. and arguing that things are not quite that bad. For example, Erikson (2007) presents evidence that Converse's finding about people's unstable opinions, the third kind of citizen ignorance, can be explained by measurement error and does not lead to any substantial conclusions about the irrationality of citizens. Oppenheimer and Edwards (2012) show how democratic procedures lead to rational results, in spite of irrationality in the individual citizen. For example, the "wisdom of crowds" ensures rational results (Oppenheimer and Edwards 2012, 186). Other authors criticize the studies because they only check people's knowledge of trivia.

This intuitive reaction, however, is rarely useful because it only leads to a dispute about the methodology of these studies and about how meaningful they really are. Instead of going into this back-and-forth about details, we should examine whether the concepts used in the studies really correspond to the phenomenon at hand in all its complexity. I argue that they are not appropriate for capturing ignorance and democracy adequately.

This strategy will also have us ask whether political knowledge really is all that relevant for participation in democracy. I do not want to suggest that it is irrelevant, rather I submit that political knowledge is merely one part of the knowledge that citizens should have. Citizens should have, in general, knowledge about the outside world and knowledge about themselves, as Offe (2003, 298) puts it. In addition, it is fairly obvious that the presentation of the studies which are taken to warrant the desired conclusion about the bad state of democracy is rather tendentious: they focus on people's ignorance and construe this ignorance as an apparent obstacle for democracy.

In contrast, when the Ipsos Mori talks of "the perils of perception," they note that ignorance is a matter of people's mistaken perception (Ipsos Mori 2016). Framing the issue in this way allows for vastly different reactions to the findings, for example, since it is not about people's ignorance but about their perception. Once we review what the evidence on *ignorance* really amounts to and include insights about the integrated view of ignorance, we will, similarly, be able to reevaluate the evidence that grounds the argument against democracy. So let's turn to the fundamental concepts of the Argument from Citizen Ignorance: democracy, ignorance and knowledge.

Democracy Is More Than Casting One's Vote in Elections

The Argument from Citizen Ignorance and authors endorsing this or similar arguments implicitly presuppose that democracy consists in elections only and therefore are impressed about findings that reveal people's ignorance of politicians and parties. But democracy does not just consist in elections, and furthermore, elections do not just consist in casting one's vote. The exchanges before voting, conversations with friends, family and strangers, reading the newspaper, watching TV, etc. are also part of the election process. And democracy itself, importantly, consists in more than voting, namely people talking to one another, exchanging "reasoned arguments, evidence, evaluation, and persuasion" (Gutmann 2007, 527) in political contexts but also at the dinner table, in small talk on the bus, at the work place, etc.

One, thus, has to take into account what Gutmann and Thompson call "middle democracy." The "land of middle democracy," as Gutmann and Thompson put it, is

> the land of everyday politics, where legislators, executives, administrators, and judges make and apply politics and laws, sometimes arguing among themselves, sometimes explaining themselves and listening to citizens, other times not. Middle democracy is also the land of interest groups, civic associations, and schools, in which adults and children develop political understandings, sometimes arguing among themselves and listening to people with different points of view other times not.
> (Gutmann and Thompson 1998, 40)

This conception takes seriously the micro level of democracy, the citizen level and the implementation of democracy in the everyday. Michelle Moody-Adams has captured these facets of democracy in the term "quotidian democracy," which recognizes that "democratic decision-making [is] a 'continuous process' in which what citizens do in the seemingly most ordinary contexts of daily life is critical to the content of democratic deliberation and to the successful functioning of democratic institutions" (Moody-Adams 2018, 194).[7]

Critics of democracy might object that these interpretations of democracy presuppose deliberative democracy, but this does not speak against these conceptions nor against using them. Instead, the onus lies with the critics; they have to explain why we should work with a limited conception of democracy as "participation in elections," and, for that matter, elections determining political representatives, rather than with my broad notion of democracy or Gutmann and Thompson's or Moody-Adams' notions. Another disadvantage of the critics' skewed picture of democracy is that it misconstrues the motivations for democracy. They presuppose that supporters of democracy are interested in democracy as producing knowledge (knowledge on a consequentialist picture). And they hold that the procedural role of knowledge for democracy entails that widespread ignorance would keep democracy from functioning properly. In particular, it would lead to bad results in elections. But citizen ignorance is not incompatible with democracy properly understood because people do not just choose and favor democracy because it is knowledge-conducive; it is not (at least not necessarily) chosen for its epistemic virtues. Other motivations like equality and individual autonomy are important driving forces for democracy.[8]

Once we are aware of the restricted notion of democracy in the Citizen Ignorance Argument and of the more adequate alternatives, we can also pay heed to other factors that influence citizens' behavior in democracy. Democracy as quotidian is continuous, flexible and pretty mundane. Factors such as being able to speak openly, being listened to respectfully, being engaged in a very material, that is, embodied, and individually experienced way become pertinent. This shift puts us on the tracks of Tocqueville's view that democracy must engage the attention and energy, that is, the mental focus and physical energy, of citizens (Tocqueville 1969). As Ben Berger puts is, for Tocqueville, political engagement that has citizens "focus on their common affairs and the business of self-government" (Berger 2011, 106) is key. This strategy also reduces the reality of ignorance in the sense of citizens being ignorant by "act[ing] at random" (Berger 2011, 107) because in this alternative, engaging conception of democracy people "are not being asked for blanket opinions on vast, complex, national and global issues ... they are close to the issues and can see the results in action" (Berger 2011, 107).[9] Of course, realizing this strategy in today's globalized, digitalized world is very different from Tocqueville's times, but democracy as engaging attention and energy of citizens can be translated into today's world. Addressing the micro level and relating it to the macro level may be one route of pursuing this aim. I return to these insights later when introducing suggestions for integrating ignorance into democracy.

Ignorance is More Than Lack of Knowledge

The second central concept at the heart of the Argument from Citizen Ignorance is *ignorance*. It is employed both by the empirical studies that are meant to support the Argument and in the Argument itself, but it is hardly ever discussed in detail.[10] The Argument and the authors who support it assume that ignorance is simply lack of knowledge with a simplistic conception of knowledge. They focus on the doxastic level of ignorance, that is, something is wrong in the beliefs of the subjects: the subject lacks a true belief, or holds a false belief to be true, or they may lack the proper justification for a true belief. But as this book and recent work in epistemology of ignorance evince, ignorance is more than lack of knowledge (e.g., Medina 2013). Ignorance also has what I have called agential and structural components. The agential component includes epistemic attitudes of the subject, both general and related to their false beliefs and true beliefs and gaps in the belief set. Epistemic attitudes may consist in awareness of gaps in one's belief set but also in epistemic virtues, for example, open-mindedness and curiosity, and epistemic vices such as close-mindedness and laziness. Real-world instances of ignorance are always composed of doxastic, agential and structural components. This also helps explain how ignorance can be actively produced and maintained. But studies on citizen ignorance and the critics of democracy do not address these additional constituents of ignorance. This is a serious shortcoming because it means that their conception of ignorance is inadequate for capturing the real-world phenomenon *ignorance* and for understanding the position of ignorance in democracies. Studies on politically motivated ignorance, the effects of science curiosity, etc. are starting points for further developments (e.g., Kahan et al. 2017).

The critics only show that people do not know political facts that would be handy in making competent political decisions. But they do not have room for versions of ignorance – including political ignorance – that are not harmful for democracy. Subjects might not know some political fact, but they might be open-minded and be interested in new information and learn more about this fact of which they are ignorant. Think of the following example: say, you do not know what the two columns on the ballot for the German general election stand for – you would fail a test about it – but this does not mean that you are unfit for being a citizen in a democratic society because being a citizen does not just consist in knowing what the two columns on the ballot stand for. And more importantly, if you are open-mindedly ignorant, you can always get the requisite information before casting your vote. Of course, if you are close-mindedly ignorant, that is, you do not know what the two columns on the ballot mean and you are generally uninterested in politics, elections, the world around you, you won't go out to get the requisite information. But the trouble does not lie in not knowing what the two columns refer to in a test, which is the kind of ignorance that is detected by the studies wielded against democracy, but *in the attitudinal component of one's ignorance*. We could complicate the picture by adding the structural components, but you get the general idea of my argument without this complication.

Critics might react to this rebuttal and the new conception of ignorance by pointing out that their studies are not just concerned with lack of factual knowledge, but that studies on people's irrationality do evince that the attitudinal level is just as fraught as the doxastic level. I have already referred to Taber and Lodge's study that had participants who had strong views on gun control and affirmative action read pro and con texts on these topics. Taber and Lodge found a prior-attitude effect, disconfirmation bias and confirmation bias as well as a polarization effect in the participants' reactions to texts that did or did not fit their own views (Taber and Lodge 2006, see also Kruglanski and Boyatzi 2012). Kahan and Corbin's findings on how active open-minded thinking magnifies polarization, similarly, puts pressure on my approach (2016).

But these and similar findings really are just grist on my mill since I have not set out to argue that citizens are not ignorant or that they do not decide using irrational heuristics. Quite to the contrary, I have started from the claim that ignorance is pervasive in democracy. I have only refined and developed the conception of ignorance in use. And as the study of ignorance in Part I has shown, we need to recognize that ignorance is even more pervasive than the supporters of the Argument from Citizen Ignorance find. Ignorance is a fact of human existence, human beings have limited cognitive capacities and are fallible. And this holds for *all* human beings, including citizens, as well as politicians, representatives and experts. But unlike the supporters of the Argument from Citizen Ignorance against Democracy, I do not think that ignorance per se is the downfall of democracy or that democracy is impossible because people, in particular citizens, are ignorant. I am arguing for a nuanced account of the place of ignorance in democracy which recognizes that ignorance encompasses several components and that political ignorance cannot be identified with lack of knowledge of political facts and the rules of the game. The Argument from Citizen Ignorance fails because it does not employ adequate conceptions of ignorance (nor of democracy) and therefore does not produce a valid conclusion.

I submit that we should accept that ignorant subjects are not foreign to democracy, and that ignorance is not just an annoying, arbitrary, deficient state of human beings. Rather, being ignorant is an integral feature of the human condition. Human beings are finite beings that do not have infallible nor unlimited cognitive capacities and, therefore, they are ignorant in certain ways and with regard to different topics. And since democracy is "government of the people, by the people, for the people," democracy will be shaped by the condition of *the people*, that is, of human beings. Therefore, democracy is bound to be affected by citizen ignorance, and that includes all members of democracy.

Once one recognizes that ignorance is pervasive in democracy and that ignorance consists in doxastic, attitudinal and structural components, one is much better positioned to formulate *which* ignorance and which components of ignorance may be threats in democracy, and to suggest tailored measures and strategies for dealing with and integrating ignorance in democracy.

Democracy contains so called *citizen ignorance* that is multiply tested in studies, but given that ignorance is natural in human beings we must also include politicians' ignorance, representatives' ignorance and experts' ignorance in any comprehensive take on ignorance in democracy. Russell Hardin (2004) is one of the few authors who mentions the issue of politicians' ignorance. Their ignorance may consist in not knowing what the interests of the citizens are "other than in broad terms" (Hardin 2004, 95), or in not knowing all the details for "devis[ing] good policies in many realms" (Hardin 2004, 85). Hardin suggests that one explanation for the latter kind of politicians' ignorance is that "much of the relevant knowledge is decentralized to smaller organizations and to citizens" (Hardin 2004, 85).[11]

Note that this is just a claim about the ever-present potential of ignorance and, at the same time, about the reality of ignorance that may or may not be manifested in myriads of ways in all human beings *qua* human beings. This is just *human ignorance*. Human beings are always ignorant even when they are knowledgeable; they are ignorant in that they do not know some important fact, for example, when the train that they need to take to be on time for a job interview leaves, or that they do not know some less important fact, for example, how many people live in New York, assuming that this information is useless for the subject in question.

If we recognize that ignorance is a natural human condition, one might employ ignorance as a human condition in a *tu quoque* argument against critics of democracy and supporters of epistocracy. Critics of democracy overlook the aforementioned fact that all human beings, and therefore all citizens, are ignorant. This means that epistocracy is also beset by a version of the Argument from Ignorance: the knowledgeable citizens, maybe the experts that the defenders of epistocracy want to install as rulers and representatives are also beset by ignorance and irrationality *qua* being human beings.

Just because they do know political facts or are experts in their particular field of expertise does not mean they are not ignorant or, for that matter, ignorant in other significant ways. They are human beings like all other citizens and therefore are necessarily ignorant in certain ways. Especially irrationality because of bias and faulty heuristics is probably prevalent with them, too. Moreover, on the suggested expanded conception of ignorance as including a doxastic component and an attitudinal component, they may be ignorant because of their particular attitudes (and epistemic vices). Experts might be more skilled at controlling for ignorance and irrationality, but they are not *guaranteed* to be correct because of their status as experts. Let me add that this observation does not entail that experts lose their special expert status. They are after all significantly more likely to be correct in their judgments and decision, but they remain fallible and subject to irrationality, since fallibility – as a facet of limited human capacities – is a fact of being a human being. Epistocracy does not come with an inherent guarantee for successful rule because of expert rule.[12]

These collected observations allow me to contextualize and defuse the Argument from Citizen Ignorance as an argument against democracy. Its empirical evidence is not irrefutably valid nor pertinent, and, most importantly, the argument employs inadequately restricted notions of ignorance and democracy. Citizen Ignorance is just an instantiation of human ignorance, a complex, but natural trait of citizens *qua* human beings, therefore, it is not a pertinent obstacle against democracy. Ignorance is an indelible part of democracy. On some reconstructions, democracy is even a tool for dealing with necessary ignorance: electing representatives is a way of taking care that somebody else fulfills tasks, like making decisions about health policies, that I cannot fulfill because I lack the knowledge, lack the time, etc. (cf. Hardin 2004). In addition, shared democratic decisions of diverse groups are much better than decisions of homogenous groups (cf. Anderson 2006).

11.3 A Vindication of Epistemically Lazy Citizens?

My emphasis on the natural place of ignorance in democracy may have given rise to a worry: my remarks may seem to imply that we should accept all ignorance in citizens of democratic communities. If all human beings are necessarily ignorant, then it seems unproblematic that citizens are ignorant about politics and various facts about the world and themselves. The objection asks whether becoming knowledgeable about politics, about the world and oneself becomes superfluous if ignorance is acceptable at this fundamental level. In effect, the charge is that I have written a defense of epistemic laziness. And this would be a frightening result. It is blatantly false that widespread ignorance about substantial facts about the world is acceptable or laudable.

The objection is helpful because it allows me to clarify my approach, and to say what I have argued and what I have not shown yet. So, in reply, I note that I have not argued that citizens are warranted in being epistemically lazy. I have just pointed out that ignorance has a natural place in democracy because being ignorant – to some degree or another – is natural in human beings and it is human beings that are the members of democracy. So there is no defense of epistemically lazy and misinformed citizens in what I have said so far.

Admittedly, it may appear like I am blessing epistemic laziness. But that is because my approach in this chapter has been mainly descriptive: I have argued that there is an important place for ignorance in democracy because human beings are necessarily ignorant. I have not talked about any normative components of ignorance and democracy. In fact, I have only developed one part of the picture of ignorance and democracy, we are still lacking the normative side in an account that acknowledges that ignorance is natural in democracy. To find material for this addition we need to go beyond political philosophy and incorporate work from social epistemology and work on ignorance. But let us start with the traditional response to the question from political philosophy.

The standard material from political philosophy for the normative side of an account of ignorance in democracy consists in educational strategies. Defenders of theories of democracy immediately present educational strategies that facilitate becoming knowledgeable citizens and, thereby, meeting the expectations. They start from the assumption that knowledge is a condition or an outcome of democracy, the roles of knowledge introduced earlier, and from this derive knowledge as a valuable aim as well as the requisite norms. Families, schools, civic associations, etc. then are taken to contribute to educating knowledgeable and knowing citizens (cf., e.g., Offe 2003, 318, Delli Carpini and Keeter 1996, 190–193, Weinshall 2003, 54).[13]

I will not go into the details of these existing proposals because these educational strategies are not the fundament of the normative account, but build on more basic, albeit largely unacknowledged normative epistemic assumptions. These normative assumptions are seldom made explicit in theory of democracy, and it is here that social epistemological work is required to spell out these fundamental normative assumptions. The key move consists in regarding the citizen as an *epistemic* agent. This approach provides the entry to the normative side of the issue of ignorance in democracy, and since I have elucidated *ignorance* and *democracy*, we are also able point to more tailored suggestions for dealing with ignorance in democracy.

The central insight for the normative side of the account of ignorance in democracy is that citizens are epistemic agents. One way to cash out this notion is via Alfred Schutz' notion of *the well-informed citizen* that he introduces in his discussion of the "social distribution of knowledge" (Schutz 1976, 120). The well-informed citizen is the ideal between what Schutz calls *the expert* and *the man on the street* (Schutz

1976, 121–122). I will bracket any qualms about Schutz's 1960s' setup because I am interested in the way that Schutz links up politics and epistemology.

> The ideal type that we propose to call the well-informed citizen (thus shortening the more correct expression: *the citizen who aims at being well informed*) stands between the ideal type of the expert and that of the man on the street. On the one hand, he neither is, nor aims at being, possessed of expert knowledge; on the other, he does not acquiesce in the fundamental vagueness of a mere recipe knowledge or in the irrationality of his unclarified passions and sentiments. To be well informed means to him to arrive at reasonably founded opinions in *fields which as he knows are at least mediately of concern to him although not bearing upon his purpose at hand*.
> (Schutz 1976, 122f., my emphasis)

Schutz's ideal of a citizen is the well-informed citizen who aims at "reasonably founded opinions."[14] This "citizen who aims at being well informed" (Schutz 1976, 122) is clearly an epistemic agent. But of course, the expert and the man on the street are also epistemic agents who meet epistemic expectations to a higher or lesser degree.

If we thus recognize that any citizen is an epistemic agent, we are automatically led to see democratic communities, constituted by citizens, as epistemic communities. On Schutz's conception, a "well-informed citizen" wants to meet epistemic expectations, wants to acquire opinions that are supported by good reasons. That means that there is a set of epistemic expectations and epistemic norms which principally concern every citizen in a democratic community *qua* being an epistemic subject.

But Schutz's distinction of the different epistemic citizens does not give us enough details of the epistemically normative side of ignorance in democracy. So let us continue from the insight that democratic communities are epistemic communities and incorporate social epistemological work on epistemic communities. Epistemic communities are also social communities, and, of course, quite trivially, democratic communities are also social communities. This collection of trivial insights is helpful because several epistemologists have examined social communities as epistemic communities, spelling out expectations and norms that the members of these communities are subject to and affirm, and on the basis of our trivial insights we can apply their theories to democratic communities.

Peter Graham develops epistemic norms as social norms (2015). He derives the norm "provide true and relevant information" (Graham 2015, 159) from Grice's principles for cooperation in conversation. This norm branches out into the two norms "believe on adequate evidence" and "inquire into relevant evidence" (Graham 2015, 159). These norms could regulate how one should tackle one's own potential ignorance, and, of course, they are reminiscent of Locke's suggestion. The Maxim-based Answer can also be applied to the case of ignorance in democratic communities. In particular, the maxims appear to be able to deal with central features of democratic discourse by inviting the epistemic agent to take the perspective of the other (second maxim) and at the same time rely on their own cognitive abilities and their beliefs and convictions (first and third maxim). So, even though Kant's maxims themselves are not norms, we can see that the maxims may be connected up with epistemic norms.

It is *epistemic norms* that provide the normative component to the picture of ignorance and democracy. Epistemic norms hold for epistemic subject *qua* members of epistemic communities, that is, social communities, and since the very same members of epistemic communities are members of democratic communities, the epistemic norms also transfer to democratic communities. And it is because epistemic norms hold for epistemic subjects as members of democratic epistemic communities that epistemic laziness is not acceptable in democracy.

Why particular epistemic norms hold can be justified in different ways. One can go back to my explanation for why Kant's maxims hold, but one may also find two promising options in social epistemology. Graham argues that epistemic norms as social norms hold because they *describe and prescribe* regularities; "social norms are regularities because norms, regularities because normative" (Graham 2015, 251). Sanford Goldberg, as we have seen in Section 9.3, argues that our epistemic expectations from one another legitimately hold because they are based on practice-generated entitlements and on moral and epistemic expectations that are based in our "institutions of morality and epistemic assessment" (Goldberg 2017b, 2879). Democratic communities would have to be shown to be constituted by practice-generated entitlements and our "institutions of morality and epistemic assessment" (Goldberg 2017b, 2879).

What are ways of dealing with ignorance in democracy when one rejects the Argument from Citizen Ignorance? One general way is to ensure that the micro level and the macro level of democracy are adequately connected, that is, that citizens and democratic structures are adequately connected. This might include forums in which citizens' positions are heard, which, of course, does not entail that the expressed views are put into practice. But it should mean addressing their concerns, explaining how policy measures fit their concerns, and explaining why they do not fit their concerns. In addition, measures should strengthen the community character of democratic communities as social communities and as epistemic communities in order to improve the social ground of the epistemic community. Facilitating exchange between the citizens will certainly prove crucial. Receptive publics (Habgood-Coote et al. 2024) and joint community service as well as non-political associations are obvious places for such discourse. In addition, projects like *Gesellschaftsdenken*,[15] and digital formats such as *Massive Open Online Deliberation Platform* (Verdiesen et al. 2016) may initiate and frame exchanges that are prepared to take seriously and address controversial disagreement, disappointment and close-mindedness. These proposals would recognize democratic communities as epistemic communities and as social communities.

From the Integrated Conception of Ignorance we can take insights for the micro level, for the individual citizen: dealing with ignorance in democracy is not restricted to the doxastic level but must include the attitudinal and structural level, too. One major aim could be to enable people to recognize and accept their own ignorance, so as to allow for open-minded ignorance. The Maxim-based Answer would support being adequately open-mindedly ignorant, because the second maxim calls for being open to the perspective of others. So one means and one aim in education is teaching Kant's maxims, making them second nature. Such epistemic abilities would also require enabling a safe environment in which one can admit to one's ignorance without feeling embarrassed, and a just society that provides conducive economic conditions for everyone. These are central components of the structural facets of ignorance. Of course, the doxastic level must be addressed, too, but it is not just about informational input. We need to always consider the attitudinal, agential and structural components of ignorance, and, as Tocqueville reminds us, ensure that people's attention and energy are engaged.[16]

Notes

1 I use the term *citizen ignorance* rather than *voter ignorance* because voting is just one part of being a member of a democratic community. Moreover, the ignorance that the critical studies purport to evince is not just restricted to voting.
2 Similar evidence in Weinshall (2003, 42).
3 See https://perils.ipsos.com/archive/index.html for previous and later 'The Perils of Perception' studies.
4 Cf. also Deutz-Schroeder and Schroeder (2008) who examine students' views on the GDR and FDR in four German federal states in a wide-ranging study.
5 For convincing criticism of the latter claim, see Hardin (2004, 78).
6 Talisse (2004) and Kaye (2015) also reject versions of the Argument from Citizen Ignorance, but their approaches are different from mine. Talisse's strategy of distinguishing belief ignorance and agent ignorance is promising, but ultimately he focuses only on deliberative democracy when we can draw

more bold conclusions for all theories of democracy. Kaye (2015) shows that ignorance is useful on a consequentialist picture of democracy, but I think that this argument leads us off track. We need to reposition ignorance in democracy at large. In discussing and rejecting the Argument from Citizen Ignorance against Democracy I also criticize the conception of ignorance that the Argument presupposes, but, unlike Talisse, I do not distinguish different kinds of ignorance; instead, I propose that we employ the Integrated Conception for democracy, too. In addition, I criticize the critics' conception of democracy in general.

7 I will not discuss the obvious connections to Dewey's theory of democracy, which Moody-Adams herself points out (Dewey 1927).

8 Kaye (2015) argues that ignorance is even unproblematic for conceptions that accept democracy on the basis of epistemic reasons.

9 Berger helpfully refers to the following passage in Tocqueville's *Democracy in America* that fits with the issue of citizen ignorance: "Here is one sort of ignorance which results from extreme publicity. Under despotisms men do not know how to act because they are told nothing; in democratic nations they often act at random because there has been an attempt to tell them everything. The former do not know; the latter forget. The main features of each picture become lost in a mass of detail" (Tocqueville 1969, 610–611).

10 Mainly it is critics of the Argument from Citizen Ignorance who discuss the term *ignorance*; see, e.g., the distinctions that Talisse introduces to reject the ignorance argument against democracy (Talisse 2004, 457–458).

11 Of course, one may also conjecture other more self-interested explanations for particular instances of ignorance, but I will refrain from entering into this discussion. The literature on incompetence and, ultimately, ignorance in the US financial crisis may serve as a starting point, e.g., Sorkin (2010) and Schiffrin (2011).

12 Thanks to Jérôme Léchot for inviting me to be clearer on what the argument means for experts.

13 For documentation of real-world applications, see, e.g., Warren and Pearse (2008) on the British Columbia Citizen's Assembly.

14 Note that these idealizations are not affected by Mills' criticism of ideal theory (Mills 2017).

15 The members of *Gesellschaftsdenken* get into conversations with people in areas of low voter turnout about values, participation and democracy; see https://gesellschaftsdenken.org/.

16 For more specific proposals we would have to study people's ignorance and their current discourses, form and content, based on the improved conception of democracy and ignorance. For example, one may want to include discussions on the effects of science curiosity on politically biased motivated reasoning (Kahan et al. 2017) or the impact of identity-related beliefs (Kahan and Corbin 2016). Florian Braun's discourse analysis of discussions about energy transition and renewable energy promises to provide fruitful insight into people's reasoning and the significance of ignorance and democracy regarding this topic (cf., e.g., Braun and Baatz 2018, Braun 2023).

12 Ignorance and Uncertainty in Medical Contexts

There are (at least) two strands to the topic of ignorance and medicine: ignorance in medical practice and ignorance in medical research. These two strands of ignorance have become glaring and pertinent during the COVID-19 pandemic. At the beginning of the pandemic, researchers did not know how COVID-19 was transmitted, they did not know the origins of the virus, they did not know which vaccines would work against the virus, etc. Some of this ignorance has been alleviated, some has changed shape and returned in the form of other questions. And at the beginning of the pandemic, medical practitioners did not know how to treat the patients best, they did not know whether they'd contract the disease, too, they also did not know how exactly the virus was transmitted, etc. I will not devote the whole chapter to the analysis of ignorance and COVID-19 because there are more general issues regarding ignorance in medical contexts. Most questions regarding COVID-19 and ignorance can be grouped with these general issues, so it is more forward-looking and more interesting to choose a broader lens and only discuss COVID-19 when it becomes relevant.[1]

This focus brings a new term into the study: uncertainty. Uncertainty is generally framed as "the subjective consciousness of ignorance" (Han 2013, 16S). Uncertainty is inherent in medical research and medical practice and has attracted increased attention in recent years – even before the COVID-19 pandemic. Relatively new methods such as evidence-based medicine, precision medicine, a shift toward shared decision-making, the relationship between generic data-driven and individual medicine, the effects of these new methods on practitioners, patients and medicine in general are some of the motivations for this increased interest.

By discussing uncertainty in medical research and practice, I can turn to discussing conscious ignorance in medical research and practice, how agents involved deal with uncertainty and how they should deal with it. I can put the previous claims and conclusions to test. In addition, medical practice highlights another facet of ignorance that I have introduced in

DOI: 10.4324/9781003375500-15

connection with symptoms of ignorance: the *affective* side of ignorance. Medical uncertainty often has affects and emotions weaved into its texture and its fundamental structure. We can thus look at how affects manifest themselves in these instances of uncertainty.

My discussion builds on current work on uncertainty and my conception of ignorance and how one should deal with ignorance. I show that work on uncertainty complements my claim that ignorance has an attitudinal component and is more than merely lacking knowledge. We also see that the Maxim-based Answer for rationally dealing with ignorance can solve issues surrounding uncertainty in patient–practitioner interaction. In fact, by examining how the Maxim-based Answer fares with dealing with uncertainty, we find out more about the scope and the functioning of the maxims. We see that the maxims are indeed not limited to conscious ignorance but are also rational ways for dealing with unconscious ignorance.

Uncertainty in medicine is a multifaceted notion because there are at least two different areas in which uncertainty is prevalent: medical research and medical (clinical) practice. I start with an example that shows how the two areas are connected, but as we will see, there are also differences in what medical agents are required to do in the different areas in dealing with uncertainty.

In medical practice, uncertainty has many faces, it can concern patients' uncertainty in what the diagnosis and the prognosis means, it can concern doctors' uncertainty about the diagnosis, or about whether they should reveal a negative prognosis to an end-of-life patient, or about how much they should tell patients about possible side-effects of a treatment or an operation or how much they should reveal of their own uncertainty. Quite fundamentally, medical uncertainty is an awareness of the limitations of one's own (patient and practitioner) or the scientific community's grasp of a phenomenon, a disease, a treatment, etc.[2] The task of dealing with these issues has become particularly pressing with the advances of modern medicine and (apparently) increasing knowledge. As Ranjana Srivastava puts it, the question is "how can doctors deal with uncertainty in a time when knowledge is plentiful? How do we educate our patients well about what we know but avoid displaying hopelessness when we don't know?" (Srivastava 2011, 2252) Again, this question also mattered greatly during the COVID-19 pandemic.

But uncertainty in medicine also appears as uncertainty in medical research, for example, in the questions of how solid the evidence in a drug trial is – questions that, again, were raised frequently regarding the COVID-19 vaccines – but also the question of how significant specific genetic mutations uncovered in genetic testing are (Tonelli and Shirts 2017), or what the implications of genomic testing for research are (Newson

218 Applications

et al. 2016). I develop these distinctions of forms of medical uncertainty by studying examples of medical uncertainty.[3]

12.1 Examples and a Typology of Uncertainty in Medical Contexts

Let's go back to the late 1980s and imagine a middle-aged female patient presenting with chest pain (angina) and shortness of breath.

> Deep negative T waves were seen on ECG. Her cardiac enzyme levels were mildly elevated. The patient was admitted with a diagnosis of acute non-ST-segment elevation myocardial infarction.
> (Virani et al. 2007, 77)

It looks like the patient has had a heart attack (an acute coronary syndrome). After one week and medical treatment the symptoms improved significantly, unlike in cases of a heart attack. At that time, in the 1980s, the physicians treating the patient would have been at a loss to understand what has happened in this case. They would be *ignorant*, maybe even clueless (Section 4.2).

In 1990, the same case (same patient, same symptoms) would have run differently. The physicians would have been able to diagnose the woman with *stress-related cardiomyopathy, Takotsobu syndrome*, also known as *broken heart syndrome*, since by 1990 *Takotsobu cardiomyopathy* (TCM) has been identified as a syndrome and taken up in medical knowledge. TCM looks like an acute coronary syndrome but differs importantly from acute myocardial infarction.

> It occurs more often in postmenopausal elderly women, is characterized by a transient hypokinesis of the left ventricular (LV) apex, and is associated with emotional or physical stress. Wall motion abnormality of the LV apex is generally transient and resolves within a few days to several weeks. The prognosis of TCM is generally good.
> (Komamura et al. 2014, 602)

With that disease entity introduced, in 1990 physicians had the concept required to put forward the right diagnosis: Takotsobu cardiomyopathy. Their ignorance was alleviated. And yet, the syndrome still remains connected to ignorance and, more specifically, to uncertainty: its pathophysiology is not clearly understood. The practitioners are aware of their ignorance, their limited understanding of the pathophysiology of the syndrome, they are uncertain, consciously ignorant. Various interpretations of the pathophysiology have been put forward, including coronary microvascular dysfunction, coronary artery spasm, catecholamine-induced myocardial stunning, reperfusion injury following acute coronary syndrome, myocardial microinfarction and abnormalities in cardiac fatty acid metabolism. Currently, catecholamine-induced cardiotoxicity and microvasculature dysfunction are the most supported theories.

(Komamura et al. 2014, 604)

Uncertainty, thus, appears in and affects medical research. This is what I propose to capture by the term *uncertainty in medical research*. Again, this type of uncertainty was particularly visible during the COVID-19 pandemic.[4]

But the syndrome is also connected to *uncertainty in medical practice* and *practitioners' uncertainty* because in the clinical presentation TCM looks like acute coronary syndrome, and so physicians have to determine whether the patient suffers from TCM or not. Recent developments in cardiac magnetic resonance imaging (MRI) contribute to reducing this instance of *diagnostic uncertainty* because

this modality allows the accurate identification of reversible myocardium damage by visualization of wall motion abnormalities in each area, quantification of ventricular function, and assessment of inflammation and fibrosis.

(Komamura et al. 2014, 604)

Technological progress in the shape of cardiac MRI, thus, has improved the grounds for diagnosing TCM, allowing physicians to deal with uncertainty in diagnosis. There is more knowledge, but in clinical life the fundamental uncertainty in a patient who presents with chest pain and short breath remains. And the introduction of TCM has produced new ignorance, even though ignorance has been minimized by introducing TCM, since it is (and remains) unknown what the causes of TCM are – an issue in etiology. In addition, *diagnostic uncertainty* can also appear as a result of how patients present themselves and their symptoms and as a result of time constraints.[5]

Paul K. J. Han presents a further layer of medical uncertainty, the question of disclosure or nondisclosure of prognosis. Han focuses in particular on disclosure or nondisclosure in end-of-life care (2016). Many agents argue in favor of disclosure of prognosis because disclosure seems constitutive of patient autonomy, "informed patient choice" (Han 2016, 567) and shared decision-making. On the other hand, as Han points out, building on work by oncologist Paul Helft, "prognostic non-disclosure is consistent with some patients' wishes, preserves hope by acknowledging uncertainty and helps patients digest difficult information over time" (Han 2016, 568). That is why one should implement "'necessary collusion': a style of communication that allows patients to dictate most of the flow of prognostic information or to avoid it" (Helft 2005, 3146). Han endorses Helft's reconstruction and undergirds his argumentation by relating how his father died from cancer and, in particular, how his father did not want to hear any precise prognosis and made plans for when he was going to be doing better.

> Throughout this time the tensions and ironies of prognostic silence loomed large. Shortly after the TARE [trans-arterial radioembolization, N.E.], and on the very weekend I gave a presentation on barriers to prognostic communication in end-of-life care at a national research conference, I visited my father and steadfastly avoided any discussion of prognosis. I struggled with my ambiguous position: as a physician I felt compelled to discuss his prognosis openly, while as a son I was all too happy to remain silent. In the end I played the part of a son – passively watching, tacitly reinforcing my father's worldview through my silence. Meanwhile, he pushed ahead through profound weakness with equally profound determination, forcing himself to eat and ambulate. There was no question that he hoped for a cure. For weeks he resisted telling even his closest relatives he had cancer; he called this his "cry of faith." Even in his final days he talked about attending events in the coming year, once he got better.
>
> (Han 2016, 570)

The open questions for the physician are whether their patient wants to know the prognosis or not, how much detail they want to know about, and whether they should (want to) know about the prognosis or not. This is another facet of *practitioner uncertainty*, in addition to diagnostic uncertainty, as mentioned in the example of TCM and acute coronary syndrome.

What I call *patients' uncertainty* is uncertainty – conscious ignorance – manifested in patients, for example, when they do not understand whether their illness is harmful or not, terminal or not, how they should deal with a particular diagnosis, or whether they should undergo genetic testing or not, whether the practitioner knows how to proceed in the case of their illness. As Han emphasizes, there is not just a cognitive dimension but also an existential dimension in these cases of patients' uncertainty: how one lives with a diagnosis, how the treatment affects one's life, one's relatives and friends (Han 2016, 571). This combination of cognitive and existential character of patients' uncertainty also explains why uncertainty can be a source of hope for patients; when there is no precise negative prognosis there is still hope for getting better. Thus, uncertainty is not always negative or harmful. Practitioners' uncertainty and patients' uncertainty are facets of *uncertainty in patient–practitioner interaction*.

Han also points to prognostic data as another source of uncertainty. First, for individual patients there are often no precise prognoses, and, second, prognostic data *qua* being made up of probabilities becomes problematic when applied to individual cases. The "precision [of evidence-based prognostic estimates] is limited by inherent shortcomings in the empirical data and statistical methods used in their estimation" (Han 2016, 571). Moreover, objective probabilities apply to groups and not to individuals and so, when one applies objective probabilities to an individual, one gets "objective single-event probability" (Han 2013, 18S) which is a "logically incoherent" idea (Hacking 2001). There is no probability for an individual case. Let's call this *uncertainty regarding prognosis*.

Patients are often unable to understand how they should read prognoses and percentages and, therefore, are more uncertain about prognoses. In reaction, one must explain what, say, probability 12 percent is. Han helpfully spells out what this means for the usefulness of objective probabilities and for understanding probabilities in medical practice:

> Importantly, the logical incoherence of objective probabilities does not undermine their potential utility in clinical decision making. Objective probabilities can inform subjective probabilities (de Finetti, 1974), and that is their principal value in health care and other decision making domains. A woman who learns from an online CPM that her lifetime risk of breast cancer is "12%," for example, ends up with an evidence-based and thus better-informed risk perception. Nevertheless, the logical incoherence of objective single-event probabilities calls for clarity and precision in their presentation and use. The woman in our example needs to be made aware that "12%" is not a literal representation of her own "true" risk but a figurative expression of scientists' confidence based on the aggregated outcomes of individuals whose characteristics are similar – but not completely equivalent – to her own. Her true risk is anyone's guess and contingent on factors beyond the available evidence that may justify higher or lower levels of confidence (Griffin & Tversky, 1992). Estimating this risk is not a strictly scientific act in which "facts" are discovered, but a social process in which personal confidence is constructed and expressed in mathematical terms.
> (Han 2013, 18S–19S)

Often, practitioners face similar issues with prognostic data as the patient in Han's example, because they, too, do not fully understand what the probabilities mean and signify. See for example Gigerenzer's research on "statistical innumeracy" among clinicians (Gigerenzer 2008b, 128). If the practitioners are aware of this limitation, this is another instance of uncertainty, if they are not aware of it, these are cases of ignorance or error.

By introducing example from medical practice and research I have distinguished

a   uncertainty in medical research
b   uncertainty regarding prognosis
c   uncertainty in patient–practitioner interaction
d   practitioner uncertainty
e   patient uncertainty.

These distinctions allow us to triangulate my conception of ignorance with uncertainty and to approach the issue of dealing with uncertainty. If one wants to find a way for dealing with patient–practitioner uncertainty, one basically asks how one should (rationally) deal with ignorance since uncertainty is a form of conscious ignorance.[6] I will argue that the Maxim-based Answer also works for the medical cases.

12.2 Dealing with Patient–Practitioner Uncertainty

Uncertainty in medicine as a form of ignorance clearly is complex and multifaceted. It has different dimensions, different topics and different concerns and manifestations. As you will have noted, this complexity fits well with the Integrated Conception of Ignorance, developed in Part 1, which emphasizes that ignorance has several components. I have argued that ignorance is more than lack of knowledge and uncertainty is also more than lack of knowledge. Han et al. argue similarly that managing uncertainty cannot be limited to providing information. This is because uncertainty may be irreducible and then it is about "cop[ing] with the consciousness of ignorance that cannot be remediated" (Han et al. 2011, 836).

By studying uncertainty, we, thus, find further evidence for the claim that ignorance is more than lack of knowledge or lack of true belief and that ignorance is not just propositional in nature. And Peels' mere list of other types of ignorance is not enough for dealing with this reality (cf. 2023, 37). The medical case reveals that ignorance has more components than propositions. On the Integrated Conception, this is an agential component (in addition to the doxastic component) and a structural component, but, of course, alternative conceptions may choose a different terminology and framing. One thing is certain from examining medical uncertainty in its different forms: ignorance is not just propositional or just doxastic. Medical uncertainty also reveals how sociopolitical structures are constitutive of ignorance. For example, physiologically female hearts are more robust than male hearts (Gerdts and Regitz-Zagrosek 2019), but more women die from heart-related diseases because there are structures that stand in the way of women getting the right medical treatment (Regitz-Zagrosek and Gebhard 2023). The social image of the typical patient with a heart disease is male. The typical female disease is breast cancer; those are the prevalent narratives. Such imageries and narratives also contribute to and constitute ignorance in medical context. That means that they are *not* just causes of ignorance (cf. Section 3.5).

Medical uncertainty also shows why the standard suggestions for dealing with ignorance in philosophy are not adequate. People do not always strive for knowledge, *pace* Aristotle, nor should they always strive for knowledge. Similarly, deontological conceptions defending duties to know fail to capture that such duties may fail to hold, as, for example, in medical contexts. No patient has a duty to know their prognosis. Of course, someone who wants to defend the view that patient autonomy is mainly cognitive may want to argue that patients have a duty to know. But I think that such a view would be a minority position. The Jamesian twin goals are also not helpful for patients dealing with ignorance and uncertainty because the patients may not want to strive for truth and avoid falsehood and they may be justified in doing so. The *right not to know* captures this possibility and even enshrines it as a right.[7] Socratic wisdom appears more promising, but the problems that led me to reject the suggestion in Part 2 come back and weaken the suggestion: it is doubtful that wisdom is an attainable goal for human beings or that it is generally attainable. It would be quite a stretch if one wanted to hold that only wise patients can deal with medical uncertainty. And maybe there would be few patients who ever meet this expectation.

But Kant's suggestion for dealing with error that I have extended to hold for ignorance in general – the Maxim-based Answer – were presented by Kant as maxims for beings who cannot be expected to achieve wisdom (Anth, AA VII, 200). That suggests that they can prove helpful for dealing with ignorance and uncertainty, in lieu of Socratic wisdom. And, in fact, the Kantian maxims are extremely fruitful for addressing medical uncertainty.

As I have noted earlier, Han (2016), Helft (2005) and others argue that sometimes uncertainty, ignorance, may be a source of hope. Han emphasizes for the case of prognostic knowledge that there is more than the cognitive perspective on such knowledge. Advocates of disclosure standardly take the cognitive perspective and cite the value of knowledge in decision-making and patient autonomy. But in patients' uncertainty there is also what Han calls the "existential perspective" on prognostic knowledge, "pertaining to how one lives and copes with the daunting, ineffable prospect of one's nonbeing" (Han 2016, 571). On this picture medical practitioners must be "flexib[le] and open, driven by a humble acknowledgment of limits in our capacity to know what is right" (Han 2016, 568).

I submit that the Maxim-based Answer provides tools and steps for practitioners for actualizing the flexibility, openness and humility required for dealing with the cognitive and existential dimension of uncertainty, that is, for dealing with patients' uncertainty and with practitioners' uncertainty. The second maxim in particular – "To think oneself (in communication with human beings) into the place of every other person" – the extended mode – is crucial in meeting Han's requirements. The physician who follows Kant's maxims in dealing with uncertainty cannot but take the patient's position or the family's position in thinking and judging. In a way, the common observation by physicians that it is important and insightful for them to be patients (from time to time) so they can be reminded and experience what it is like to be a patient is the enacted, pragmatic equivalent to Kant's second maxim of taking the other's position in thinking. What physicians as patients experience is patients' uncertainty. And I suggest that when the physicians are patients they experience in particular the existential component of patients' uncertainty, not so much the cognitive component because it is often very probable that they understand most of the theoretical, medical details that their colleagues are communicating to them.[8]

The first maxim is also particularly useful for practitioners having to deal with uncertainty in patient–practitioner interaction. I have started with Srivastava's question of how doctors can "deal with uncertainty in a time when knowledge is plentiful" (2011, 2252) and her answer reveals why and how the first maxim and the third maxim that are rather self-centered are crucial for practitioners in dealing with patient uncertainty and with their own (practitioner) uncertainty. Srivastava suggests that in dealing with patients' and practitioners' uncertainty, doctors should acknowledge their own feelings and they should have compassion and patience for themselves (2011, 252–253). She hopes that

> believing that it's OK to feel lost in the murkiness of data or that we're not alone in grappling with fundamental matters like the unfairness of suffering might allow us to appreciate that there are some aspects of our work over which we have less control than others. This appreciation, in turn, can help us communicate more effectively with our patients.
> (Srivastava 2011, 2253)

Such self-directed thoughts require that one take oneself seriously as an agent, an epistemic agent and an emotional agent. And doing so, in turn, can be translated or realized in following the first and the third maxim.

One underlying problem in expressing practitioners' uncertainty is that patients may not want to know about practitioner uncertainty. Research suggests that verbal expressions of practitioners' uncertainty, in particular, may have negative effects on patients' confidence in their physicians (Ogden et al. 2002, 172; see also McGovern and Harmon 2017). Ogden et al. (2002) studied how patients and practitioners evaluated the effects of verbal expressions of uncertainty vs. behavioral expressions of uncertainty. Apparently, some behavioral expressions of uncertainty, for example, looking something up in book or on the computer, do not have quite as strong negative repercussions as most verbal expressions. Verbal expressions studied were

> "said I'm not sure about this," "said I need to find out more," "said let's see what happens," "said I don't know," "said, I haven't come across this before" and "said I think this might be."
>
> (Ogden et al. 2002, 172)

Behavioral expressions studied were:

> "used a book to find out about a condition," "asked another GP for advice," "asked a nurse for advice," "referred you/them to a hospital," "used a computer to find information about a condition."
>
> (Ogden et al. 2002, 172)

The evaluations of the patients and GPs in the studies suggest that "while verbal expressions are detrimental, behavioral expressions may be positive" (Ogden et al. 2002, 175). Practitioners, in fact, underestimated how detrimental verbal expressions of uncertainty may be. But Ogden et al. also note that the context in which the practitioner and the patient interact may influence the effects of expressions of uncertainty (2002, 175).[9]

Regardless of these results, the Maxim-based Answer is also applicable for patients in dealing with patient–practitioner uncertainty. They should rely on themselves, listen to their own thoughts, think consistently. And in addition, they should take the position of others in thinking. For example, parents who think about doing a genetic screening of their unborn child would have to take the position of the child and potential siblings – if they wanted to deal with uncertainty in the most sensitive way, and, according to Kant, in a way that comes to close to wisdom. This does not mean that the epistemic agent should believe what the others are saying, blindly defer to others, or not listen to what they themselves think and feel. The three modes of thought (the enlightened, the extended and the consequent mode of thought) must be balanced. And the balancing may very well be different in different contexts. In effect, I suggest that the Maxim-based

Answer fundamentally allows agents to realize the relational nature of medical issues.[10]

12.3 Dealing with Prognosis Uncertainty

Until now, I have focused on patient uncertainty, practitioner uncertainty and patient–practitioner uncertainty. But uncertainty about prognosis and uncertainty about medical research are also central facets of medical uncertainty. How does the Maxim-based Answer fare with these varieties of uncertainty? Uncertainty about prognosis is crucial in patient uncertainty and practitioner uncertainty, so to some extent I have already addressed this variety of uncertainty, but it is still worth looking at it in more detail because there is a special character to uncertainty about prognosis. It leads to another central conception in medical uncertainty, *uncertainty tolerance*.

Han et al. suggest that uncertainty about prognosis can be a form of scientific *certainty* and there is uncertainty about prognosis because of all three sources of uncertainty: probability, ambiguity and complexity. Yet, uncertainty about prognosis is also problematic because it is difficult to represent. Remember Han's remarks about how objective probabilities and subjective probabilities need to be triangulated and explained properly (Han 2013, 18S–19S). Han also calls for practitioners to improve how they present and represent probabilities to patients so that the patients are better equipped and enabled to understand probabilities in prognoses. For example, for picturing randomness there are attempts to use "icon array-based presentations" (Han 2013, 20S) that are dynamic and can therefore change which and how many individuals are affected. Note that such improved representations do not get rid of uncertainty about prognosis, but they are a first step toward understanding what uncertainty about prognosis consists in, what one is uncertain about.

This first step might be thought to be conducive to building what researchers have called *uncertainty tolerance*, a balance between negative and positive responses to uncertainty. More and more research tries to get at this concept. Yet, a meta-study by Strout et al. (2018) reveals that this research is often of low methodological quality (2018, 1521) and that findings are often contradictory (2018, 1522–1525). Strout et al. emphasize that uncertainty tolerance can be either a state or a trait (Strout et al. 2018, 1519) and they propose the following definition that covers different understandings of uncertainty tolerance that are in use. Uncertainty tolerance is "the set of negative and positive psychological responses – cognitive; emotional; and behavioral – provoked by the conscious awareness of ignorance about particular aspects of the world" (Strout et al. 2018, 1519).

Part of the explanation for the inconsistent data is that the studies – 67 in total in the meta-study of Strout et al. – used different measures as well as different scales to examine uncertainty tolerance (2018, 1521) and they differed in what outcomes they focused on – "trainee-centered, provider-centered, patient-centered" and "cognitive, emotional and behavioral" (Strout et al. 2018, 1521). The insights about uncertainty tolerance of providers, that is, medical practitioners, that are most consistent link high uncertainty tolerance and openness toward applying "new medical interventions" (Strout et al. 2018, 1532). Further consistent connections are found between uncertainty tolerance and emotional well-being.[11] I do not think that the current state of research warrants any strong empirical, scientific conclusions about uncertainty tolerance. But we can certainly employ the concept, the idea and explicate it ourselves.

The Maxim-based Answer builds on an autonomous agent, one who thinks for herself but also thinks from the perspective of others. I surmise that this approach can be constitutive of being able to deal with uncertainty about prognosis. Since such uncertainty is largely ineradicable for individuals – because prognosis as objective probability conceptually cannot say anything definitive, certain about the individual case – the solution cannot lie in trying to overcome it, but only in how one approaches this uncertainty. Of course, the right kind of information would (dis)solve uncertainty about prognosis, but it is conceptually not available, so this option is not relevant. An agent who is epistemically autonomous is able to take steps toward modulating her stance toward uncertainty, toward a balance of positive and negative reactions to uncertainty, for example, "thoughts and feelings of opportunity and hope; information seeking and decisions making" (positive reactions) and "thoughts and feelings of vulnerability; information and decision avoidance" (largely negative reactions) (Strout et al. 2018, 1519).

But as Han's intervention about the cognitive and existential perspective on prognosis and uncertainty reveals (2016), in medical contexts the issue is not purely cognitive. Existential considerations also factor into how one deals with uncertainty and, thus, also into developing uncertainty tolerance. In this book I cannot discuss how existential and cognitive considerations are connected, in this realm or in general, whether they are compatible or incommensurable. Let me just highlight that relational conceptions of autonomy may be able to develop answers to these questions because relational autonomy "highlights the social dimensions of *individual* agency" (Westlund 2012, 61, emphasis in original).

There are a number of practical suggestions for dealing with medical uncertainty in the literature, for example, Srivastava's suggestions mentioned earlier. Han's study of "conceptual, methodological, and ethical problems in communicating uncertainty in clinical evidence" (2013)

228 Applications

concludes with four suggestions for how one should approach communicating uncertainty. "Determine the right type and amount of uncertainty information to communicate" (Han 2013, 28S), "improve conceptual understanding of uncertainty in clinical evidence" (Han 2013, 29S), "standardize the language and methods used to represent and communicate uncertainty" (Han 2013, 29S), "promote patient centeredness in the communication of uncertainty" (Han 2013, 29S). Such practical suggestions might also ultimately improve uncertainty tolerance, though, of course, adequately communicating uncertainty does not guarantee that the subject deals with uncertainty adequately.

12.4 Dealing with Uncertainty in Medical Research

Finally, what about uncertainty in medical research? This form of uncertainty can affect researchers, patients and practitioners – most recently felt in the COVID-19 pandemic. As is well recognized by now, medical progress does not inevitably or steadily lead to less uncertainty in medical research. Instead uncertainty in (and about) medical research remains a constant (not just regarding COVID-19). Some researchers working on human genes openly admit that they are uncertain about the effects and implications of their research, for example, Jennifer Doudna working on CRISPR (2015). Or obstetrician-gynecologist Louise King notes how for many surgeries in reproductive medicine, it is not clear whether the surgery is effective because there are not enough studies on the particular kind of surgery (King 2017, 53S). And Tonelli and Shirts show that precision medicine cannot rely on traditional population-based evidence and instead needs to employ mechanistic reasoning as a workaround. Genetic testing often uncovers so-called variants of uncertain significance (VUS) (Tonelli and Shirts 2017, 1649), genetic mutations which only occur in one individual, or maybe at most in her family and some relatively recent ancestors. Tonelli and Shirts note that on the standard population-based methodology, these mutations, in fact, are "variants of *unknowable* significance" (2017, 1649, my emphasis) because one cannot apply the standard methodology to cases of extremely rare, even singular, mutations. Related issues appear for randomized clinical drug trials: in the case of a variant of uncertain significance there are never enough participants to do a randomized clinical trial for a drug that is studied as medication.

For my study it is highly interesting to see how practitioners and researchers deal with this instance of something unknowable. Tonelli and Shirts convincingly argue that precision medicine that deals with the individuality of patients must include mechanistic reasoning and methodologies to deal with VUS. Mechanistic reasoning functions as a workaround for such uncertainty. The solution is also related to the method *Use a*

Proxy, a scientific method that I have mentioned in the Introduction. Yet, mechanistic reasoning is not strictly identical to a proxy, it works more like an Argument from Analogy method. Mechanistic reasoning allows researchers and practitioners to deal with VUS because

> simple mechanistic reasoning alone may be enough to reclassify a VUS as either benign or pathogenic using a variety of allelic considerations, for instance, a variant that clearly causes a known effect, such as loss of gene function, that is in the same gene domain as all other pathogenic variants.
>
> (Tonelli and Shirts 2017, 1649)

So for researchers, a way for dealing with uncertainty, that is, dealing with conscious ignorance is to use mechanistic reasoning, to employ analogies or to use proxies. These tools (or: methods) are all workarounds for continuing one's research despite some gap in information, data, evidence and the like. Of course, these tools only work for conscious ignorance. You cannot develop and use a workaround if you do not know that you need one. – If you accidentally use a workaround and do not know that you are using a workaround, this does not count as using a workaround since you do not know that you are using a workaround.

The tools for dealing with conscious ignorance also fit well with the paradigms of conscious ignorance, for example, a scientist who uses a proxy for getting closer to understanding whether a drug works against a rare genetic disorder, is investigatively ignorant. She wants to know more about the issue that she is ignorant about.

This brings me to the question of how medical researchers deal with *unconscious ignorance* and how they should deal with it. Of course, the question is beset with the issue of first-personal limitations in dealing with ignorance. If I do not know that I do not know that *p*, I am unconsciously ignorant, then I cannot explicitly tackle and address my unconscious ignorance. At first glance it may seem that the Maxim-based Answer does not work this time, but I do suggest that the three maxims are also useful for covering such cases. The enlightened, the extended and the consequent mode of thought are a great starting point for tackling unconscious ignorance as a possibility (and maybe also as an actuality): in particular the first two maxims, thinking for oneself and taking up the perspective of others, are valuable guides in addressing unconscious ignorance. Mainly, because by trusting oneself and taking the perspective of others seriously one has a mechanism – or even method – for filtering and detecting what one does not know. It is what I have called a diagnostic tool for ignorance. On this picture, the three maxims work like a sieve or a filter for unconscious ignorance that is caught in the sieve if it is, so to say, big enough and, thereby, becomes conscious.[12]

You might think that following the Maxim-based Answer has a similar effect to just being aware of one's own fallibility, but the maxims are more precise than mere awareness of one's own fallibility. This is because one's awareness of one's fallibility does not, in the same way, work like a sieve or filter. Staying with the picture, we can say that awareness of one's fallibility produces divisions or mesh that are too coarse-grained and, therefore, do not adequately filter the input. The maxims do not just work for dealing with conscious ignorance but also for tackling unconscious ignorance, the possibility of ignorance.

Notes

1 See also El Kassar (2022) for COVID-19 and ignorance.
2 This is what Gorovitz and MacIntyre call *ignorance*, arguing against the alternative term *ineptitude* in their contribution on medical fallibility (1975, 14).
3 See also Wilkesmann and Steden (2019) for a broad edited collection on ignorance in medicine and care.
4 But see also my (2022) highlighting that there is not just ignorance but also knowledge in medical researchers.
5 Thanks to Vanessa Rampton for discussions about this example and medical uncertainty.
6 Incidentally, it is an interesting combination of the first- and third-person perspectives on ignorance that may also be taken to include the second-person perspective. I cannot address these implications in this context.
7 Cf. the updated collection on the right to know and the right not to know by Chadwick et al. (2014).
8 One might go so far as to suggest that one should change the order of the three maxims in patient–practitioner interaction so that the second maxim is the first maxim. I do not think that this is necessary; the practitioner also has to think for herself, and one may even argue that she has to start with thinking for herself.
9 See, e.g., Cousin et al. (2013), Epstein (2006) for follow-up research and McGovern and Harman (2017) for an overview.
10 See Sherwin (1998) and Nelson (2013) for how relational conceptions of autonomy are relevant in medical contexts.
11 For more connections that have been found but are often contradictory, see Strout et al.'s (2018) helpful review study in full.
12 See Paul Kockelman's (2013) insightful study of sieves in the digital age.

Outlook

I always feel that it is a good sign when at the end of a talk, of a conversation, of an article, of a book, there is still more to say, more to ask, more to discuss and more to think about. So, I am glad that at the end of this book there are many follow-up questions and new questions. Let me just briefly note some of my questions and thoughts before closing.

I would like to see whether my proposal for dealing with one's own ignorance is applicable to dealing with *other people's ignorance*. As I have noted earlier, my hunch is that the Maxim-based Answer – *modulo* some changes – also works for other people. The maxims might be used as a *touchstone* to examine other people's ignorance and to see, for example, whether one needs to do something about their ignorance.

I would also like to connect my insights with work on what Jane Friedman has called "junk beliefs" and "interest-driven epistemology." By discussing what Gilbert Harman's "clutter avoidance" really requires, she shows that we need to include the "*costs* of believing some things and so knowing" (Friedman 2018, 582, my emphasis) in our studies into epistemic norms and obligations. Clearly, these considerations are also highly relevant for dealing with ignorance and for approaching one's own ignorance. Relatedly one may also examine the relation between the Maxim-based Answer and epistemic norms. As I have noted earlier, we may continue to see that the borders between epistemic and practical considerations become porous.

I would also like to see where my conception leads us with respect to collective ignorance or ignorance of group agents. There seems to be something like collective ignorance, for example, in communities suppressing, forgetting, ignoring certain facts, events and memories (cf. Peels 2023). The relation between forgetting, memories and ignorance, of course, is another large topic related to ignorance that inspires philosophical work. Does the Integrated Conception also apply to such ignorance? Can we adapt it, or would we have to develop another conception?

Ignorance and the good life is another topic that I have only briefly touched upon and need to consider further. Hazlett (2013) has argued that knowledge is not all that important to a good life, and it would be worthwhile to approach the question from ignorance and with a view to the insights gathered in this study. The good life could also be considered as a standard for what one needs to know and where ignorance is valuable and acceptable – I only need to know what is required for a good life. Though this suggestion definitely looks too self-centered to be viable.

There are also further fields of application for the Integrated Conception of Ignorance and the Maxim-based Answer that I would like to consider. For example, ignorance is a crucial issue in deep learning and artificial intelligence because human beings do not know, cannot know how the deep learning mechanism works; it can only perceive its results. There are a number of questions related to how we should deal with systems that leave us thus ignorant as to their own procedures and their effects.

And, finally, ignorance, and dealing with one's own ignorance, is hugely relevant for educational contexts (cf. Peels and Pritchard 2021). Can we teach students to rationally deal with their own ignorance? One option might be to teach an "epistemic meta-competence" – one of the goals of Barzilai and Chinn's epistemic education (2018). This meta-competence makes students aware of "legitimate uncertainty" and "lead[s] them to calibrate their confidence and regulate their behavior accordingly, e.g., proceeding with greater caution or withholding judgment altogether" (Barzilai and Chinn 2018, 363). The Three Maxims might be a part of this meta-competence.

You may find that this book on ignorance is too optimistic, too light, when the effects of ignorance may be detrimental and our being ignorant in one way or another seems largely unavoidable. But my attitude toward ignorance during my work on this book has indeed been one of optimism, not naïve optimism that underestimates ignorance but reflective optimism, as I have called it earlier. Let me close by trying to illustrate this attitude. A view on the ambivalence of knowledge that Georg Henrik von Wright attributes to Johann Wolfgang von Goethe, to my mind, perfectly captures my optimism and respect in dealing with ignorance. Von Wright's article addresses the question "So knowledge is power – but is it good for man to know?" by examining three myths – Adam and Eve, Prometheus and Faust (von Wright 1993). Von Wright describes Goethe's perspective in *Faust* as follows:

> Goethe's view is clear. The power that human knowledge provides is not as such an evil. It becomes an evil if man in his delight at 'wie herrlich weit wir es gebracht' [how marvellously far we have come] stops to enjoy the fruits of his work without realizing its incompleteness

or feeling the yearning for something better. Then man perishes. As long as his unease haunts him, he has hope.

(von Wright 1993, 150, translation in original)

It is this combination of yearning for something better, this unease about dangers, and this hope that constitute the reflective optimism that I take to be a valuable attitude toward ignorance and the question of how we should rationally deal with it.

References

I refer to texts by Kant using the abbreviations of the Kant-Forschungsstelle (with one exception: *Jäsche Logic*).

AA	*Akademie-Ausgabe*
Anthr	*Anthropology from a Pragmatic Point of View*

        Anthropology from a Pragmatic Point of View. In: *Anthropology, History, and Education*. 2007. Edited by Günter Zöller and Robert B. Louden. Cambridge Edition of the Works of Immanuel Kant in Translation. Cambridge: Cambridge University Press.

        In: *Der Streit Der Fakultäten, Anthropologie in Pragmatischer Hinsicht*. Vol. VII. Kant's Gesammelte Schriften (Akademie Ausgabe). Berlin: De Gruyter.

CPJ   *Critique of the Power of Judgment*

        Critique of the Power of Judgment. 2000. Translated by Paul Guyer and Eric Matthews. The Cambridge Edition of the Works of Immanuel Kant. Cambridge: Cambridge University Press.

        In: *Kritik Der Praktischen Vernunft, Kritik Der Urteilskraft*. Edited by Königlich preussische Akademie der Wissenschaften. Vol. V. Kant's Gesammelte Schriften (Akademie Ausgabe). Berlin: De Gruyter.

CPR   *Critique of Pure Reason*

        Critique of Pure Reason. 2009. Edited by Paul Guyer and Allen W. Wood. The Cambridge Edition of the Works of Immanuel Kant. Cambridge: Cambridge University Press.

        Kritik Der Reinen Vernunft (2. Aufl. 1787). Edited by Königlich preussische Akademie der Wissenschaften. Vol. III. Kant's Gesammelte Schriften (Akademie Ausgabe). Berlin: De Gruyter.

G   *Groundwork of the Metaphysics of Morals*

        Groundwork of the Metaphysics of Morals. In *Practical Philosophy*, 2006. Edited by Mary J. Gregor, 37–108. The Cambridge Edition of the Works of Immanuel Kant. Cambridge: Cambridge University Press.

        In: *Die Religion Innerhalb Der Grenzen Der Blossen Vernunft, Die Metaphysik Der Sitten*. 1968. Vol. VI. Kant's Gesammelte Schriften (Akademie Ausgabe). Berlin: De Gruyter.

HN	*Handschriftliche Notizen* In: *Handschriftlicher Nachlass: Logik*. 1924. Vol. XVI. Kant's Gesammelte Schriften (Akademie Ausgabe). Berlin: De Gruyter.
JL	*Jäsche Logic* *Lectures on Logic*. 1992. Edited by J. Michael Young. The Cambridge Edition of the Works of Immanuel Kant. Cambridge: Cambridge University Press.
LE	*Lectures on Ethics* *Lectures on Ethics*. 1997. Edited by Peter Heath and J. B. Schneewind. The Cambridge Edition of the Works of Immanuel Kant. New York: Cambridge University Press. In: *Moralphilosophie*. Vol. XXVII. Kant's Gesammelte Schriften (Akademie Ausgabe). Berlin: De Gruyter.
MM	*The Metaphysics of Morals* In: *Die Religion Innerhalb Der Grenzen Der Blossen Vernunft, Die Metaphysik Der Sitten*. 1968. Vol. VI. Kant's Gesammelte Schriften (Akademie Ausgabe). Berlin: De Gruyter. "The Metaphysics of Morals." In *Practical Philosophy*, 2006. Edited by Mary J. Gregor, 353–604. The Cambridge Edition of the Works of Immanuel Kant. Cambridge: Cambridge University Press.
OOT	"What Does It Mean to Orient Oneself in Thinking?" "What Does It Mean to Orient Oneself in Thinking?" In *Religion and Rational Theology*, 1996. Edited by Allen W. Wood and George di Giovanni, 1–18. Cambridge: Cambridge University Press. "Was heisst: Sich im Denken Orientieren?" In: *Abhandlungen Nach 1781*. Vol. VIII. Kant's Gesammelte Schriften (Akademie Ausgabe). Berlin: De Gruyter.
WIE	"An Answer to the Question: What Is Enlightenment?" "An Answer to the Question: What Is Enlightenment?" In *Practical Philosophy*, 2006. Edited by Mary J. Gregor, 11–22. The Cambridge Edition of the Works of Immanuel Kant. Cambridge: Cambridge University Press. «Beantwortung der Frage: Was ist Aufklärung?» In *Abhandlungen Nach 1781*. Vol. VIII. Kant's Gesammelte Schriften (Akademie Ausgabe). Berlin: De Gruyter.

Ackerman, Phillip L., Margaret E. Beier and Kristy R. Bowen. 2002. "What We Really Know about Our Abilities and Our Knowledge." *Personality and Individual Differences* 33 (4): 587–605. https://doi.org/10.1016/S0191-8869(01)00174-X.

Adler, Hans, and Rainer Godel, eds. 2010. *Formen des Nichtwissens der Aufklärung*. Laboratorium Aufklärung, Bd. 4. München: Fink.

Ahlstrom-Vij, Kristoffer. 2013a. *Epistemic Paternalism: A Defence*. Houndmills: Palgrave Macmillan.

———. 2013b. "In Defense of Veritistic Value Monism." *Pacific Philosophical Quarterly* 94 (1): 19–40. https://doi.org/10.1111/j.1468-0114.2012.01442.x.

―――. 2013c. "Why We Cannot Rely on Ourselves for Epistemic Improvement." *Philosophical Issues* 23 (1): 276–96. https://doi.org/10.1111/phis.12014.
Alcoff, Linda Martin. 2007. "Epistemologies of Ignorance: Three Types." In *Race and Epistemologies of Ignorance*, edited by Nancy Tuana and Shannon Sullivan, 39–57. New York: State University of New York Press.
Alcoff, Peter. 2015. "Epistemic Normativity and Social Norms." In *Epistemic Evaluation: Purposeful Epistemology*, edited by David K. Henderson and John Greco, 247–73. Oxford: Oxford University Press.
Al Farābī, Abū-Naṣr Muḥammad Ibn-Muḥammad. 1986. "Kitāb Al-Burhān (Demonstration)." In *Kitāb Al-Burhān Wa-Kitāb al-Sharā'iṭ al-Yaqīn (Book of Demonstration and Book of Conditions of Certainty)*, edited by Majid Fakhry, 19–96. Beirut: Dar el-Machreq.
―――. 1998. *On the Perfect State*. Translated by Richard Walzer [S.l.]: Chicago, IL: Great Books of the Islamic World.
Al Fārābī, Abū-Naṣr Muḥammad Ibn-Muḥammad, Ilai Alon, and Shukri B. Abed. 2002. *Al-Fārābī's philosophical lexicon =: Qāmūs al-Fārābī al-falsafī*. Vol. 2. 2 vols. Cambridge: E.J.W. Gibb Memorial Trust.
―――. 2002. *Al-Fārābī's Philosophical Lexicon = Qāmūs al-Fārābī al-falsafī*. Edited by Ilai Alon. Vol. 2. 2 vols. Cambridge: E.J.W. Gibb Memorial Trust.
Al-Ghazālī. 2005. "The Rescuer from Error." In *Medieval Islamic Philosophical Writings*, edited by Muhammad Ali Khalidi, 59–98. Cambridge Texts in the History of Philosophy. Cambridge: Cambridge University Press. https://doi.org/10.1017/CBO9780511811050.007.
Altanian, Melanie. 2021. "Remembrance and Denial of Genocide: On the Interrelations of Testimonial and Hermeneutical Injustice." *International Journal of Philosophical Studies* 29 (4): 595–612. https://doi.org/10.1080/09672559.2021.1997397.
Anderson, Elizabeth. 2006. "The Epistemology of Democracy." *Episteme* 3 (1–2): 8–22. https://doi.org/10.3366/epi.2006.3.1-2.8.
―――. 2010. *The Imperative of Integration*. Princeton, NJ: Princeton University Press.
―――. 2012. "Epistemic Justice as a Virtue of Social Institutions." *Social Epistemology* 26 (2): 163–73. https://doi.org/10.1080/02691728.2011.652211.
Annas, Julia. 2008. "The Sage in Ancient Philosophy." In *Anthropine Sophia: Studi Di Filologia e Storiografia Filosofica in Memoria Di Gabriele Giannantoni*, edited by Gabriele Giannantoni and Francesca Alesse, 11–28. Elenchos : Collana Di Testi e Studi Sul Pensiero Antico 50. Napoli: Bibliopolis.
Anson, Ian G. 2018. "Partisanship, Political Knowledge, and the Dunning-Kruger Effect: Partisanship, Political Knowledge, and the Dunning-Kruger Effect." *Political Psychology* 39 (5): 1173–92. https://doi.org/10.1111/pops.12490.
Aristoteles. 1960. *Posterior Analytics: Topica*. Translated by Hugh Tredennick and Edward Seymour Forster. Vol. 391. The Loeb Classical Library. London: Heinemann.
―――. 1995a. *The Complete Works of Aristotle: The Revised Oxford Translation*. Vol. 1. Edited by Jonathan Barnes. Princeton, NJ: Princeton University Press.

———. 1995b. *The Complete Works of Aristotle: The Revised Oxford Translation*. Vol. 2. Edited by Jonathan Barnes. Princeton, NJ: Princeton University Press.
St. Augustine. 1993. *On Free Choice of the Will*. Translated by Thomas Williams. Indianapolis: Hackett.
Baehr, Jason. 2011. *The Inquiring Mind*. Oxford: Oxford University Press. www.oxfordscholarship.com/view/10.1093/acprof:oso/9780199604074.001.0001/acprof-9780199604074.
———. 2014. "Sophia: Theoretical Wisdom and Contemporary Epistemology." In *Virtues and Their Vices*, edited by Kevin Timpe and Craig A. Boyd, 302–23. Oxford: Oxford University Press. https://doi.org/10.1093/acprof:oso/9780199645541.003.0015
———., ed. 2016. *Intellectual Virtues and Education: Essays in Applied Virtue Epistemology*. Routledge Studies in Contemporary Philosophy 75. New York: Routledge.
Bailey, Alison. 2007. "Strategic Ignorance." In *Race and Epistemologies of Ignorance*, edited by Shannon Sullivan and Nancy Tuana, 77–94. New York: State University of New York Press.
Baltes, Paul B., and Ursula M. Staudinger. 2000. "Wisdom: A Metaheuristic (Pragmatic) to Orchestrate Mind and Virtue toward Excellence." *American Psychologist* 55 (1): 122–36. https://doi.org/10.1037//0003-066X.55.1.122
Baron, Jonathan. 2008. *Thinking and Deciding*, 4th ed. New York, NY: Cambridge University Press.
Baron, Marcia. 2016. "Justification, Excuse, and the Exculpatory Power of Ignorance." In *Perspectives on Ignorance from Moral and Social Philosophy*, edited by Rik Peels, 53–76. New York: Routledge. www.taylorfrancis.com/books/e/9781317369554/chapters/10.4324%2F9781315671246-10.
Barzilai, Sarit, and Clark A. Chinn. 2018. "On the Goals of Epistemic Education: Promoting Apt Epistemic Performance." *Journal of the Learning Sciences* 27 (3): 353–89. https://doi.org/10.1080/10508406.2017.1392968
Bates, David. 1996. "The Epistemology of Error in Late Enlightenment France." *Eighteenth-Century Studies* 29 (3): 307–27.
Battaly, Heather. 2008. "Virtue Epistemology." *Philosophy Compass* 3 (4): 639–63. https://doi.org/10.1111/j.1747-9991.2008.00146.x
Bennett, Karen. 2017. *Making Things Up*, 1st ed. Oxford: University Press. https://doi.org/10.1093/oso/9780199682683.001.0001
Berger, Ben. 2011. *Attention Deficit Democracy: The Paradox of Civic Engagement*. Princeton, NJ: Princeton University Press.
Berker, Selim. 2013. "The Rejection of Epistemic Consequentialism." *Philosophical Issues* 23: 363–87. https://doi.org/10.1111/phis.12019
Berlin-Brandenburgischen Akademie der Wissenschaften. n.d. "Un-." In *Digitales Wörterbuch Der Deutschen Sprache*. Accessed August 8, 2019. www.dwds.de/wb/un-.
Blumenberg, Hans. 1985. *The Legitimacy of the Modern Age*. Studies in Contemporary German Social Thought. Cambridge, MA: MIT Press.
Bondy, Patrick. 2018. "Knowledge and Ignorance, Theoretical and Practical." *Social Epistemology Review and Reply Collective* 7 (12): 9–14.

References

Bonitz, Hermann. 1849. *Aristotelis Metaphysica*, 2nd ed. Bonn: A. Marcus.
Booth, Anthony Robert. 2017. "Islamic Philosophy and Politics." In *Analytic Islamic Philosophy*, edited by Anthony Robert Booth, 171–99. London: Palgrave Macmillan. https://doi.org/10.1057/978-1-137-54157-4
Bortolotti, Lisa. 2015. "The Epistemic Innocence of Motivated Delusions." *Consciousness and Cognition* 33 (May): 490–99. https://doi.org/10.1016/j.con cog.2014.10.005
Bortolotti, Lisa, and Ema Sullivan-Bissett. 2017. "How Can False or Irrational Beliefs Be Useful?" *Philosophical Explorations* 20 (sup1): 1–3. https://doi.org/10.1080/13869795.2017.1287290
Brandt, Reinhard. 1981. "Materialien Zur Entstehung Der Kritik Der Reinen Vernunft (John Locke Und Johann Schultz)." In *Beiträge Zur Kritik Der Reinen Vernunft, 1781–1981*, edited by Gerhard Lehmann, Ingeborg Heidemann and Wolfgang Ritzel, 37–68. Berlin: W. de Gruyter.
———. 1999. *Kritischer Kommentar Zu Kants Anthropologie in Pragmatischer Hinsicht (1798)*. Kant-Forschungen, Bd. 10. Hamburg: F. Meiner Verlag.
Braun, Florian. 2014. *Wissenschaft Als Selbstzweck. Eine Wissenschaftsphilosophische Untersuchung Zu Aristoteles' Und Hegels Ideal Der Selbstgenügsamen Erkenntnis*.
———. 2023. *Klimaverantwortung und Energiekonflikte: eine Argumentationsanalyse von Abwägungen zu Windkraftanlagen*. 1. Auflage. Schriftenreihe "Wissenschafts- und Technikforschung" Neue Folge, Band 23. Baden-Baden: Nomos.
Braun, Florian, and Christian Baatz. 2018. "Klimaverantwortung Und Energiekonflikte Eine Klimaethische Betrachtung von Protesten Gegen Energiewende-Projekte." In *Reflexive Responsibilisierung*, edited by Anna Henkel, Nico Lüdtke, Nikolaus Buschmann and Lars Hochmann, 31–48. Bielefeld: transcript Verlag. https://doi.org/10.14361/9783839440667-002
Brennan, Jason. 2016. *Against Democracy*. Princeton, NJ: Princeton University Press.
Bright, Stephen B., and James Kwak. 2023. *The Fear of Too Much Justice: Race, Poverty, and the Persistence of Inequality in the Criminal Courts*. New York: The New Press.
Brogaard, Berit. 2016. "Ignorance and Incompetence: Linguistic Considerations." In *The Epistemic Dimensions of Ignorance*, edited by Martijn Blaauw and Rik Peels, 57–80. Cambridge: Cambridge University Press. https://doi.org/10.1017/9780511820076.004
Bromberger, Sylvain. 1992. *On What We Know We Don't Know: Explanation, Theory, Linguistics, and How Questions Shape Them*. Chicago, IL: University of Chicago Press, Center for the Study of Language and Information, and Leland Stanford Junior University.
Brown, Jonathon D., and Rebecca J. Rogers. 1991. "Self-Serving Attributions: The Role of Physiological Arousal." *Personality and Social Psychology Bulletin* 17 (5): 501–06. https://doi.org/10.1177/0146167291175004
Bruner, Justin P. 2013. "Policing Epistemic Communities." *Episteme* 10 (4): 403–16. https://doi.org/10.1017/epi.2013.34

References

Cambiano, Giuseppe. 2012. "The Desire to Know Metaphysics A1." In *Aristotle's Metaphysics Alpha*, edited by Carlos Steel, 1–42. Oxford: Oxford University Press. https://doi.org/10.1093/acprof:oso/9780199639984.003.0001.
Carabotti, Marilia, Annunziata Scirocco, Maria Antonietta Maselli, and Carola Severi. 2015. "The Gut-Brain Axis: Interactions between Enteric Microbiota, Central and Enteric Nervous Systems." *Annals of Gastroenterology : Quarterly Publication of the Hellenic Society of Gastroenterology* 28 (2): 203–9.
Carter, J. Adam, and Emma C. Gordon. 2014. "Openmindedness and Truth." *Canadian Journal of Philosophy* 44 (2): 207–24. https://doi.org/10.1080/00455091.2014.923247
Carter, K. Codell, and Barbara R. Carter. 2005. *Childbed Fever: A Scientific Biography of Ignaz Semmelweis, with a New Introduction by the Authors*. New Brunswick, NJ: Transaction.
Cassam, Quassim. 2016. "Vice Epistemology." *The Monist* 99 (2): 159–80. https://doi.org/10.1093/monist/onv034
———. 2019. *Vices of the Mind: From the Intellectual to the Political*, 1st ed. Oxford: Oxford University Press.
Castellio, Sebastian. 1563/2015. *Die Kunst des Zweifelns und Glaubens, des Nichtwissens und Wissens. De arte dubitandi et confidendi, ignorandi et sciendi*. Edited by Hans-Joachim Pagel and Wolfgang Friedrich Stammler. Translated by Werner Stingl. Bibliothek historischer Denkwürdigkeiten. Essen: Alcorde Verlag.
Çayir, Kenan. 2014. *Who Are We? Identity, Citizenship and Rights in Turkey's Textbooks*. İstanbul: Tarih Vakfı History Foundation Publ.
Chadwick, Ruth F., Mairi Levitt and Darren Shickle, eds. 2014. *The Right to Know and the Right Not to Know: Genetic Privacy and Responsibility*, 2nd ed. Cambridge Bioethics and Law. Cambridge: Cambridge University Press.
Chignell, Andrew. 2007. "Kant's Concepts of Justification." *Noûs* 41 (1): 33–63. https://doi.org/10.1111/j.1468-0068.2007.00637.x
Chisholm, Roderick M. 1966. *Theory of Knowledge*, 1st ed. Englewood Cliffs, NJ: Prentice-Hall.
———. 1977. *Theory of Knowledge*, 2nd ed. Englewood Cliffs, NJ: Prentice-Hall.
———. 1989. *Theory of Knowledge*, 3rd ed. Prentice Hall Foundations of Philosophy Series. Englewood Cliffs, NJ: Prentice Hall.
Clifford, William Kingdon. 1999. "The Ethics of Belief." In *The Ethics of Belief and Other Essays*, edited by Tim Madigan, 70–96. Great Books in Philosophy. Amherst, NY: Prometheus Books.
Coates, Ta-Nehisi. 2017. *Between the World and Me*. New York: Random House.
Code, Lorraine. 1991. *What Can She Know? Feminist Theory and the Construction of Knowledge*. Ithaca, NY: Cornell University Press.
———. 2004. "The Power of Ignorance." *Philosophical Papers* 33 (3): 291–308. https://doi.org/10.1080/05568640409485144
———. 2014a. "Culpable Ignorance?" *Hypatia* 29 (3): 670–76. https://doi.org/10.1111/hypa.12071
———. 2014b. "Ignorance, Injustice and the Politics of Knowledge." *Australian Feminist Studies* 29 (80): 148–60. https://doi.org/10.1080/08164649.2014.928186

240 References

Cohen, Leah Hager. 2013. *I Don't Know: In Praise of Admitting Ignorance (Except When You Shouldn't)*. New York: Riverhead Books.

Conrad, Elfriede. 1994. Kants Logikvorlesungen Als Neuer Schlüssel Zur Architektonik Der Kritik Der Reinen Vernunft: Die Ausarbeitung Der Gliederungsentwürfe in Den Logikvorlesungen Als Auseinandersetzung Mit Der Tradition. Forschungen Und Materialien Zur Deutschen Aufklärung, Bd. 9. Stuttgart-Bad Cannstatt: Frommann-Holzboog.

Converse, Philip E. 2006. "The Nature of Belief Systems in Mass Publics (1964)." *Critical Review* 18 (1–3): 1–74. https://doi.org/10.1080/08913810608443650.

Cook, J. Thomas. 2007. *Spinoza's Ethics: A Reader's Guide*. Continuum Reader's Guides. London: Continuum.

Cousin, Gaetan, Marianne Schmid Mast, and Nicole Jaunin-Stalder. 2013. "When Physician-Expressed Uncertainty Leads to Patient Dissatisfaction: A Gender Study." *Medical Education* 47 (9): 923–31. https://doi.org/10.1111/medu.12237

Cross, Charles, and Floris Roelofsen. 2018. "Questions." In *The Stanford Encyclopedia of Philosophy*, edited by Edward N. Zalta. Stanford: Metaphysics Research Lab, Stanford University. https://plato.stanford.edu/archives/spr2018/entries/questions/

Davidson, Donald. 2001a. "On the Very Idea of a Conceptual Scheme (1974)." In *Inquiries into Truth and Interpretation*, 183–98. Oxford: Clarendon Press.

———. 2001b. "Radical Interpretation." In *Inquiries into Truth and Interpretation*, 125–40. Oxford: Clarendon Press.

Delli Carpini, Michael X., and Scott Keeter. 1996. *What Americans Know about Politics and Why It Matters*. New Haven, CT: Yale University Press.

DeNicola, Daniel R. 2017. *Understanding Ignorance: The Surprising Impact of What We Don't Know*. Cambridge, MA: MIT Press.

Descartes, René. 2017. *Meditations on First Philosophy: With Selections from the Objections and Replies*, 2nd ed. Edited by John Cottingham and Bernard Williams. Cambridge Texts in the History of Philosophy. Cambridge: Cambridge University Press.

Deutz-Schroeder, Monika, and Klaus Schroeder. 2008. Soziales Paradies Oder Stasi-Staat? Das DDR-Bild von Schülern-Ein Ost-West-Vergleich. 1. Aufl. Berlin & München, Bd. 6. Stamsried: Vögel.

Dewey, John. 1927. *The Public and Its Problems*. New York : Holt.

Dorr, Cian. 2003. "Vagueness without Ignorance." *Philosophical Perspectives* 17 (1): 83–113. https://doi.org/10.1111/j.1520-8583.2003.00004.x

Dotson, Kristie. 2011. "Tracking Epistemic Violence, Tracking Practices of Silencing." *Hypatia* 26 (2): 236–57. https://doi.org/10.1111/j.1527-2001.2011.01177.x

Doudna, Jennifer. 2015. "Perspective: Embryo Editing Needs Scrutiny." *Nature* 528 (7580): S6–S6. https://doi.org/10.1038/528S6a

Dovidio, John F., Angelika Love, Fabian M. H. Schellhaas, and Miles Hewstone. 2017. "Reducing Intergroup Bias through Intergroup Contact: Twenty Years of Progress and Future Directions." *Group Processes & Intergroup Relations* 20 (5): 606–20. https://doi.org/10.1177/1368430217712052

Dudenredaktion. n.d. "Halbwissen" on *Duden online*. www.duden.de/rechtschreibung/Halbwissen

Dunning, David. 2011. "The Dunning–Kruger Effect." *Advances in Experimental Social Psychology* 44: 247–96. https://doi.org/10.1016/B978-0-12-385 522-0.00005-6
———. 2012. *Self-Insight: Roadblocks and Detours on the Path to Knowing Thyself*. New York and Hove: Psychology Press.
Elga, Adam. 2005. "On Overrating Oneself ... and Knowing It." *Philosophical Studies* 123 (1–2): 115–24. https://doi.org/10.1007/s11098-004-5222-1
El Kassar, Nadja. 2018. "What Ignorance Really Is. Examining the Foundations of Epistemology of Ignorance." *Social Epistemology* 32 (5): 300–10. https://doi.org/10.1080/02691728.2018.1518498
———. 2019a. "A Critical Catalogue of Ignorance. A Reply to Patrick Bondy." *Social Epistemology Review and Reply Collective* 8 (2): 49–51.
———. 2019b. "The Irreducibility of Ignorance. A Reply to Peels." *Social Epistemology Review and Reply Collective* 8 (2): 31–38.
———. 2022. "Wissen, Unwissenheit Und Ignoranz: Corona Als Chance Und Herausforderung Für Den Epistemologischen Diskurs." In *Wissensproduktion Und Wissenstransfer in Zeiten Der Pandemie*, edited by Pedro Schmechtig and Rico Hauswald, 371–402. Baden-Baden: Karl Alber.
———. Forthcoming. "Non-ideal Theory and Ignorance." In *Routledge Handbook of Non-ideal Theory*, edited by Hilkje C. Hänel and Johanna Müller. London: Routledge.
Epstein, Ronald M. 2006. "Making Communication Research Matter: What Do Patients Notice, What Do Patients Want, and What Do Patients Need?" *Patient Education and Counseling* 60 (3): 272–78. https://doi.org/10.1016/j.pec.2005.11.003
Erikson, Robert S. 2007. "Does Public Ignorance Matter?" *Critical Review* 19 (1): 23–34. https://doi.org/10.1080/08913810701499619
Essed, Philomena, and Isabel Hoving. 2014. "Innocence, Smug Ignorance, Resentment: An Introduction to Dutch Racism." In *Dutch Racism*, edited by Philomena Essed and Isabel Hoving, 9–3ß. Rodopi: Brill. https://doi.org/10.1163/9789401210096_002
Fassio, Davide, and Robin McKenna. 2015. "Revisionary Epistemology." *Inquiry* 58 (7–8): 755–79. https://doi.org/10.1080/0020174X.2015.1083468
Feldman, Richard. 2000. "The Ethics of Belief." *Philosophy and Phenomenological Research* 60 (3): 667–95. https://doi.org/10.2307/2653823
———. 2002. "Epistemological Duties." In *The Oxford Handbook of Epistemology*, edited by Paul K. Moser, 362–83. Oxford: Oxford University Press. https://doi.org/10.1093/0195130057.001.0001
Ferrier, James F. 1854. *The Theory of Knowing and Being*. Edinburgh: William Blackwood and Sons.
Fine, Kit. 2018. "Ignorance of Ignorance." *Synthese* 195 (9): 4031–45. https://doi.org/10.1007/s11229-017-1406-z
Finetti, Bruno de. 1974. *Theory of Probability*. Vol. 1. New York: John Wiley.
Firestein, Stuart. 2012. *Ignorance: How It Drives Science*. Oxford: Oxford University Press.

Fiske, Susan T., and Shelley E. Taylor. 2013. *Social Cognition: From Brains to Culture*, 2nd ed. Los Angeles: Sage.

Frankfurter Allgemeine Zeitung. 2008. "Erschreckendes Unwissen. 'Die DDR War Keine Diktatur.' " July 25.

Fricker, Miranda. 2007. *Epistemic Injustice: Power and the Ethics of Knowing*. Oxford: Oxford University Press.

Friedman, Jane. 2013. "Suspended Judgment." *Philosophical Studies: An International Journal for Philosophy in the Analytic Tradition* 162 (2): 165–81.

———. 2018. "Junk Beliefs and Interest-Driven Epistemology." *Philosophy and Phenomenological Research* 97 (3): 568–83. https://doi.org/10.1111/phpr.12381

Fuhrer, Therese. 2010. "Ignorantia." In *Augustinus-Lexikon. Volume 3: Figura(e)—Mensura*, edited by Cornelius Mayer, 491–95. Basel: Schwabe.

Gadamer, Hans-Georg. 2013. *Truth and Method*. First paperback edition. Translation revised by Joel Weinsheimer and Donald G. Marshall. The Bloomsbury Revelations Series. London: Bloomsbury.

Gamper, Michael. 2010. "Nicht-Wissen und Literatur. Eine Poetik des Irrtums bei Bacon, Lichtenberg, Novalis, Goethe." *Internationales Archiv für Sozialgeschichte der deutschen Literatur* 34 (2): 92–120. https://doi.org/10.1515/iasl.2009.016

Garrett, Don. 2013. Representation, Misrepresentation, and Error in Spinoza's Philosophy of Mind. Vol. 1. Edited by Michael Della Rocca. Oxford: Oxford University Press. https://doi.org/10.1093/oxfordhb/9780195335828.013.009

Geisenhanslüke, Achim. 2011. *Dummheit Und Witz: Poetologie Des Nichtwissens*. München: Wilhelm Fink.

Gelman, Andrew. 2021. "Can the 'Dunning-Kruger Effect' Be Explained as a Misunderstanding of Regression to the Mean?" *Statistical Modeling, Causal Inference and Social Science Blog*. October 12. https://statmodeling.stat.columbia. edu/2021/10/12/can-the-dunning-kruger-effect-be-explained-as-a-misunderstanding-of-regression-to-the-mean

Gerdts, Eva, and Vera Regitz-Zagrosek. 2019. "Sex Differences in Cardiometabolic Disorders." *Nature Medicine* 25 (11): 1657–66. https://doi.org/10.1038/s41 591-019-0643-8

Gettier, Edmund. 1963. "Is Justified True Belief Knowledge?" *Analysis* 23 (6): 121–23.

Gigerenzer, Gerd. 2002. *Adaptive Thinking: Rationality in the Real World*. Evolution and Cognition. Oxford: Oxford University Press.

Gigerenzer, Gerd. 2008a. *Rationality for Mortals: How People Cope with Uncertainty*. Evolution and Cognition. Oxford: Oxford University Press.

———. 2008b. "Understanding Risks in Health Care." In *Rationality for Mortals: How People Cope with Uncertainty*, 127–35. Evolution and Cognition. Oxford: Oxford University Press.

Gignac, Gilles E., and Marcin Zajenkowski. 2020. "The Dunning-Kruger Effect Is (Mostly) a Statistical Artefact: Valid Approaches to Testing the Hypothesis with Individual Differences Data." *Intelligence* 80 (May): 101449. https://doi.org/10.1016/j.intell.2020.101449

Ginsborg, Hannah. 2006. "Aesthetic Judgment and Perceptual Normativity." *Inquiry* 49: 403–37.
Goldberg, Sanford C. 2017a. "A Proposed Research Program for Social Epistemology." In *Social Epistemology and Epistemic Agency: Decentralizing Epistemic Agency*, edited by Patrick J. Reider, 3–20. London: Rowman & Littlefield.
———. 2017b. "Should Have Known." *Synthese* 194 (8): 2863–94. https://doi.org/10.1007/s11229-015-0662-z
———. 2018. *To the Best of Our Knowledge: Social Expectations and Epistemic Normativity*, 1st ed. Oxford: Oxford University Press.
Goldman, Alvin I. 1999. *Knowledge in a Social World*. Oxford University Press. https://doi.org/10.1093/0198238207.001.0001
Goldman, Alvin I., and Erik J. Olsson. 2009. "Reliabilism and the Value of Knowledge." In *Epistemic Value*, edited by Duncan Pritchard, Adrian Haddock and Alan Millar, 19–41. Oxford: Oxford University Press.
Gorovitz, Samuel, and Alasdair Macintyre. 1975. "Toward a Theory of Medical Fallibility." *Hastings Center Report* 5 (6): 13–23. https://doi.org/10.2307/3560992
Gosepath, Stefan. 1992. *Aufgeklärtes Eigeninteresse: Eine Theorie Theoretischer Und Praktischer Rationalität*. 1. Aufl. Frankfurt am Main: Suhrkamp.
———. 2002. "Practical Reason: A Review of the Current Debate and Problems." *Philosophical Explorations* 5 (3): 229–38. https://doi.org/10.1080/10002002108538735
Graham, David A. 2014. "Rumsfeld's Knowns and Unknowns: The Intellectual History of a Quip." *The Atlantic*. March 27. www.theatlantic.com/politics/archive/2014/03/rumsfelds-knowns-and-unknowns-the-intellectual-history-of-a-quip/359719/
Graham, Peter. 2015. "Epistemic Normativity and Social Norms." In *Epistemic Evaluation: Purposeful Epistemology*, edited by David K. Henderson and John Greco, 247–73. Oxford: Oxford University Press.
Greco, John. 2009. "Knowledge and Success from Ability." *Philosophical Studies* 142 (1): 17–26. https://doi.org/10.1007/s11098-008-9307-0
Griffin, Dale, and Amos Tversky. 1992. "The Weighing of Evidence and the Determinants of Confidence." *Cognitive Psychology* 24 (3): 411–35. https://doi.org/10.1016/0010-0285(92)90013-R
Gross, Matthias. 2010. Ignorance and Surprise: Science, Society, and Ecological Design. Cambridge, MA: MIT Press. https://doi.org/10.7551/mitpress/9780262013482.001.0001
———. 2016. "Risk as Zombie Category: Ulrich Beck's Unfinished Project of the 'Non-Knowledge' Society." Edited by Anna Stavrianakis and Mark B Salter. *Security Dialogue* 47 (5): 386–402. https://doi.org/10.1177/0967010616645020
Gross, Matthias, and Linsey McGoey, eds. 2015. *Routledge International Handbook of Ignorance Studies*. Routledge International Handbooks. London: Routledge.

Gutmann, Amy. 2007. "Democracy." In *A Companion to Contemporary Political Philosophy*, edited by Robert E. Goodin, Philip Pettit and Thomas Pogge, 521–31. Oxford: Blackwell.

Gutmann, Amy, and Dennis F. Thompson. 1996. *Democracy and Disagreement*. Harvard: Harvard University Press.

Haas, Jens, and Katja Maria Vogt. 2015. "Ignorance and Investigation." In *Routledge International Handbook of Ignorance Studies*, edited by Matthias Gross and Linsey McGoey, 17–24. New York: Routledge.

Habgood-Coote, Joshua, Natalie Alana Ashton, and Nadja El Kassar. 2024. "Receptive Publics." *Ergo an Open Access Journal of Philosophy* 11 (5). https://doi.org/10.3998/ergo.5710

Hacking, Ian. 2001. *An Introduction to Probability and Inductive Logic*. Cambridge: Cambridge University Press.

Han, Paul K. J. 2013. "Conceptual, Methodological, and Ethical Problems in Communicating Uncertainty in Clinical Evidence." *Medical Care Research and Review* 70 (1suppl): 14S–36S. https://doi.org/10.1177/1077558712459361

———. 2016. "The Need for Uncertainty: A Case for Prognostic Silence." *Perspectives in Biology and Medicine* 59 (4): 567–75. https://doi.org/10.1353/pbm.2016.0049

Han, Paul K. J., William M. P. Klein and Neeraj K. Arora. 2011. "Varieties of Uncertainty in Health Care: A Conceptual Taxonomy." *Medical Decision Making* 31 (6): 828–38. https://doi.org/10.1177/0272989X10393976

Hardin, Russell. 2004. "Representing Ignorance." *Social Philosophy and Policy* 21 (1): 76–99. https://doi.org/10.1017/S0265052504211049

Harman, Elizabeth. 2011. "Does Moral Ignorance Exculpate?" *Ratio* 24 (4): 443–68. https://doi.org/10.1111/j.1467-9329.2011.00511.x

Harman, Gilbert. 1986. *Change in View: Principles of Reasoning*. Cambridge, MA: MIT Press.

Harvin, Cassandra Byers. 1996. "Conversations I Can't Have." *On the Issues: The Progressive Woman's Quarterly* 5 (2): 15–16.

Haslanger, Sally. 1999. "What Knowledge Is and What It Ought to Be: Feminist Values and Normative Epistemology." *Noûs* 33: 459–80. https://doi.org/10.1111/0029-4624.33.s13.20

———. 2006. "I—Sally Haslanger What Good Are Our Intuitions?" *Aristotelian Society Supplementary Volume* 80 (1): 89–118. https://doi.org/10.1111/j.1467-8349.2006.00139.x

———. 2013. *Resisting Reality Social Construction and Social Critique*. Oxford: Oxford University Press.

———. 2017. "Racism, Ideology, and Social Movements." *Res Philosophica* 94 (1): 1–22. https://doi.org/10.11612/resphil.1547

———. 2018. "Feminist Metaphysics." In *The Stanford Encyclopedia of Philosophy*, edited by Edward N. Zalta. Stanford: Metaphysics Research Lab, Stanford University. https://plato.stanford.edu/archives/fall2018/entries/feminism-metaphysics/

Hazlett, Allan. 2013. *A Luxury of the Understanding: On the Value of True Belief*. Oxford: Oxford University Press.

Helft, Paul R. 2005. "Necessary Collusion: Prognostic Communication with Advanced Cancer Patients." *Journal of Clinical Oncology* 23 (13): 3146–50. https://doi.org/10.1200/JCO.2005.07.003

Hertwig, Ralph, and Christoph Engel. 2021. "Homo Ignorans: Deliberately Choosing Not to Know." In *Deliberate Ignorance*, edited by Ralph Hertwig and Christoph Engel, 3–17. The MIT Press. https://doi.org/10.7551/mitpress/13757.003.0011

Heuser, Uwe Jean. 2018. "Was Wissen Sie Über Wirtschaft?" *Die Zeit*, February 1.

Heuser, Uwe Jean, and Susan Djahangard. 2018a. "Was Wissen Die Deutschen Über Wirtschaft?" *Die Zeit*, February 8.

———. 2018b. "Durchblick Schafft Vertrauen." *Die Zeit*, February 22.

Hewstone, Miles, Mark Rubin and Hazel Willis. 2002. "Intergroup Bias." *Annual Review of Psychology* 53 (1): 575–604. https://doi.org/10.1146/annurev.psych.53.100901.135109

Hodges, Wilfrid, and Therese-Anne Druart. 2019. "Al-Farabi's Philosophy of Logic and Language." In *The Stanford Encyclopedia of Philosophy*, edited by Edward N. Zalta, Summer 2019. Metaphysics Research Lab, Stanford University. https://plato.stanford.edu/archives/sum2019/entries/al-farabi-logic/

Hoek, Wiebe van der, and Alessio Lomuscio. 2004. "A Logic for Ignorance." In *Declarative Agent Languages and Technologies*, edited by João Leite, Andrea Omicini, Leon Sterling and Paolo Torroni, 97–108. Heidelberg: Springer

Hofer, Gabriela, Valentina Mraulak, Sandra Grinschgl and Aljoscha C. Neubauer. 2022. "Less-Intelligent and Unaware? Accuracy and Dunning–Kruger Effects for Self-Estimates of Different Aspects of Intelligence." *Journal of Intelligence* 10 (1): 10. https://doi.org/10.3390/jintelligence10010010

Hon, Giora. 1995. "Going Wrong: To Make a Mistake, to Fall into Error." *Review of Metaphysics* 49 (193): 3–20.

———. 2009. "Error: The Long Neglect, the One-Sided View, and a Typology." In *Going Amiss in Experimental Research*, edited by Giora Hon, Jutta Schickore and Friedrich Steinle, 11–26. Dordrecht: Springer. https://doi.org/10.1007/978-1-4020-8893-3_2

Huber, Franz. 2016. "Formal Representations of Belief." In *The Stanford Encyclopedia of Philosophy*, edited by Edward N. Zalta. Stanford: Metaphysics Research Lab, Stanford University. https://plato.stanford.edu/archives/spr2016/entries/formal-belief

İnan, İlhan. 2012. *The Philosophy of Curiosity*. Routledge Studies in Contemporary Philosophy 34. New York: Routledge.

Innerarity, Daniel. 2013. *Demokratie des Wissens: Plädoyer für eine lernfähige Gesellschaft*. Sozialtheorie. Bielefeld: Transcript.

Ipsos Mori. 2016. "Perceptions Are Not Reality: What the World Gets Wrong | Ipsos." December 14, 2016. www.ipsos.com/en-uk/perceptions-are-not-reality-what-world-gets-wrong

James, William. 2014. *The Will to Believe and Other Essays in Popular Philosophy*. Cambridge: Cambridge University Press.

Jimmy Kimmel Live. 2014. *Lie Witness News: SXSW Edition*. www.youtube.com/watch?v=frjaQ17yAww&feature=youtu.be. Accessed June 6, 2019.

Jüngel, Eberhard. 2005. "Der Mensch Im Schnittpunkt von Wissen, Glauben, Tun Und Hoffen. Die Theologische Fakultät Im Streit Mit Der Durch Immanuel Kant Repräsentierten Philosophischen Fakultät." In *Kant Im Streit Der Fakultäten*, edited by Volker Gerhardt and Thomas Meyer, 1–38. Berlin: De Gruyter.
Kahan, Dan M. 2016. "The Politically Motivated Reasoning Paradigm, Part 1: What Politically Motivated Reasoning Is and How to Measure It." In *Emerging Trends in the Social and Behavioral Sciences*, edited by Robert A. Scott and Stephan M. Kosslyn, 1–16. Hoboken, NJ: John Wiley & Sons. https://doi.org/10.1002/9781118900772.etrds0417
———. 2017. "The Expressive Rationality of Inaccurate Perceptions." *Behavioral and Brain Sciences* 40. https://doi.org/10.1017/S0140525X15002332
Kahan, Dan M., and Jonathan C. Corbin. 2016. "A Note on the Perverse Effects of Actively Open-Minded Thinking on Climate-Change Polarization." *Research & Politics* 3(4). https://doi.org/10.1177/2053168016676705
Kahan, Dan M., Asheley Landrum, Katie Carpenter, Laura Helft and Kathleen Hall Jamieson. 2017. "Science Curiosity and Political Information Processing." *Political Psychology* 38 (S1): 179–99. https://doi.org/10.1111/pops.12396
Kahneman, Daniel. 2013. *Thinking, Fast and Slow*. First paperback edition. New York: Farrar, Straus and Giroux.
Kaye, Simon T. 2015. "Democracy despite Ignorance: Questioning the Veneration of Knowledge in Politics." *Critical Review* 27 (3–4): 316–37. https://doi.org/10.1080/08913811.2015.1111681
Keefe, Jennifer. 2007. "James Ferrier and the Theory of Ignorance." *The Monist* 90 (April): 297–309. https://doi.org/10.2307/27904033
Kennedy, Helena. 2019. "Opinion: The Mockery of Naomi Wolf's Book Error Disguises the Real Outrage We Should Feel." *The Independent*. June 28. www.independent.co.uk/voices/naomi-wolf-outrages-gay-rights-book-error-a8979646.html
Kerwin, Ann. 1993. "None Too Solid: Medical Ignorance." *Knowledge* 15 (2): 166–185. https://doi.org/10.1177/107554709301500204
———. 2015. "Fictional Reflections: Taking It Personally: Medical Ignorance." In *Routledge International Handbook of Ignorance Studies*, 378–84. Routledge.
Khalidi, Muhammad Ali, ed. 2005. "Introduction." In *Medieval Islamic Philosophical Writings*, x–xl. Cambridge Texts in the History of Philosophy. Cambridge: Cambridge University Press.
King, Louise P. 2017. "Should Clinicians Set Limits on Reproductive Autonomy?" *Hastings Center Report* 47 (S3): S50–S56. https://doi.org/10.1002/hast.796
Kirkpatrick, Elizabeth M., and Peter Mark Roget, eds. 1998. *Roget's Thesaurus*, New ed. London: Penguin Books.
Klein, Peter D. 2008. "Useful False Beliefs." In *Epistemology: New Essays*, edited by Quentin Smith, 25–63. Oxford: Oxford University Press.
Klein, Roberta Cutler. 1987. "Are We Morally Obligated to Be Intellectually Responsible?" *Philosophy and Phenomenological Research* 48 (1): 79. https://doi.org/10.2307/2107707
Kockelman, Paul. 2013. "The Anthropology of an Equation: Sieves, Spam Filters, Agentive Algorithms, and Ontologies of Transformation." *HAU: Journal of Ethnographic Theory* 3 (3): 33–61. https://doi.org/10.14318/hau3.3.003
Köhl, Harald. 1990. *Kants Gesinnungsethik*. Berlin: De Gruyter.

Kolodny, Niko, and John Brunero. 2018. "Instrumental Rationality." In *The Stanford Encyclopedia of Philosophy*, edited by Edward N. Zalta. Stanford: Metaphysics Research Lab, Stanford University. https://plato.stanford.edu/archives/win2018/entries/rationality-instrumental/

Komamura, Kazuo. 2014. "Takotsubo Cardiomyopathy: Pathophysiology, Diagnosis and Treatment." *World Journal of Cardiology* 6 (7): 602. https://doi.org/10.4330/wjc.v6.i7.602

Korsgaard, Christine. 1997. "The Normativity of Instrumental Reason." In *Ethics and Practical Reason*, edited by Garrett Cullity and Berys Gaut, 215–54. Oxford: Clarendon Press.

Kourany, Janet A., and Martin Carrier, eds. 2019. *Science and the Production of Ignorance: When the Quest for Knowledge Is Thwarted*. Cambridge, MA: MIT Press.

Kricheldorf, Hans R. 2016. *Getting It Right in Science and Medicine*. Cham: Springer. https://doi.org/10.1007/978-3-319-30388-8

Krueger, Joachim. 1998. "Enhancement Bias in Descriptions of Self and Others." *Personality and Social Psychology Bulletin* 24 (5): 505–16. https://doi.org/10.1177/0146167298245006

Kruglanski, Arie W., Donna M. Webster, and Adena Klem. 1993. "Motivated Resistance and Openness to Persuasion in the Presence or Absence of Prior Information." *Journal of Personality and Social Psychology* 65 (5): 861–76. https://doi.org/10.1037/0022-3514.65.5.861

Kruglanski, Arie W., and Lauren M. Boyatzi. 2012. "The Psychology of Closed and Open Mindedness, Rationality, and Democracy." *Critical Review* 24 (2): 217–32. https://doi.org/10.1080/08913811.2012.711023

Kunda, Ziva. 1990. "The Case for Motivated Reasoning." *Psychological Bulletin* 108 (3): 480–98. https://doi.org/10.1037/0033-2909.108.3.480.

Kusch, Martin. 2010. "Social Epistemology." In *Routledge Companion to Epistemology*, edited by Sven Bernecker and Duncan Pritchard, 873–84. London: Routledge.

Lea, Richard. 2019. "Naomi Wolf Admits Blunder over Victorians and Sodomy Executions." *The Guardian*, May 24. www.theguardian.com/books/2019/may/24/naomi-wolf-admits-blunder-over-victorians-and-sodomy-executions

Le Morvan, Pierre. 2011a. "Knowledge, Ignorance and True Belief." *Theoria* 77 (1): 32–41. https://doi.org/10.1111/j.1755-2567.2010.01083.x

———. 2011b. "On Ignorance: A Reply to Peels." *Philosophia* 39 (2): 335–44. https://doi.org/10.1007/s11406-010-9292-3

———. 2012. "On Ignorance: A Vindication of the Standard View." *Philosophia* 40 (2): 379–93. https://doi.org/10.1007/s11406-011-9330-9

———. 2013. "Why the Standard View of Ignorance Prevails." *Philosophia* 41 (1): 239–56. https://doi.org/10.1007/s11406-013-9417-6

Le Morvan, Pierre, and Rik Peels. 2016. "The Nature of Ignorance: Two Views." In *The Epistemic Dimensions of Ignorance*, edited by Martijn Blaauw and Rik Peels, 12–32. Cambridge: Cambridge University Press.

Lincoln, Abraham. 1953. "Address Delivered at the Dedication of the Cemetery at Gettysburg." In *The Collected Works of Abraham Lincoln*, edited by Roy P. Basler, 17–23. New Brunswick: Rutgers University Press.

Lippmann, Walter. 1922. *Public Opinion.* New York: Macmillan.
Locke, John. 1979. *An Essay Concerning Human Understanding.* Edited by P. H. Nidditch. The Clarendon Edition of the Works of John Locke. Oxford: Clarendon Press and Oxford University Press.
———. 1996. *Some Thoughts Concerning Education: And, of the Conduct of the Understanding.* Edited by Ruth Weissbourd Grant and Nathan Tarcov. Indianapolis, IN: Hackett.
Löwenstein, David. 2017. *Know-How as Competence: A Rylean Responsibilist Account.* Studies in Theoretical Philosophy, vol. 4. Frankfurt am Main: Vittorio Klostermann.
Marshall, George. 2015. *Don't Even Think about It: Why Our Brains Are Wired to Ignore Climate Change.* Paperback edition. London: Bloomsbury.
Mason, Elinor. 2015. "Moral Ignorance and Blameworthiness." *Philosophical Studies* 172 (11): 3037–57. https://doi.org/10.1007/s11098-015-0456-7
———. 2017. "Moral Incapacity and Moral Ignorance." In *Perspectives on Ignorance from Moral and Social Philosophy,* edited by Rik Peels, first edition, 30–52. Routledge Studies in Contemporary Philosophy 85. New York: Routledge.
McDowell, John. 1996. *Mind and World: With a New Introduction.* Cambridge, MA: Harvard University Press.
McGoey, Linsey. 2012. "The Logic of Strategic Ignorance." *British Journal of Sociology* 63 (3): 533–76. https://doi.org/10.1111/j.1468-4446.2012.01424.x
McGovern, R., and D. Harmon. 2017. "Patient Response to Physician Expressions of Uncertainty: A Systematic Review." *Irish Journal of Medical Science (1971 -)* 186 (4): 1061–65. https://doi.org/10.1007/s11845-017-1592-1
McKay, Ryan T., and Daniel C. Dennett. 2009. "The Evolution of Misbelief." *Behavioral and Brain Sciences* 32 (6): 493–510. https://doi.org/10.1017/S0140525X09990975
McKenna, Robin. 2023. *Non-ideal Epistemology.* Oxford: Oxford University Press.
Medina, José. 2013. *The Epistemology of Resistance: Gender and Racial Oppression, Epistemic Injustice, and Resistant Imaginations.* Studies in Feminist Philosophy. Oxford: Oxford University Press.
Meier, Georg Friedrich. 2015. *Vernunftlehre.* Edited by Robert Theis and Werner Schneiders. Nachdruck with an introduction by Riccardo Pozzo. Gesammelte Werke / Christian Wolff. Abt III, Materialien Und Dokumente, Band 144. Hildesheim: Georg Olms Verlag.
Meier-Oeser, Stephan. 2001. "Unwissen." In *Historisches Wörterbuch Der Philosophie,* edited by Karlfried Gründer, Joachim Ritter and Gottfried Gabriel, 341–48. Darmstadt: Schwabe.
Melville, Herman. 1985. *Billy Budd, Sailor and Other Stories.* Edited by Harold Beaver. Penguin Classics. London: Penguin Books.
Meylan, Anne. 2024. "In Defence of the Normative Account of Ignorance." *Erkenntnis* 89 (1): 207–21. https://doi.org/10.1007/s10670-022-00529-7
Mills, Charles. 1997. *The Racial Contract.* Ithaca, NY: Cornell University Press.
———. 2007. "White Ignorance." In *Race and Epistemologies of Ignorance,* edited by Shannon Sullivan and Nancy Tuana, 11–38. New York: State University of New York Press.

———. 2015. "Global White Ignorance." In *Routledge International Handbook of Ignorance Studies*, edited by Matthias Gross and Linsey McGoey, 217–27. Routledge International Handbooks. London: Routledge.

———. 2017. "'Ideal Theory' as Ideology." In *Black Rights/White Wrongs: The Critique of Racial Liberalism*, 72–90. Transgressing Boundaries. New York: Oxford University Press.

Milton, John. 1667/2003. *Paradise Lost*. Edited by John Leonard. Penguin Classics. London: Penguin Books.

Moody-Adams, Michelle. 2018. "Democratic Conflict and the Political Morality of Compromise." In *Compromise*, edited by Jack Knight, 186–219. Nomos, LIX. New York: New York University Press.

Moretti, Luca, and Tommaso Piazza. 2018. "Defeaters in Current Epistemology: Introduction to the Special Issue." *Synthese* 195 (7): 2845–54. https://doi.org/10.1007/s11229-017-1551-4

Morris, Errol. 2013. *The Unknown Known*. Radius-TWC.

Nelson, Erin. 2013. *Law, Policy and Reproductive Autonomy*. Oxford; Portland, Oregon: Hart Publishing.

Newson, Ainsley J., Samantha J. Leonard, Alison Hall and Clara L. Gaff. 2016. "Known Unknowns: Building an Ethics of Uncertainty into Genomic Medicine." *BMC Medical Genomics* 9 (1): 57. https://doi.org/10.1186/s12920-016-0219-0.

Nicolai De Cusa. 1440. *De docta ignorantia. Die belehrte Unwissenheit*. Edited by Hans Gerhard Senger. Translated by Paul Wilpert. Latin-German. Hamburg: Meiner.

Nietzsche, Friedrich. 2002. *Beyond Good and Evil: Prelude to a Philosophy of the Future*. Edited by Rolf-Peter Horstmann and Judith Norman. Cambridge Texts in the History of Philosophy. Cambridge: Cambridge University Press.

Norlock, Kathryn J. 2019. "Perpetual Struggle." *Hypatia* 34 (1): 6–19. https://doi.org/10.1111/hypa.12452

Nottelmann, Nikolaj. 2016. "The Varieties of Ignorance." In *The Epistemic Dimensions of Ignorance*, edited by Rik Peels and Martijn Blaauw, 33–56. Cambridge: Cambridge University Press. https://doi.org/10.1017/9780511820076.003

Nozick, Robert. 1990. *Examined Life: Philosophical Meditations*. New York: Simon & Schuster.

O'Connor, Cailin, and James Owen Weatherall. 2018. *The Misinformation Age: How False Beliefs Spread*. New Haven, CT: Yale University Press.

Offe, Claus. 2003. "Micro-Aspects of Democratic Theory. What Makes for the Deliberative Competence of Citizens?" In *Herausforderungen Der Demokratie. Zur Integrations- Und Leistungsfähigkeit Politischer Institutionen*, 297–320. Frankfurt am Main: Campus Verlag.

Ogden, Jane, Kaz Fuks, Mary Gardner, Steve Johnson, Malcolm McLean, Pam Martin, and Reena Shah. 2002. "Doctors Expressions of Uncertainty and Patient Confidence." *Patient Education and Counseling* 48 (2): 171–76. https://doi.org/10.1016/S0738-3991(02)00020-4

Olsson, Erik J., and Carlo Proietti. 2016. "Explicating Ignorance and Doubt: A Possible Worlds Approach." In *The Epistemic Dimensions of Ignorance*, edited

250 References

by Rik Peels and Martijn Blaauw, 81–95. Cambridge: Cambridge University Press. https://doi.org/10.1017/9780511820076.005

O'Neill, Onora, ed. 2015. "Orientation in Thinking: Geographical Problems, Political Solutions." In *Constructing Authorities: Reason, Politics and Interpretation in Kant's Philosophy*, 153–69. Cambridge: Cambridge University Press. https://doi.org/10.1017/CBO9781316337141.011

Oppenheimer, Danny, and Mike Edwards. 2012. *Democracy despite Itself: Why a System That Shouldn't Work at All Works so Well*. Cambridge, MA: MIT Press.

Peels, Rik. 2010. "What Is Ignorance?" *Philosophia* 38 (1): 57–67. https://doi.org/10.1007/s11406-009-9202-8

———. 2011. "Ignorance Is Lack of True Belief: A Rejoinder to Le Morvan." *Philosophia* 39 (2): 345–55. https://doi.org/10.1007/s11406-010-9301-6

———. 2012. "The New View on Ignorance Undefeated." *Philosophia* 40 (4): 741–50. https://doi.org/10.1007/s11406-012-9364-7

———. 2014a. "Against Doxastic Compatibilism." *Philosophy and Phenomenological Research* 89 (3): 679–702. https://doi.org/10.1111/phpr.12040

———. 2014b. "What Kind of Ignorance Excuses? Two Neglected Issues." *Philosophical Quarterly* 64 (256): 478–96. https://doi.org/10.1093/pq/pqu013

———. 2023. *Ignorance: A Philosophical Study*. New York: Oxford University Press.

Peels, Rik, and Martijn Blaauw. 2016. "Introduction." In *The Epistemic Dimensions of Ignorance*, edited by Rik Peels and Martijn Blaauw, 1–11. Cambridge: Cambridge University Press. https://doi.org/10.1017/9780511820076.001

Peels, Rik, and Duncan Pritchard. 2021. "Educating for Ignorance." *Synthese* 198 (8): 7949–63. https://doi.org/10.1007/s11229-020-02544-z

Pettigrew, Richard. 2016. "Jamesian Epistemology Formalised: An Explication of 'The Will to Believe.'" *Episteme* 13 (3): 253–68. https://doi.org/10.1017/epi.2015.44

Plato. 1993. *Philebus*. Translated by Dorothea Frede. Indianapolis, IN: Hackett.

———. 1997. *Complete Works*. Edited by John M. Cooper. Indianapolis, IN: Hackett.

———. 2010. *Meno and Phaedo*. Edited by D. N. Sedley. Cambridge Texts in the History of Philosophy. Cambridge: Cambridge University Press.

Pohlhaus, Gaile. 2012. "Relational Knowing and Epistemic Injustice: Toward a Theory of Willful Hermeneutical Ignorance." *Hypatia* 27 (4): 715–35. https://doi.org/10.1111/j.1527-2001.2011.01222.x

Pozzo, Riccardo. 2015. "Introduction." In *Vernunftlehre*, by Georg Friedrich Meier, edited by Robert Theis and Werner Schneiders, 5*–22*. Gesammelte Werke / Christian Wolff. Abt III, Materialien Und Dokumente, Band 144. Hildesheim: Georg Olms Verlag.

Prien, Bernd. 2006. Kants Logik Der Begriffe: Die Begriffslehre Der Formalen Und Transzendentalen Logik Kants. Kantstudien. Ergänzungshefte 150. Berlin: De Gruyter.

Pritchard, Duncan. 2013. "Epistemic Paternalism and Epistemic Value." *Philosophical Inquiries* 1 (2). https://doi.org/10.4454/philinq.v1i2.53

Pritchard, Duncan. 2016. "Ignorance and Epistemic Value." In *The Epistemic Dimensions of Ignorance*, edited by Rik Peels and Martijn Blaauw, 132–43. Cambridge: Cambridge University Press. https://doi.org/10.1017/9780511820076.008
———. 2021a. "Ignorance and Inquiry." *American Philosophical Quarterly* 58 (2): 111–24. https://doi.org/10.2307/48613999.
———. 2021b. "Ignorance and Normativity." *Philosophical Topics* 49 (2): 225–44.
Proctor, Robert. 2008. "Agnotology: A Missing Term to Describe the Cultural Production of Ignorance (and Its Study)." In *Agnotology: The Making and Unmaking of Ignorance*, edited by Robert Proctor and Londa L. Schiebinger, 1–33. Stanford: Stanford University Press.
Proctor, Robert, and Londa L. Schiebinger, eds. 2008. *Agnotology: The Making and Unmaking of Ignorance*. Stanford: Stanford University Press.
Radbruch, Jonas. 2018. "Alle Sind Mitte." *Die Zeit*, February 15.
Ravetz, Jerome R. 1993. "The Sin of Science: Ignorance of Ignorance." *Knowledge* 15 (2): 157–65. https://doi.org/10.1177/107554709301500203
Regitz-Zagrosek, Vera, and Catherine Gebhard. 2023. "Gender Medicine: Effects of Sex and Gender on Cardiovascular Disease Manifestation and Outcomes." *Nature Reviews. Cardiology* 20 (4): 236–47. https://doi.org/10.1038/s41569-022-00797-4
Rescher, Nicholas. 2009. *Ignorance: On the Wider Implications of Deficient Knowledge*. Pittsburgh: University of Pittsburgh Press.
Riggs, Wayne. 2003. "Balancing Our Epistemic Goals." *Noûs* 37 (2): 342–52. https://doi.org/10.1111/1468-0068.00442
———. 2016. "Open-Mindedness, Insight, and Understanding." In *Intellectual Virtues and Education: Essays in Applied Virtue Epistemology*, edited by Jason S. Baehr, 18–37. Routledge Studies in Contemporary Philosophy 75. New York: Routledge.
———. 2018. "Open-Mindedness." In *The Routledge Handbook of Virtue Epistemology*, edited by Heather Battaly, 1st ed., 141–54. London: Routledge. https://doi.org/10.4324/9781315712550
Ritter, Joachim. 1927. *Docta Ignorantia: Die Theorie Des Nichtwissens Bei Nicolaus Cusanus*. Leipzig: Verlag von B.G. Teubner.
Rives, Amélie. 1892. "Innocence versus Ignorance." *North American Review* 155 (430): 287–92.
Roberts, Robert C., and W. Jay Wood. 2007. *Intellectual Virtues: An Essay in Regulative Epistemology*. New York: Clarendon Press.
Ronell, Avital. 2002. *Stupidity*. Urbana, IL: University of Illinois Press.
Rosen, Gideon. 2004. "Skepticism about Moral Responsibility." *Philosophical Perspectives* 18: 295–313.
Rosenfeld, Sophia A. 2011. *Common Sense: A Political History*. Cambridge, MA: Harvard University Press.
Ryan, Sharon. 2003. "Doxastic Compatibilism and the Ethics of Belief." *Philosophical Studies: An International Journal for Philosophy in the Analytic Tradition* 114 (1/2): 47–79.
———. 2018. "Wisdom." In *The Stanford Encyclopedia of Philosophy*, edited by Edward N. Zalta. Stanford: Metaphysics Research Lab, Stanford University. https://plato.stanford.edu/archives/fall2018/entries/wisdom.

References

Schickore, Jutta. 2005. "'Through Thousands of Errors We Reach the Truth'—but How? On the Epistemic Roles of Error in Scientific Practice." *Studies in History and Philosophy of Science Part A* 36 (3): 539–56. https://doi.org/10.1016/j.shpsa.2005.06.011

Schiffrin, Anya, ed. 2011. *Bad News: How America's Business Press Missed the Story of the Century*. New York: New Press.

Schüling, Hermann. 2009. *Der Irrtum. Sein Umfeld, Seine Formen, Entwicklungen Und Ursachen*. Vol. 11. System Und Evolution Des Menschlichen Erkennens: Ein Handbuch Der Evolutionären Erkenntnistheorie, Bd. 46. Hildesheim: G. Olms.

Schumpeter, Joseph A. 1976. *Capitalism, Socialism and Democracy*. New York: Harper Perennial.

Schutz, Alfred. 1976. "The Well-Informed Citizen." In *Collected Papers II*, edited by Arvid Brodersen, 120–34. The Hague: Martinus Nijhoff.

Schwartz, Alexandra. 2016. "The 'Unmasking' of Elena Ferrante." *New Yorker*, October 3. www.newyorker.com/culture/cultural-comment/the-unmasking-of-elena-ferrante

Schwarz, Balduin. 1976. "Irrtum." In *Historisches Wörterbuch Der Philosophie*, edited by Karlfried Gründer, 589–606. Darmstadt: Schwabe.

———. 2009. "Der Irrtum in Der Philosophie." In *Anthologie Der Realistischen Phänomenologie*, edited by Josef Seifert and Cheikh Mbacké Gueye, 497–516. Heusenstamm: Ontos.

Shelby, Tommie. 2014. "Racism, Moralism, and Social Criticism." *Du Bois Review: Social Science Research on Race* 11 (1): 57–74. https://doi.org/10.1017/S1742058X14000010

Sherwin, Susan. 1998. "A Relational Approach to Autonomy in Health Care." In *The Politics of Women's Health: Exploring Agency and Autonomy*, edited by Susan Sherwin, 19–47. Philadelphia: Temple University Press.

Silva Jr., Paul, and Robert Weston Siscoe. 2024. "Ignorance and Awareness." *Noûs* 58 (1): 225–43. https://doi.org/10.1111/nous.12450

Smith, Angela M. 2005. "Responsibility for Attitudes: Activity and Passivity in Mental Life." *Ethics* 115 (2): 236–71. https://doi.org/10.1086/426957

Smithson, Michael. 1989. *Ignorance and Uncertainty: Emerging Paradigms*. Cognitive Science. New York: Springer.

———. 1993. "Ignorance and Science: Dilemmas, Perspectives, and Prospects." *Knowledge* 15 (2): 133–56. https://doi.org/10.1177/107554709301500202

———. 2015. "Afterword: Ignorance Studies. Interdisciplinary, Multidisciplinary, and Transdisciplinary." In *Routledge International Handbook of Ignorance Studies*, edited by Matthias Gross and Linsey McGoey, 385–99. Routledge International Handbooks. London: Routledge.

Somin, Ilya. 2016. *Democracy and Political Ignorance: Why Smaller Government Is Smarter*, 2nd ed. Stanford, CA: Stanford Law Books, an imprint of Stanford University Press.

Sorkin, Andrew Ross. 2010. *Too Big to Fail: The Inside Story of How Wall Street and Washington Fought to Save the Financial System—and Themselves*. Updated and with a new afterword. London: Penguin Books.

Srivastava, Ranjana. 2011. "Dealing with Uncertainty in a Time of Plenty." *New England Journal of Medicine* 365 (24): 2252–53. https://doi.org/10.1056/NEJMp1109456

Stanovich, Keith E., and Richard F. West. 1997. "Reasoning Independently of Prior Belief and Individual Differences in Actively Open-Minded Thinking." *Journal of Educational Psychology* 89 (2): 342–57. https://doi.org/10.1037/0022-0663.89.2.342

Strout, Tania D., Marij Hillen, Caitlin Gutheil, Eric Anderson, Rebecca Hutchinson, Hannah Ward, Hannah Kay, Gregory J. Mills and Paul K. J. Han. 2018. "Tolerance of Uncertainty: A Systematic Review of Health and Healthcare-Related Outcomes." *Patient Education and Counseling* 101 (9): 1518–37. https://doi.org/10.1016/j.pec.2018.03.030

Sunstein, Cass R. 1991. "Preferences and Politics." *Philosophy and Public Affairs* 20 (1): 3–34.

Taber, Charles S., and Milton Lodge. 2006. "Motivated Skepticism in the Evaluation of Political Beliefs." *American Journal of Political Science* 50 (3): 755–69. https://doi.org/10.1111/j.1540-5907.2006.00214.x

Talisse, Robert B. 2004. "Does Public Ignorance Defeat Deliberative Democracy?" *Critical Review* 16 (4): 455–63. https://doi.org/10.1080/08913810408443619

Taylor, Shelley E., and Jonathon D. Brown. 1988. "Illusion and Well-Being: A Social Psychological Perspective on Mental Health." *Psychological Bulletin* 103 (2): 193–210. https://doi.org/10.1037/0033-2909.103.2.193

———. 1994. "Positive Illusions and Well-Being Revisited: Separating Fact from Fiction." *Psychological Bulletin* 116 (1): 21–27. https://doi.org/10.1037/0033-2909.116.1.21

Thomas Aquinas. 1912–1936. *Summa Theologica*. Translated by Fathers of the English Dominican Province. Second revised edition. 22 vols. London: Benziger Brothers.

Timmermann, Jens. 2018. "Autonomy, Progress and Virtue: Why Kant Has Nothing to Fear from the Overdemandingness Objection." *Kantian Review* 23 7(3): 379–97. https://doi.org/10.1017/S1369415418000201

Tocqueville, Alexis de. 1969. *Democracy in America*. Edited by J. P. Mayer. Translated by George Lawrence. New York: Harper Perennial Modern Classics.

Tonelli, Mark R., and Brian H. Shirts. 2017. "Knowledge for Precision Medicine: Mechanistic Reasoning and Methodological Pluralism." *JAMA* 318 (17): 1649–50. https://doi.org/10.1001/jama.2017.11914

Townley, Cynthia. 2011. *A Defense of Ignorance: Its Value for Knowers and Roles in Feminist and Social Epistemologies*. Lanham: Lexington Books.

Treeck, Werner van. 2015. *Dummheit: Eine Unendliche Geschichte*. Stuttgart: Reclam.

Tuana, Nancy. 2006. "The Speculum of Ignorance: The Women's Health Movement and Epistemologies of Ignorance." *Hypatia* 21 (3): 1–19. https://doi.org/10.1111/j.1527-2001.2006.tb01110.x

Tugendhat, Ernst. 1993. *Vorlesungen über Ethik*. Suhrkamp-Taschenbuch Wissenschaft 1100. Frankfurt am Main: Suhrkamp.

———. 2010. "Retraktationen Zur Intellektuellen Redlichkeit." In *Anthropologie Statt Metaphysik, Zweite erweiterte Auflage*, 85–113. München: C.H. Beck.

Tversky, Amos, and Daniel Kahneman. 1974. "Judgment under Uncertainty: Heuristics and Biases." *Science* 185 (4157): 1124–31. https://doi.org/10.1126/science.185.4157.1124

Ungar, Sheldon. 2008. "Ignorance as an Under-Identified Social Problem." *British Journal of Sociology* 59 (2): 301–26. https://doi.org/10.1111/j.1468-4446.2008.00195.x

Unger, Peter K. 1975. *Ignorance: A Case for Scepticism.* Oxford: Oxford University Press.

Valentini, Laura. 2012. "Ideal vs. Non-Ideal Theory: A Conceptual Map: Ideal vs Non-Ideal Theory." *Philosophy Compass* 7 (9): 654–64. https://doi.org/10.1111/j.1747-9991.2012.00500.x

Van Dormael, Jaco. 2015. *Le Tout Nouveau Testament.* Le Pacte.

Van Woudenberg, René. 2009. "Ignorance and Force: Two Excusing Conditions for False Beliefs." *American Philosophical Quarterly* 46 (4): 373–86.

Verdiesen, Ilse, Martijn Cligge, Jan Timmermans, Lennard Segers, Virginia Dignum and Jeroen van den Hoven. 2016. "MOOD: Massive Open Online Deliberation Platform—A Practical Application." *Proceedings of 22nd European Conference on Artificial Intelligence.* https://ceur-ws.org/Vol-1668/paper1.pdf

Virani, Salim S., A. Nasser Khan, Cesar E. Mendoza, Alexandre C. Ferreira and Eduardo de Marchena. 2007. "Takotsubo Cardiomyopathy, or Broken-Heart Syndrome." *Texas Heart Institute Journal* 34 (1): 76–79.

Vogt, Katja Maria. 2015. *Belief and Truth: A Skeptic Reading of Plato.* Oxford: Oxford University Press.

Warren, Mark E., and Hilary Pearse, eds. 2008. *Designing Deliberative Democracy: The British Columbia Citizens' Assembly.* Cambridge: Cambridge University Press. https://doi.org/10.1017/CBO9780511491177

Watterson, Bill. 1993. *Calvin and Hobbes. Is It a Right to Remain Ignorant?* 05 January 1993, www.gocomics.com/calvinandhobbes/1993/01/05. Accessed: 12 June 2024.

Weiner, Drew S., and Corey L. Guenther. 2018. "Self-Enhancement Bias." In *Encyclopedia of Personality and Individual Differences*, edited by Virgil Zeigler-Hill and Todd K. Shackelford, 1–7. Cham: Springer. https://doi.org/10.1007/978-3-319-28099-8_1905-1

Weinshall, Matthew. 2003. "Means, Ends, and Public Ignorance in Habermas's Theory of Democracy." *Critical Review* 15 (1–2): 23–58. https://doi.org/10.1080/08913810308443573

Wekker, Gloria. 2016. *White Innocence: Paradoxes of Colonialism and Race.* Durham: Duke University Press.

Wesche, Tilo. 2011. *Wahrheit Und Werturteil: Eine Theorie Der Praktischen Rationalität.* Philosophische Untersuchungen 27. Tübingen: Mohr Siebeck.

Westlund, Andrea C. 2012. "Autonomy in Relation." In *Out from the Shadows. Analytical Feminist Contributions to Traditional Philosophy*, edited by Sharon L. Crasnow and Anita M. Superson, 59–81. Oxford: Oxford University Press. https://doi.org/10.1093/acprof:oso/9780199855469.001.0001

Westover, Tara. 2018. *Educated: A Memoir*, 1st ed. New York: Random House.

Whitcomb, Dennis. 2010. "Curiosity Was Framed." *Philosophy and Phenomenological Research* 81 (3): 664–87.

Whiting, Daniel. 2013. "The Good and the True (or the Bad and the False)." *Philosophy* 88 (2): 219–42. https://doi.org/10.1017/S0031819113000260

Wierenga, Edward. 2018. "Omniscience." In *The Stanford Encyclopedia of Philosophy*, edited by Edward N. Zalta. https://plato.stanford.edu/entries/omniscience/
Wilholt, Torsten. 2019. "On Knowing What One Does Not Know: Ignorance and the Aims of Research." In *Science and the Production of Ignorance: When the Quest for Knowledge Is Thwarted*, edited by Janet Kourany and Martin Carrier, 195–218. Cambridge, MA: MIT Press.
Wilkesmann, Maximiliane, and Stephanie Steden, eds. 2019. *Nichtwissen stört mich (nicht): zum Umgang mit Nichtwissen in Medizin und Pflege*. Wiesbaden: Springer VS.
Williams, Bernard. 2004. *Truth & Truthfulness: An Essay in Genealogy*. Princeton, NJ: Princeton University Press.
Williams, Patricia J. 1998. *Seeing a Color-Blind Future: The Paradox of Race*. The 1997 BBC Reith Lectures. New York: Noonday Press.
Williamson, Timothy. 1996. *Vagueness*. Problems of Philosophy. New York: Routledge.
Wingert, Lutz. 1997. "Gott Naturalisieren? Anscombes Problem Und Tugendhats Lösung." *Deutsche Zeitschrift Für Philosophie* 45 (4): 501–8.
———. 2019. "Regeln Für Die Wahrheitssuche? Über Epistemische (Erkenntnisbezogene) Normen." Unpublished manuscript.
Wolterstorff, Nicholas. 1994. "Locke's Philosophy of Religion." In *The Cambridge Companion to Locke*, edited by Vere Chappell, 172–98. Cambridge Companions to Philosophy. Cambridge: Cambridge University Press. https://doi.org/10.1017/CCOL0521383714.008
———. 1996. *John Locke and the Ethics of Belief*. Cambridge Studies in Religion and Critical Thought 2. Cambridge: Cambridge University Press.
Wright, G. H. von. 1993. The Tree of Knowledge and Other Essays. Vol. 11. Philosophy of History and Culture. Leiden: E.J. Brill.
Zagzebski, Linda. 1996. *Virtues of the Mind: An Inquiry into the Nature of Virtue and the Ethical Foundations of Knowledge*. New York: Cambridge University Press.
———. 2003. "Intellectual Motivation and the Good of Truth." In *Intellectual Virtue: Perspectives from Ethics and Epistemology*, edited by Linda Zagzebski and Michael DePaul, 135–54. Oxford: Oxford University Press.
Zimmerman, Michael J. 1997. "Moral Responsibility and Ignorance." *Ethics* 107 (3): 410–26.
———. 2008. Living with Uncertainty: The Moral Significance of Ignorance. Cambridge Studies in Philosophy. Cambridge: Cambridge University Press. https://doi.org/10.1017/CBO9780511481505

Index

absence of belief 79–83
acceptance (dealing with ignorance) 147–148
active ignorance 51, 52, 60
actively upheld false outlooks 51–52
adequacy conditions 56–58
affective side of ignorance 97–100, 217
agential conceptions of ignorance 47–53
agnostic position 182
agnotology 21
Al Fārābī, Abu-Nasr Muhammad Ibn-Muhammad 15
Al-Ghazālī 15
Alcoff, Linda 21, 53–55
alethic ignorance 39
alethic obligation to God 154–158
ambivalence of knowledge 232–233
ameliorative epistemology 11
amoralist approach 186
analytical epistemology 18–19
Anderson, Elizabeth 55, 112, 115–116
anger 100
Annas, Julia 140–141
Aristotle: desire to know 124–132; nature of human beings 121, 124; theoretical wisdom 148
arrogance 94–96
attitudinal component of ignorance 78, 208, 210, 217

Baehr, Jason 136
Baltes, Paul 137–138, 140
behavioral expressions of uncertainty 225
belief acquisition 156–157
belief maintenance 156–157

beliefs: absence of 79–83; holding a false belief 9–10, 85–89; open-minded thinking 116–117; rationality norm 123; suspending 83–84
benign ignorance 112
Bennett, Karen 62–63
bias: faulty inferences 112; in politics 78–79, 202; and stereotypes 115–116
Bildung 128–129
blameless ignorance 46
bliss 98
Blumenberg, Hans 14–15
Bonitz, Hermann 125, 127
Brennan, Jason 199, 201
building relations 62

Cambiano, Giuseppe 125–126
Castellio, Sebastian 15
caution (dealing with ignorance) 147–148
Chisholm, Roderick 151
Christianity: alethic obligation to God 154–158; original sin 13–14
citizen ignorance 199–200, 204–214
Clifford, William 143, 150, 152–153
climate change 116–117, 189
close-mindedly ignorant 91–94, 101–102
cluelessness 81–83
"clutter avoidance" 93, 153, 231
cognitive fallibility 74
cognitively preferred ignorance 93
Cohen, Leah Hager 99
collective ignorance 231
common ignorance 163

common language, argument from 41–42
complete ignorance 80–81, 102
conscious ignorance 229
consequentialist approach 143–148
Converse, Philip 202, 204
COVID-19 pandemic, 8; medical uncertainty 216–218, 228
curiosity 94–96, 97

deep ignorance 80, 81, 102
deliberate ignorance 76–77, 113
deliberative democracy 206
democracy: definition 200; epistemic communities 189; open-minded thinking 116–117; pervasiveness of ignorance in democracy 23, 199–214
deontological approach: epistemic duties 150–154; epistemic duties as other-regarding duties 158–161; of Kant 162–170; Locke's alethic obligation to God 154–158
Descartes, René 15–16, 83–84
desire to know 22, 124–131
diagnostic uncertainty 219, 226–228
disbelieving ignorance 80
dogmatism 92
Dotson, Kristie 51, 60
doxastic ignorance 39
Dunning-Kruger effect 74–76

education 211
Edwards, Mike 202, 204
elections, voting in 78–79, 200, 205–206
Elga, Adam 75, 122–123
elitism 191
embarrassment 99
emotions 97–100
empirical conceptions of ignorance 29–32
the Enlightenment 16
entitlement (epistemic duties) 159–160
epistemic communities 213–214
epistemic duties: deontological approach 148, 150–151; James' twin goals 143; as other-regarding duties 158–161
epistemic fallibility 74
epistemic laziness 210–214

epistemic norms 186–189, 213
epistemic rationality 122
epistemologies of ignorance 53–55, 207
epistemology: analytical 18–19; feminist 18, 21; ignorance as part of 19–22; James' twin goals 144, 146–147; socio-epistemological assumptions 10–11
Erkenntnis 163, 164
error: avoiding and dealing with 165; causes of 110–112; deontological approach 165–166; as form of ignorance 9–10, 87; James' twin goals 143–148; Maxim-based Answer (Kant) 174–175; as a symptom of ignorance 86–88
excuse: ignorance as an 46
expertise 209–210, 211–212

factual ignorance 10
fallibility 74–75
false beliefs: absence of 79–80; causes of ignorance 109–110; as form of ignorance 9–10, 92; philosophical traditions 15–16; symptoms of ignorance 85–89
falsehood 5; argument from ignorance of 43–44; practical wisdom 139
faulty reasoning 110–112
fearful ignorance 99–100
Feldman, Richard 147, 158–160
feminist epistemology 18, 21
Ferrier, James 16
formal ignorance 163
Fricker, Miranda 60, 123
Friedman, Jane 83–84, 231

Gadamer, Hans-Georg 128
Gamper, Michael 87
Gettier-type ignorance 39–40, 45
Gigerenzer, Gerd 75
Goldberg, Sanford 144, 150, 186–187, 213
the good life 232
Graham, Peter 212–213
group agents, ignorance of 231

Haas, Jens 4, 68–69, 160
Halbwissen 70, 83, 86, 88–89, 102
Han, Paul K. J. 219–222, 223–224, 226, 227

258   Index

happiness 98
Harman, Gilbert 93, 153, 231
Harvin, Cassandra Byers 84–85, 114
Haslanger, Sally 37, 61
Helft, Paul 219–220
heuristics 75, 78–79, 112, 202
historical context, ignorance 11–12, 24
history of philosophy 12–19, 121
history of science 16–17
Hon, Giora 87
hope 96
horizon 71–74, 162–165
human progress 131
humility 94–96, 134–135

ideology and ignorance 61
ignorance: adequacy conditions 56–58; agential conceptions 47–53; approaching 3–5; caring about 1–3; causes of 108–117; degrees of 47, 84; in epistemology 19–22; history of philosophy 12–19; integrated conception 58–64; logical conceptions and empirical conceptions 29–32; meaning of 1–2, 5, 37–38; nature of 24; in philosophy 22–23; prevalence 70–79; reductionist propositional conceptions 38–47; structural conceptions 53–56; subjects and objects of 5–10; symptoms 68–70, 100–103; syndrome framework 32–34; types of 6–10, 13, 15
ignorance of falsehoods argument 43–44
Ignoranz 3–4
illusion, and error 165
indifferent ignorance 93, 102
integrated conception of ignorance 58–64; two objections against 63–64
intellectual honesty 177–180, 183–186
intellectual humility 134–135
"interest-driven epistemology" 231
interrogative attitude 83–84
investigative ignorance 89–90
"issue public" heuristic 202

James, William 131, 143–148, 151, 153

"junk beliefs" 231
justificational ignorance 39

Kahneman, Daniel 75, 112
Kant, Immanuel: conception of error 87–88; dealing with error and the *sensus communis* 165–170, 173–176; the horizon 71–74, 162–165; human progress 131; maxims 166–170
Kaye, Simon T. 203
Klein, Roberta Cutler 151
knowledge: and democracy 203–204, 207–208; desire to know 22, 124–131; epistemic actions 160; factual ignorance 10; narrow conceptions of 57; our relationship to 2
'known unknowns' 6
Köhl, Harald 173–174
Kruglanski, Arie W. 79

laziness 94–96, 210–214
Le Morvan, Pierre 19, 20, 39–47
legitimate uncertainty 232
Lincoln, Abraham 200
Lippmann, Walter 200
Locke, John 16, 110–112, 154–158, 167–168
Lodge, Milton 78, 106, 208
logical conceptions of ignorance 29–32

material ignorance 163
Maxim-based Answer: advantages of 180–181; avoiding error 23; citizen ignorance 213, 214; developing 173–176; medical context 217, 223–226; motivations and intellectual honesty 177–180, 183–186; objections against 182–192; other people's ignorance 231; *sensus communis* 169–170, 173–176; the three maxims 166–170; unconscious ignorance 229–230
McDowell, John 128–129
McGoey, Linsey 144
mechanistic reasoning 228–229
medical context: COVID-19 pandemic 216–218, 228; dealing with patient-practitioner uncertainty

217, 222–226; dealing with prognosis uncertainty 226–228; errors and false belief 9; examples and a typology of uncertainty 218–222; ignorance and uncertainty 23; ignorance in medical practice 216–218; ignorance in medical research 216–218, 219, 228–230; propositional ignorance 8
Medina, José 51, 52–53, 60
meta-competence 232
meta-ignorance 74–75
Meylan, Anne 47–48, 49–51
Mills, Charles 18, 51–52, 53, 60
moral ignorance 10
moral philosophy 19, 21
morality 185–186
Mori, Ipsos 201, 205
motivated ignorance 113, 114–117
motivations for intellectual honesty 177–180, 183–186

naïve optimists 182–183
"nature of times" heuristic 78–79, 202
neutral conception of ignorance 57
New View of ignorance 38–39, 44–47, 55, 59–60
Nicholas of Cusa 15
Nichtwissen 3–4
Nietzsche, Friedrich 17–18
non-ideal epistemology 12
non-ideal pessimism 12
non-reflective cluelessness 82–83, 102
Norlock, Kathryn 12
normative ignorance 10
Normative View of ignorance 48–51
Nozick, Robert 139

Offe, Claus 203–204
Ogden, Jane 225
Olsson, Erik 29, 30–31
O'Neill, Onora 175
open-minded thinking 116–117
open-mindedly ignorant 89–91, 101
Oppenheimer, Danny 202, 204
optimism, reflective vs. naïve 182–183, 232
orientation in thinking 166
original sin 13–14
overdemandingness 190–192

passion 111
patient-practitioner uncertainty 217, 220–221, 222–226; *see also* medical context
Peels, Rik 4, 18–19, 20, 38–47, 58–63, 79–80
pessimism 182–184
phronimos 129, 132, 140, 148
Pohlhaus, Gaile 18, 51, 115
politically motivated reasoning 116–117
politics: bias in 78–79, 202; epistemic norms 189; ignorance and uncertainty 23; open-minded thinking 116–117; pervasiveness of ignorance in democracy 199–214
populist politics 200
post-conceptual ignorance 43–44
practical ignorance 10
practical philosophy 189
practical rationality 122
practical wisdom 130, 135–136, 139, 141
practice-generated entitlement 159–160
pre-conceptual ignorance 43–44
preferred ignorance 92–94, 101, 112
presumed knowledge 95, 102, 112
prevalence of ignorance 70–79
primordia naturalia 70
Pritchard, Duncan 19, 46, 47–51, 134–135, 144, 146–147, 164
privilege 99
probabilities 221–222, 226
prognosis uncertainty 220–222, 223–224, 226–228; *see also* medical context
Proietti, Carlo 29, 30–31
propositional ignorance 8, 58–59, 80–81
proxy method 229
psychological states 96–97

questions, as symptoms of ignorance 84–85

race: motivated ignorance 114–115; white ignorance 51–52
rationality: 18, 122–123, 128, 136, 177 epistemic and practical 122
reasoning, faulty 110–112

reductionist propositional conceptions of ignorance 38–47, 58
reflective cluelessness 82–83
reflective ignorance 89–90, 101, 146
reflective optimism 12, 182, 183–184, 232
religion: alethic obligation to God 154–158; knowledge of God 15; original sin 13–14
Rescher, Nicholas 73–74
revisionary epistemology 10–11
Riggs, Wayne 146–147, 148
Roberts, Robert 129–130, 139, 190–191
Rumsfeld, Donald 6
Ryan, Sharon 135, 136–137

St Augustine 14–15, 70
sanctioning (epistemic norms) 186–187
Schickore, Jutta 80
Schumpeter, Joseph 199, 200
Schutz, Alfred 211–212
science: errors and false belief 8–9; history of 16–17; scientific ignorance 53, 163; scientist's approach to ignorance 90; sources of error 80; *see also* medical context
second nature 128–129
self-confidence 99
self-evaluation bias 76, 122–123
self-standing phenomenon, ignorance as 56–57
sensus communis 165–166, 169–170, 173–176
shame 99
Shelby, Tommie 61
Shirts, Brian H. 228–229
social context: citizen ignorance 199–200, 212–213; in medicine 222–223
socio-epistemological assumptions 10–11
Socrates 12–13, 121, 132–136, 150, 164, 180
Socratic ignorance 121–122, 132–141
Socratic wisdom 132–141
Somin, Ilya 199
Spinoza, Baruch 15–16
Srivastava, Ranjana 217, 224, 227–228

Standard View of ignorance 39, 40–44, 47, 55
statistical innumeracy 221–222
Staudinger, Ursula 137–138, 140
stereotypes 115–116
stigmatization 115–116
structural conceptions of ignorance 53–56
stupidity 5, 13
Sunstein, Cass 203
surprise 96
suspending belief 83–84
syndrome framework 32–34

Taber, Charles S. 208
Takotsobu cardiomyopathy (TCM) 218
theoretical wisdom 135–136, 141, 148
Thomas Aquinas 14
Tonelli, Mark R. 228–229
trivial ignorance 63, 74, 77–78
trust 96–97
truth: human nature 17; James' twin goals 143–148; relationship to ignorance 5
Tuana, Nancy 54, 92
Tugendhat, Ernst 167, 177–180, 183–187
Tversky, Amos 75, 112
"twin goals" (James) 143–148

uncertainty, overlap with ignorance 23
uncertainty tolerance 226–228
unconscious ignorance 229–230
Unger, Peter 18
unified account argument 40–41
Unkenntnis 3–4
unwanted knowledge 113
Unwissen 3–4, 33
Unwissenheit 3, 33, 36, 165
Use a Proxy method 229

vicious ignorance 77–79, 89–96
virtue epistemology 5–6
virtuous ignorance 89–96
Vogt, Katja Maria 4, 65, 68–70, 89, 91–92, 95, 103, 160
von Wright, Georg Henrik 232–233

well-informed citizens 211–212
well-informed preferred ignorance 92–93
Wesche, Tilo 187
White ignorance 51–52, 59–60, 61–62
widespread vicious ignorance 77–79

wisdom, properties of 137–138
Wittgensteinian approach 56
Wolterstorff, Nicholas 154, 155–157
Wood, W. Jay 129–130, 139, 190–191

Printed in the United States
by Baker & Taylor Publisher Services